SEA POWER
IN THE 1970s

Conference on Problems of Naval
Armaments, Ithaca, n.y., 1972.

SEA POWER
IN THE 1970s

George H. Quester, Editor

Sponsored by the Cornell University

Program on Peace Studies

DUNELLEN

New York • London

Distributed by Kennikat Press • Port Washington, N.Y.

International Standard Book Number 0-8046-7088-9

Library of Congress Catalogue Card Number 73-88666

Printed in the United States of America

UNIVERSITY PRESS OF CAMBRIDGE, MASS SERIES
CONSULTING EDITOR: EUGENE H. NELLEN

Library of Congress Cataloging in Publication Data

Conference on Problems of Naval Armaments, Ithaca,
    N.Y., 1972.
    Sea power in the 1970s.

    Includes bibliographical references and index.
    1. Navies—Congresses. 2. Sea-power—Congresses.
I. Quester, George H. II. Cornell University.
Program on Peace Studies. III. Title.
VA40.C66 1972   359   73-88666
ISBN 0-8046-7088-9

Editor's Notes

Soviet competition with the United States on the high seas is not an old phenomenon, having emerged only in the late 1960s. As such, it can be given too much or too little attention, and its implications for detente and arms control can be misunderstood in various ways. The papers presented in this book are intended to discuss some problems the two super-powers will confront in managing their oceanic confrontation through the 1970s. Papers were originally prepared for a Conference on Problems of Naval Armaments convened in Ithaca, New York, in April 1972 by the Cornell University Program on Peace Studies. While each of these papers has been revised somewhat in response to comments exchanged at the Conference, they were and are intended to offer discordant viewpoints. No effort has been made to align them with any single interpretation of the naval arms control problem.

In Chapter 1 John T. Hayward (Vice Admiral, U.S. Navy, retired) presents a case for increased U.S. naval preparedness which, in many ways, reflects the views of officers currently serving in the U.S. Navy who share a sense of alarm about the growth of the Soviet Navy. Chapter 2 expresses my somewhat contrary view that naval armaments in the future will have a symbolic function not directly related to any likely war-fighting role.

Chapter 3, by Arnold Kuzmack of the Brookings Institution, is a modified version of an article which appeared in *Military Review*, February 1972, questioning the cost-effectiveness and survivability of aircraft carriers. Chapter 4, by Barry Blechman of the Brookings Institution, separates reality from myth on the Soviet naval programs of the 1960s and 1970s; a longer version of this paper is slated to appear as a monograph in the series of the Brookings Institution.

The next three chapters discuss particular theaters of the Soviet-United States confrontation. In Chapter 5 Curt Gasteyger of the Atlantic Institute surveys the force deployments in the Mediterranean and the uses to which they might be put politically. Chapter 6, by Professor Jack Spence of the University of Swansea, Wales, discusses similar questions for the Indian Ocean. Chapter 7, by Professor T. B. Millar of Australian National University, then surveys the far eastern region from Singapore into the Pacific Ocean.

Chapter 8, by Michael Rosenthal of the Cornell University Program on Science, Technology and Society and Program on Peace Studies, presents some proposals on improved ground-rules for the procurement or deployment of the two superpowers' strategic-missile firing submarines.

Chapter 9, by Gerard J. Magone, Senior Fellow of the Woodrow Wilson International Center for Scholars, finally presents an analysis of trends in the international law of the sea, trends which may have relevance to preventing wars and moderating conflicts in the future.

The Cornell University Program on Peace Studies is committed to research and teaching on the moderation or prevention of war. The Conference on Problems of Naval Armaments was the second conference sponsored by the Program, having been preceded a year earlier by a Conference on Nuclear Proliferation. The following scholars from the Cornell Program, and from other universities, participated in the Conference:

Cornell Participants

Peter Auer, Aerospace Engineering
John Barceló, Law
Hans Bethe, Physics
Milton Esman, Government and Center
    for International Studies
Edward Fox, History
Harrop Freeman, Law
Cynthia Frey, Government
David Karns, Government
Peggy Karns, Government
Franklin Long, Chemistry and Program
    on Science, Technology and Society
Omi Marwah, Peace Studies Program

David Mozingo, Government and China Program
George Quester, Government
Richard Rosecrance, Government
Michael Rosenthal, Program on Science,
    Technology and Society and Peace Studies Program
Myron Rush, Government and Soviet Studies
Martin Sherwin, Program on Science,
    Technology and Society
Norman Uphoff, Government

Visiting Participants

Charles D. Allen, United States Arms Control
    and Disarmament Agency
Rolf Bjornerstedt, United Nations Secretariat
William Coogan, United States General Accounting Office
John P. Coyle, Department of the Navy
Curt Gasteyger, Atlantic Institute
John T. Hayward, General Dynamics Corporation
Morton Halperin, The Brookings Institution
Arnold Kuzmack, The Brookings Institution
Gerard J. Mangone, Woodrow Wilson International Center for Scholars
T. B. Millar, Australian National University
Peter Sharfman, United States Arms Control
    and Disarmament Agency
Ian Smart, International Institute of Strategic Studies
Jack Spence, University College of Swansea, Wales

Contents

1

The Case for a Modernized U.S. Navy

John T. Hayward

The world long remembers the picture of the surrender ceremony on the deck of the U.S.S. Missouri on that lovely day in September 1945. It not only brought to a close World War II, but it marked the zenith of the naval might of the United States. We were supreme on the surface, below the sea, and in the air above it. It will be twenty-seven years ago this year, and much has gone on in the world, and this anniversary of this event may well mark the fact that the once supreme maritime strength of the U.S. has been eclipsed by the U.S.S.R. The U.S., in fact, may become number two. One must trace the events in these intervening years as well as look a little bit at the history "of the bear who walks like a man" but who has now put out to sea.

The Russian Navy had its beginnings in the seventeenth century under Peter the Great who imported foreign naval officers to staff Russian ships and set up a shipbuilding industry. When he died in 1725 interest in the Russian Navy lagged. The eighteenth century found Catherine the Great building up Russian seapower. Her victory at Tchesme in the Aegean Sea stunned Europe. Better known to most U.S. Naval Officers is the fact that Contre Admiral Ivanovich Pavel Jones was none other than our own John Paul Jones of Bon Homme Richard fame. She was the only one to ever confer the rank of Admiral on this superb Naval Officer. From this battle until 1807 the Russians kept a Naval Squadron in the Mediterranean, so their presence there today is not a new element in Russian history. Tsar Alexander's treaty with Napoleon forced it to withdraw. The nineteenth century and the early twentieth century culminated in defeat by Togo at Tushima. World War I followed by the Kronstadt Mutiny made the Navy practically nonexistent. World War II found it with 533 warships, including four cruisers, 37 destroyers and 206 submarines; yet it never really fought at sea. The Germans even claimed that the Russians had laid down keels for two 35,000-ton battleships. The fact remains that the Navy fought under the command of the Army and 600,000 fought ashore as Naval Infantry. The role of the Navy was particularly one of defense of the flanks of the Army at the Coasts.

This undistinguished history of the use of maritime power by the U.S.S.R. makes one wonder why we should be concerned. The present record will show why. Let us quote the Commander in Chief of the Soviet Navy, Admiral Sergei Gorshkov, describing Soviet seapower in 1972. "Our fleet can not only break the attack of an aggressor but also inflict annihilating blows in distant oceans and deep in enemy territory . . ." and then added, "the flag of the Soviet Navy now proudly flies over the oceans of the world. Sooner or later, the United States will have to understand that it no longer has mastery of the seas." If there is one way to appreciate the U.S.S.R. approach to maritime power it is by seeing the totality of their approach. They pursue all elements that go to make up seapower. Soviet planning takes into account all phases from marine biology to the deployment of naval vessels. It includes oceanography, fishing, electronic detection technology, as well as shipbuilding.

The new Soviet Navy is the most modern in the world. It covers everything from helicopter carriers to nuclear submarines. It is designed primarily against the strengths of the U.S. Navy and has acquired many of the techniques employed by the U.S.N. Only a few of these ships are 20 years or older, in contrast to a large portion of the U.S. naval combatant fleet. Its numbers are impressive when one considers its modernity. It now consists of 20 to 24 cruisers, two helicopter carriers, 110 to 120 destroyers and frigates, 92 ocean-going escorts plus a great number of fast patrol boats armed with surface-to-surface missiles and support ships for its forces. When one adds its nuclear submarine fleet to this, one can't help but assume the Russian strategy on the sea is no longer tied to the defense of the flanks of the Army. A look at the diversity and scope of its shipyards shows that between 1947 and 1957 the Russians built 19 cruisers, 104 destroyers and 348 submarines. They can now produce one nuclear submarine a month.

This becomes even more impressive when one looks at the other elements that go into their total approach to maritime power. The modest merchant fleet of the early fifties had only 487 vessels approaching about two million deadweight tons. At the time of the Cuban crisis in 1962 it had grown to a total of almost six million deadweight tons. Now it is in the neighborhood of 14.8 million with a projected growth in the year 1980 to 27.2 million deadweight tons in about 4,000 ships. It is interesting to note that their tanker fleet has had the fastest rate of growth in its numbers of any in the world. The Soviets now have the largest number of tankers on order in the world. While they use many foreign yards, about fifty per cent of their ships are built at home. They have in the neighborhood of 35 modern shipyards.

The Soviet fishing fleets in fact cover the seas of the world and are highly effective in extending Russian influence. Fishing development has been offered to many countries of the third world. The ports they use extend from Cuba to Ceylon. The fleet is in the neighborhood of six million gross tons in about 4,000 seagoing vessels. The aggressive tactics of these fishing fleets are of considerable concern to our relatively small fishing efforts. The use of modern large refrigerator mother-ships has revolutionized the approach in the far reaches of the ocean. It is in fact a sea-based fishing complex. Remember that the Russians prior to W.W. II were just coastal fishermen. They now roam the world and no place is too far for them to fish. The International Geophysical Year of 1957 and '58 saw them complete the largest oceanographic program of any nation. As in all Soviet enterprises, military considerations are given high priority and all their oceanographic research feeds into the Soviet Navy. It is large and effective. As in the other maritime fields this effort is gaining in momentum and capability.

The above brief discussion of the total approach to the maritime problem by the U.S.S.R. clearly shows their determination to exploit the potential of sea power for their national objectives.

It is necessary to review briefly the U.S. Navy and the U.S. approach to the maritime question since September 2, 1945. The events following September brought the unification of the armed services, although some people referred to it as the multiplication of forces because the U.S.A.F. was created as a separate service. The idea prevalent at the time was that the bomber with the atomic weapon made all other forces obsolete. Who needed a U.S. Navy? What for? There were no navies to fight. The Navy since W.W. II has fought land wars, such as ground support in Korea, the present effort in South East Asia. A cheaper way of getting tactical air support for our ground forces was the role of the C.V.A. Our aircraft and weapons were designed for this. Sea control did not sell Congress for appropriations for ships in those days.

Who remembers that we spent $550,000,000 for air bases in Morocco but wouldn't build the first C.V.A., the United States. Its cancellation led to the resignation of the Secretary of the Navy John Sullivan. We no longer have the bases in Morocco and some day the planes with the hammer and sickle on their wings may fly against us from them. The U.S.S. United States would still be ours and flying the U.S. flag if we had built her. This was not just true of aircraft carriers, for our nuclear submarines were also influenced by this syndrome that we didn't need a Navy. There were no ships to sink, so we justified and built them to sink Russian submarines, and we have no real anti-shipping torpedoes today. We have no surface-to-surface missiles either, nor did we modernize our guns for use at sea. The influence of politics on weapon systems was all too apparent. The so-called "Revolt of the Admirals" and the emotions on the C.V.A. left their mark over the years. Even today we have supposedly responsible Senators still arguing the usefulness in our spectrum of maritime power of the nuclear-powered aircraft carrier. There is nothing that has occurred over the last 27 years that has changed the usefulness of the aircraft carrier. Certainly it is an attractive target, as it always has been. It is no more vulnerable than any air field and has the advantage that it can move.

The following table is taken from the 1971 Brookings Institution report on the problem of Naval Force Levels and Modernization.[1] The remarks that accompany it are from the same report:

Table 1. Distribution of Ships by Age and Category, 1980[a]

	Number of ships by age				
Ship Category	Under 20 years	20-29 years	30 years or more	All ages	Percentage 30 years old or more
Carriers	7	4	10	21	48
Attack submarines	62	18	42	122	34
Cruiser-destroyer forces	124	40	114	278	41
Amphibious assault ships	60	32	35	127	28
Mine countermeasure ships	—	61	1	62	2
Underway replenishment ships	25	15	42	82	51
Fleet support ships	10	—	87	97	90
All categories	288	170	331	789	42

[a]Assumes no new ship construction after fiscal 1971 program. Data as of July, 1970.

"Table 1 illustrates the modernization problem facing the Navy. Under the assumption (for purposes of exposition) that there is no new ship construction after the fiscal 1971 program and that the ship retirements announced as of July 1970 take place, there will be 331 ships, out of a total of 789 ships in the Navy, thirty years old or older in 1980.[6] If modernization is to be completed by then, either these ships will have to be replaced or force levels will have to be reduced. If they are all to be replaced, on a one-for-one basis, more than 60 ships would have to be funded each year for the next five years or so. By contrast, five ships were funded in fiscal 1969, 10 in 1970, 15 in 1971, and funding for 19 is requested in the President's 1972 budget. The Defense Department had not, however, adopted lower force levels for planning purposes until the 1972 budget; nor had it indicated the strategic rationale for the lower force levels that would result from a continuation of current funding levels.

"Table 1 shows that the impact of block obsolescence is very uneven. The amphibious assault forces and attack submarines are relatively modern, whereas 90 percent of the fleet support ships will be overage by 1980. The last ship in this category to be built is a submarine rescue ship (A.S.R.) in the fiscal 1968 program. Some ships were included in the 1969 and 1970 budget requests and were approved by Congress, but they were later cancelled to fund cost overruns on other ships. None were included in the President's 1971 budget, but some are included in his 1972 budget. Such anomalous situations arise from a shipbuilding budget that is inadequate to modernize approved future force levels."

This gives some idea of the magnitude of the problem in the naval ship area if we are to meet the challenge of the years ahead. When one looks at our Merchant Marine the situation is even worse. A look at history suggests that a nation that builds ships, engages in mercantile shipping, collects revenue therefrom and keeps the sealanes open for commerce has been internationally influential and economically affluent. Any idea that this component of maritime power can be divorced from the overall maritime resources is not valid. Mr. MacNamara as well as Secretary of the Navy Ignatius in their testimony before Congress in the '60s attempted to create the belief the Navy was not concerned with the Merchant Marine strength of the United States. They gave no support for revitalizing our Merchant Marine. They did not understand the totality of the problem of the maritime resources of a nation.

Now the order of the day for the last third of the century is certainly change. It is the common denominator of this complex world of ours today. So it is necessary that we examine in detail how our maritime resources and in particular how our Navy interfaces with the changes. It is only natural if everything else changes, such as our moral values, political ideas and social approaches to education, that one must look closely at such classical ideas as Mahan's on seapower. We know all too well there are no such things as absolutes in life. Even such a cornerstone as the idea that the velocity of light is constant is under fire by present-day physicists. There are such questions as nuclear parity or inferiority. Where is the Soviet expansion going? What are its objectives; What is its strategy?

What are the elements that make up the principal threats to the U.S. and the free world? Are they political, technical or economic, or maybe a combination of all three? What I am trying to bring out is the world of the seventies is altered. This is a time of vast, utterly unprecedented change. The post-war order of international relations is gone. This has put the whole post war United States foreign policy into question and as such has a direct bearing on sea power. Many things have all ready disappeared in the "winds of change." The idea of Communism as a monolithic structure, the belief by our Allies in our strength, the value of the dollar and the rise of isolationism all have appeared on the scene. The appeal of unilateral disarmament to the great numbers of educated in our country cannot be discounted. It is well for us in the U.S. to remember Charles Colton's words, "To know the pain of power, we must go to those who have it; to know its pleasures, we must go to those who are seeking it; the pains of power are real, its pleasures imaginary." No one need look past our South East Asian experience to agree with the above. Our concern over national unity, political stability and law and order has brought about an apparent loss of national confidence. Have we really lost our sense of direction, our resolve; is the U.S. headed for a real breakdown as so many people believe these days?

It would be foolish to consider our question about the U.S. Navy without the backdrop of the national situation and the fact that what we do in this area must have an interface with all these changes in our national thinking. This atmosphere of thinking makes it mandatory for us to examine in depth our planning and to discard many of our older thoughts and ideas.

While all these changes are taking place within our national approach to our problems it is still true that the view one holds of the external world will have a large influence upon how we assess the role of military force in general and the Navy in particular, in dealing with anticipated international politico-military problems. It is probably best to discuss these areas as we discuss the various roles we expect Naval and Maritime forces to play in the years to come.

Let us start with the generally accepted classical definition of national strategy. It is the use by a nation of its political, economic, technical and military forces in peace as well as war to achieve its national objectives and to lessen the impact of any defeat it is unfortunate enough to sustain. As we all know the most difficult thing to achieve in our land is a consensus on our national objectives; the chorus of discordant voices in our democracy makes it a very difficult task. However, there is one national objective on which I am sure we can get almost one hundred per cent agreement. It is that no one wants a nuclear war.

So we come to the first and probably the most important role and that is the deterrent one played by our seagoing forces. I believe in his foreign policy report of 1970 to Congress the President describes our national objective in this area as he sees it. His statement is "The overriding purpose of our strategic posture is political and defensive; to deny other countries the ability to impose their will on the U.S. and its allies under the weight of strategic military superiority. We must insure that all potential aggressors see unacceptable risks in contemplating nuclear attack, or nuclear blackmail or acts which could escalate to strategic nuclear war, such as a conventional attack on Europe." The continuing trend in this country and abroad raises serious doubts whether this purpose can be attained in the '70s. The fact that we will be in a second-rate position strategically in the mid-seventies appears to be fully justified. The impact of this changing balance of power is hard to pin down at the moment for it is bound to have its effect throughout all the tasks facing our naval forces. One must realize the balance of these nuclear forces has neutralized to some extent the diplomatic influence of such weapons, though the Cuban crisis is still present in our memories. The Proxmires and Fulbrights cannot repeal the fact that hostile powers are pursuing programs that can alter the balance of power and leave the U.S. isolated. One must remember that when even in a state of admitted strategic inferiority to the U.S. the U.S.S.R. has periodically pressed forward such policies as its present Mideast encouragement to the Arab states. Inferiority certainly must have set definite limits to just what risks they would take. It is disturbing to think what risks they would take with strategic superiority.

I certainly do not agree with the MacNamara-Nitze thesis that the assured destruction capability of our nuclear forces made it unnecessary for us to continue to build up our triad approach to our strategic systems. Never forget that it is what the Russians think, not what you and I believe, that goes into the deterrent equation. The future may find that in order to bargain in a crisis you must have strength in your strategic systems. Inferiority may have serious political implications. When one looks at the overall yield of our stockpile and sees that the greater portion is still bomber delivered one has reason for deep thought on our systems. Is 25 megatons equal to one megaton? Ask the Russians, for they seem to

believe in 5 to 25. I hope we proceed with the U.L.M.S.,
follow on to our present Polaris/Poseidon system and that we
have a 5 megaton warhead, and the opposition know it. The
reverberations of this situation are passed through the rest of
the spectrum of Naval forces. It is not only logical, but a
must, that for the future deterrent posture of the U.S. our
major systems be at sea. Even if we started today to build our
forty-second ballistic missile submarine the Russians would
have over 70 by the time we had our forty-second finished
and operational. As I stated years ago, before Congress, let's
make it neither "Fortress America" nor "Target U.S.A.," and
that means to go to sea.

The A.B.M. may be a useful ploy in negotiations with the
U.S.S.R. but as a viable use of our scarce resources to protect
our vulnerable land-based missiles it doesn't make sense
technically nor as a strategic approach. It is apparent the use
of conventional Naval forces across the whole spectrum of
conflict is of vital concern in a world of nuclear deterrence. A
quick thrust by conventional forces and a *fait accompli* leave
the choice of escalation up to the opposition. A well-planned
nibbling technique in many areas of the world can be
successful in the nuclear age. Remember from your war-gam-
ing experience that very basic equation: Objective to be
gained is equal to the value of the objective minus the cost.
The numbers of values put into this will vary with each
nation. We must never forget that it is what the enemy thinks
the cost to himself will be, not what you or I do. It is hard
from a credibility point of view to convince the world you
would risk destruction of our own land for many of the
smaller countries or places we are committed to assist. These
facts all lead to the conclusion that one needs modern naval
forces, employing all the conventional weapons available, to
be able to project our power across the seas quickly and
effectively in the years to come.

One of the roles of naval power is that of overseas presence
in all parts of the world. This area is in the political
component of that all-inclusive definition of national strategy

I gave you. Overseas presence in peacetime is a major diplomatic task for U.S. naval forces. The Soviets have made excellent use of their forces in this area by close coordination with diplomatic aims. They have a total approach encompassing military, economic and foreign policy. The use of their maritime resources to expand Soviet influence in Somalia is a classic example. Their worldwide fishing and merchant fleets along with their modern naval forces give the Soviets a commanding presence overseas and influence in parts of the world they never had before.

Let us look briefly at the task that confronts the United States. Generally we must make a total approach to the maritime strength of the U.S. It is quite obvious the U.S. is coming home from across the sea. I am sure this decade will find a great number of our deployed forces such as in Western Europe and Korea back in the continental U.S. Specifically the modernization of our Navy should be pursued with the idea of obtaining the best system to do the following tasks:

    (a) Deterrence
    (b) Sea control
    (c) Projection of our power across the sea
    (d) Overseas presence

There is a great tendency in the Navy today to forget the hard lesson of the war at sea in W.W. II. They also have a way of perpetuating things that shouldn't be. The task is to know the difference. Remember that war was fought on the seven seas. One salient fact came out of that struggle, and that was that the decision in the air determined who was going to control the surface of the sea. Technological progress in the area of missiles and "smart" weapons have added to rather than detracted from the strength of the aircraft. Nothing in the last 27 years has changed these facts and so one needs modern aircraft based at sea as modern platforms. Nuclear propulsion has really increased the potentiality of the carrier as a platform. When one looks at the present program of the U.S.N. in building new ships and allocating its scarce resources, one can not be overly impressed that it will meet the tasks in the eighties. It is obvious that, outside of the deterrent mission, our Navy is too preoccupied with defense and is prone to forget the real reason for a force is their offensive striking power. Electronic counter measures will kill no one and will scare no one! The proposed frigate program seems tailored to the Battle of the Atlantic. One must never forget aircraft sink ships, and missile-carrying submarines can stand off and pick a typical Atlantic convoy to pieces. These ships outside of mere numbers really don't fit my idea of modernizing the Navy. A look at the 963 also leaves one unimpressed—8200 tons and a five-inch gun! A study of the fiscal picture shows many diluting projects with little real payoff, resulting in an increasing inability to buy the things most needed for a modern Navy. I realize this is a subject that can be debated and will probably be discussed in detail in Congress as well as the Executive Branch. I only hope they let the Navy decide and build the ships they believe they need. The civilian masterminding of this over the last 27 years has led to such things as the 1052 class as well as no modern gas turbine ships in the combatant fleet. The Navy has the greatest background of knowledge in this area and should be allowed to do what is required.

Our approach with the other components of maritime power is separate in a way from the tasks of the Navy but is part of the total approach. The President's approach to revitalize our Merchant Marine really has the chance to succeed. Construction subsidies as well as operational ones have the ability to again make us competitive. The fact that even a Vietnam conflict has been sustained by the U.S. flag merchant fleet carrying 98 percent of the material and over two thirds of the military personnel has not really penetrated to the average American. These old ships shortly will pass from the scene. The picture on the commercial and economic side is just as dim. We must proceed to build and operate a modern merchant fleet.

Our scientific and oceanographic programs have been centralized, as a result of the Marine Resources and Engineering Development Act which was Public Law 89-454 passed by the 89th Congress in June 1966. The establishment of a National Council on Marine Resources and Engineering, in the Executive Office of the President, has strengthened our National Effort in this field.

The realities of the tasks in the maritime area in the years to come will become very apparent in the unceasing struggle in the world. The ability to do the tasks of deterrent, sea control and the projection of power plus the overseas presence role will be required if we are to effectively perform our mission. The tools will change as our technology advanced, but the overall requirements for the capabilities will remain. Seapower still does count. It is no longer the final arbiter of relations between nations, but is of such vital importance that no major country can afford to leave command of any important ocean in the hands of a potential adversary. This is the unending struggle, and it explains why the Russians have made such efforts in the last ten years to match our naval strength. So we must approach our problem of modernizing the Navy with a clear idea of the objectives of this task. There is no question that a total approach must be made by the U.S. in exploiting and development of its total maritime power. If we are to survive as a world power in the last third of the twentieth century we had better get about our task.

NOTES

1. Arnold Kuzmack, *Naval Force Levels and Modernization* (Washington, Brookings, 1971), pp. 8-9.

2 Naval Arms Races: Functional or Symbolic?

George H. Quester

Six or eight years ago, it was generally agreed that the United States together with its allies possessed an overwhelming superiority in the kinds of naval force which had been used in World War II. It was also generally thought that such force would be of limited and diminishing importance for any political and military interactions likely in the future. Such strength, to be sure, had been of immense importance in blockading or quarantining Cuba in the missile crisis, and it had facilitated interventions by United States forces in the Dominican Republic, in Southeast Asia, and in the Middle East. Yet the mere absence of a naval challenge from the Soviet bloc, and the enormous destructive force of the nuclear weapons in the air and land forces, suggested more nostalgia than real military function in the Navy's conventional firepower.

All of such reasoning has now come under challenge, if only because the Soviet Union has chosen to invest substantially in more modern versions of the very classes of ships that were being pooh-poohed, and to deploy such ships into the Mediterranean Sea, the Pacific and Indian Oceans, and at a token level, even into the Caribbean.[1] Even if the Soviet Navy has not really grown in tonnage, it has indeed developed a capability for operating at much longer distances from its home ports.

Surface Navies

A stream of excited statements has thus emerged from
various Western sources, alarmed about the substantial
increase of Soviet naval power along N.A.T.O.'s "southern
flank." The Soviet Navy, to be sure, has not yet invested in
aircraft carriers comparable to those of the U.S., British or
French navies, but it has deployed two helicopter carriers,
and even these represent a noticeable expansion from what
had been a zero base. More attention is devoted to destroyers
and cruisers, most of them fitted with surface-to-surface
missiles, an area of weaponry in which the West had lagged
until recently. When aircraft based on friendly shore bases on
the Mediterranean coasts are totalled in, the firepower of the
Soviet fleet in the area does not exceed that of the U.S. Sixth
fleet, but the comparison is not ludicrous anymore. Some
analysts have noted that even the Italian fleet, also a part of
N.A.T.O., after all, exceeds the largest tonnage of Soviet
ships yet to enter the Mediterranean; but these ships, like
those of the United States, are older than their Soviet
opposite numbers, and not as well equipped in surface-to-
surface missile firepower.

Yet all such comparisons of tonnage or conventional
firepower, as if World War II were to be fought over again,
may miss the point. The U.S. Sixth Fleet carries nuclear
weapons, and so presumably does the Soviet Mediterranean
fleet. It is thus very unlikely that a naval war could be fought
in the area without such weapons coming into use, even
leaving aside the tactical nuclear weapons that could be
delivered by the aircraft of either side based within flying
range of the Mediterranean. To a lesser extent, the same
likelihood of nuclear escalation would seem to hover over
naval engagements in the Indian Ocean, or the Atlantic or
Pacific.

The shadow of possible or probable use of nuclears thus at
least alters much of naval strategy as it would have been
applied in 1944. Large concentrated convoys would be

terribly inviting targets for the use of a single bomb, and thus might have to be foregone. Concentrations for amphibious assaults such as the storming of Normandy would similarly be too tempting as targets for tactical nuclear weapons. If the Lanchester Square Law ever applied to naval operations (suggesting that concentrations of firepower are much more effective than dispersed units, so that one should "never divide the fleet"), the nuclear weapon seems to upset this, serving as a "great equalizer" which could destroy any fleet of cruisers that was collected to concentrate its firepower. Some interesting speculation has come forth on whether nuclear weapons will assist one side or the other in the murkier realm of submarine and anti-submarine warfare. Nuclear warheads on torpedoes might, as suggested above, make convoys easily destructible for any U-boat, but perhaps the same warheads will be harnessable as very effective depth charges, making it much easier for a surface vessel to destroy a submarine.

Yet any such revision of comparative firepower figures, or of naval strategy, again may miss the point of what naval confrontations are all about in the nuclear age. To use nuclear weapons at sea, or to engage in combat operations which would probably risk their use, would be to upset a very serious nuclear allergy, with risks of fallout and destruction in the countries abutting the seas involved, with great risks of escalation to World War III. Nuclear naval warfare is unlikely to happen precisely because it is so dangerous, and naval warfare is unlikely to happen because it is so likely to become nuclear.

Given all the attention that has been paid to "limited war" in the last fifteen years, this might seem excessively pessimistic on the risks of escalation in a war involving ships carrying nuclear weapons. We do not even know as a matter of public record which ships of the nuclear powers carry such weapons on board; for example, Russian ships in the Mediterranean, or U.S. ships shelling the coast of North Vietnam? As the retaliatory missile forces of each side have become more secure against preemptive attack in the 1960s, some of the stimulus to such an escalation has been reduced in any event, as "shoot first, ask questions later" is no longer a necessary policy for the strategic forces of either side.

Yet escalation threshholds are in the eyes of the beholder, and the risk of an unauthorized firing of a nuclear weapon still has some extra inhibiting effect wherever such weapons are known to be deployed. Could the Russians really be sure that some Artillery Captain would not fire off a tactical nuclear warhead in defense of Bavaria, even if the President of the United States had forbidden it? The weapons are deployed far enough forward to pose the risk. If an attempt were made to sink an American ship carrying nuclear warheads, could the opposing side really be sure that such warheads would not come into use? The world has seen a surprising degree of conventional-war exemption for military forces which are nuclear equipped. Is it the defenses of the U.S. carriers in the South China Sea that protect them against surface-to-surface missile attack, or is it their "trip-wire" role, which perhaps dissuades the Russians from ever equipping Hanoi with this ability to sink such ships?

Even if nuclear weapons were not based on board the aircraft carriers of the U.S. Navy, thus making these ships trip wires as much as bases of military power, the mere size of such ships, their large crews and enormous financial costs, will make it unthinkable that an enemy could be allowed to sink one without the most serious risk of escalation to serious warfare. Because nuclear war between the U.S. and Soviet Union is always a background possibility, it is thus not even crucial for such atomic weapons to be physically present in the area, to inhibit the naval operations which are so often discussed. The simple fact that large ships rather than small are required to handle airplanes ties the commitment of the United States together into a bundle that cannot be ignored.

The military strength of a naval force thus cannot so easily be fractionated when it is embarked at sea. When it is disembarked, when Marines are landed, or airplanes are launched on missions over some country, the American presence conversely can be much more fractionated. Individual planes can be shot down by some hostile protégé of the U.S.S.R.; individual soldiers or Marines can be killed, without a risk of World War III; it may even be Russians manning the surface-to-air missile (S.A.M.) sites that bring individual planes down. Back on the large ships that carry them, still escorted by destroyers and cruisers at close range, the planes and ships become part of a package that sinks or swims as a unit, so that few can dare try to sink it.

The naval forces of the nuclear powers must therefore be analyzed in terms of two distinct forms of impact. They may still be very functional for the military and political futures of the countries along whose shores they sail; they constitute a mobile military base which requires little or no acquiescence from the countries exposed, or from their neighbors. Fleets can serve as a mobile artillery platform, capable of raining down shells in support of one faction or another in any civil war or international war. They serve as floating airbases which can supply the same kind of support further inland. They represent transient barracks, housing infantry which could storm ashore to help one side win a battle; they finally at least provide a floating magazine of military equipment, which might more handsomely equip any local army the fleet is supporting. Even the possibility of such intervention imposes a shadow of external influence over the countries involved.

At sea, at the same moment, the principal impact of navies will have become symbolic rather than functional, a trip wire of national commitment which perhaps may be interposed to prevent the onshore use of the other side's fleet, but is unlikely to be used militarily in attacking that force. The significance of a fleet deployed into any sea may thus lie less in the number of guns or sea-to-sea missiles it carries than in the number of ships which simply might be maneuvered into the other fleet's way, always carrying the symbolic threat of escalation to a much greater conflict. For the symbolic purpose noted here, the Russians perhaps could just as easily have deployed all their schoolchildren on board cruise liners in the Mediterranean, in a "campus afloat" program which just happened to get in the way when American carriers were meaning to launch air patrols over the Middle East, or when an American attack transport was planning to enter a harbor. To risk the accidental sinking of such a cruise ship might pose the same symbolic dangers of severe Russian reaction as in a collision with a Russian cruiser or helicopter carrier.

Of course, the sanctuary for big ships of big powers at sea can be overstated. It is not as secure, for example, as the sanctuary accorded the cities of the super-powers; an American aircraft carrier might thus be attacked even when the U.S.S.R. remained unwilling to start a missile war exchanging city for city. Yet some of the symbolic sanctuary covers the ships also, if only because the risk then of further escalation to a city-destroying World War III could never be so totally ruled out.

The cruise ships carrying Russian schoolchildren are also not quite as analogous to contemporary fleets as is the U.S. garrison in West Berlin. We at least pretend that we are fixated on the fighting ability of the garrison and the carriers. The garrison maneuvers with its tanks within the confines of Berlin and tries to keep up its marksmanship. Pretending to be expecting combat makes the "trip wire" all the more effective, since tokens of commitment come to be less credible once they are openly discussed as such. Yet if Presidents and Generals must pretend that the West Berlin garrison is intended for the defense of the city, we know in reality that it serves mainly as a symbol to activate other retaliation in the contingency of a Russian attack. The deterrent backing the U.S. Navy similarly functions more reliably if Presidents and Admirals at least pretend that they are contemplating major naval battles with the Russians, while they may really be reminding Moscow of a more horrendous threat.

Are aircraft carriers of the U.S. Navy really as sinkable,

therefore, as this analysis suggests, remaining afloat mainly due to Russian restraint in fear of escalation and retaliation? American naval officers of course are prone to deny this vulnerability, just as they are prone to support their requests for equipment, and alarm at Russian acquisitions, in terms of a war as it would have been fought in 1944. To pretend that weapons will be functional, and will be used functionally rather than symbolically, is a normal part of the international bargaining and deterrence process, and of the domestic scramble for funds. Yet Russian reconnaissance aircraft regularly find and overfly U.S. aircraft carriers to suggest the carriers' vulnerability. American aircraft are conversely dispatched to meet and escort in the reconnaissance bombers, perhaps to show that they would never have reached the carrier in a war situation to complete their attack.[2] News reports indicate, however, that some of the reconnaissance bombers occasionally reach their "target" before being met; the use of nuclear air-to-surface missiles, moreover, would very plausibly reduce the survivability of targets as large as naval ships.

In political crises of the future, the first fleet to reach the port of the country undergoing turmoil may thus be very significant. This will not be because there are so many operational military advantages to being first into port, for there indeed may be more disadvantages than advantages within the confines of a harbor. Rather, being first into port can confront the opposing navy with the choice of staying away or risking the symbolic and real collisions which might escalate to full-scale hostilities. There will always be a risk of escalation to a World War III in such games of political pressure, but it will be far more probable that an aversion to World War III will cause the slower side to concede the local political issue by default, to the "first fleet into port." The number of ships on each side thus retains importance, if only because the side with the most ships can interpose the most trip wires in the most places, winning the most political contests by default. We have not been arguing here that no "naval arms race" is being run; rather the race is under way, but on a different racetrack from the one usually described.

As numbers still make a difference, so does location. Even when warships were being deployed in genuine expectation of combat, prior to the nuclear era, states never had total "control of the seas," in that they could muster a numerical superiority everywhere. Ever since 1945, the Russians presumably had a likely superiority in the Black Sea, and the U.S. will probably always have one within the Caribbean. The importance of geography and location is illustrated by the obvious Russian concern to get the Suez Canal opened, since its closing prevents the Soviet Navy from extending its competition with Western fleets easily from the Mediterranean into the Red Sea.

The comparative size of two fleets in any particular sea, e.g. the Mediterranean, is thus significant for a series of reasons. First and foremost, the "Naval Ordinance" remains important as long as regimes along the banks of the sea regard it as important. Much of what happens in politics amounts to self-confirming propositions, and the governments on each side have to be aware of this. Second, the larger the number of ships deployed by any particular navy, the better its chance of reaching some crisis point in time to effect the political outcome, by landing marines, supplying air cover, etc. Third, the larger the number of ships on the other side, the better its chance of blocking and non-violently interfering with such operations. Finally, if a naval war were still to come, despite all the risks of further escalation, the larger navy would probably suffer fewer losses than the smaller. It is being argued here that the most important functions of navies now will rest within the first three categories, rather than the final category of actual combat. The use of navy may thus be primarily to get into another navy's way, not to shoot at it or sink it, but to block it so that fears of shootings and sinkings will divert it from its chosen course.

Some of this purpose may be linked to the tests of resolve that have occurred regularly between ships of the two fleets in the years since World War II, as Soviet destroyers have gotten in the way of American or British aircraft carriers, as American and Soviet ships have almost literally played games of "chicken" which scrape the paint, or more, off one of the ships. Some of such incidents may simply reflect the personal machismo of the naval commanders involved; at other times, it may have been the result of genuine confusions and differences about the laws of the sea, with each side resenting a possibly high-handed redefinition of the rules by the adversary. Some of this may have thus been frivolous and purposeless. Yet it is also a symptom of the navies' recognition that they may have to win political battles in the future without ever activating their weapons.

Lest the practice of such tactics get out of hand in some wider process of escalation or simple misunderstanding, an agreement was initiated during President Nixon's summit visit to Moscow by which each side in effect promised to desist from some of the "shouldering" and "bumping" practices of the past. Yet it is hardly clear that this agreement would be repeated on both sides if a serious crisis got under way. It might be bad "arms control" to require that the Russian and American fleets be left with only two choices, full respect for the rules of the sea or all-out combat.

The symbolic significance of navies (at sea) and the functional significance of navies (on land) are of course not totally separable. If a Russian destroyer sailed into the path of American aircraft carriers while they were attempting to launch an aircraft mission, they would in effect be applying the symbolic impact to interfere with the functional. An attempt to use ships close in to shore might similarly strain the distinction thus far drawn. Many of the ships used here might be smaller (landing craft, mine sweepers, ships the size of the Pueblo, etc.) and thus reflect less of any total national commitment to avenge their loss. The range of coastal artillery is not unlimited, and the sense of aggression in the sinking of such a ship would thus be less aggravated. Minefields also can be left in place in such coastal waters, which leaves the "last clear choice" to the ships which get involved, and with the responsibility for any sinkings.

Whether this coastal zone extends to three miles or twelve miles may become a function of changing notions of international law. It is interesting to note Communist Chinese behavior in 1958 during the shelling of Quemoy, when the United States decided in a very limited fashion to demonstrate its resolve to keep the island replenished with supplies. American L.S.T. ships, not the largest in any navy, but not the smallest either, carried the supplies to within three miles of Quemoy, whereupon smaller amphibious-tracked vehicles of the Chinese Nationalist armed forces went the rest of the way to the island. Confronted by this challenge, the Chinese Communists did not shell the American vessels, but only the Nationalist vehicles.[3]

Larger American ships regularly come close to the Chinese border by sailing in and out of Hong Kong. While Peking has occasionally protested, it has never interfered with these ships. The seizure of the Pueblo off the coast of North Korea, probably outside the 12-mile limit, was facilitated by the small size of the ship, physically as well as symbolically. Indeed if the ship had not had a name, but only a designation such as PC-131, the American reaction would probably have been less severe.

The Tonkin Gulf incident which led to the first American air attacks against North Vietnam have been much debated on whether Hanoi's naval craft indeed attacked the American destroyers as much as the U.S. official account claimed. Yet the incident serves admirably as an illustration of that symbolic impact of naval presence which persists separately from the functional impact. Had Hanoi's agents merely attacked a group of American advisers within South Vietnam, it would have been difficult, albeit not impossible, to have mobilized American opinion in support of such retaliation. A destroyer is still a big enough ship, however, so that the mere prospect of its sinking can seem to call for retaliation of a qualitatively enhanced sort. The destroyer, unlike landing craft or coastal vessels, is at least an "ocean-going" warship, suggesting a discreteness and apartness which an enemy had to go out of its way to violate. It allegedly stayed out to sea far enough (certainly beyond the 12-mile limit) so that the enemy could leave it alone.[4] Whether Hanoi thus committed a blunder in giving President Johnson an excuse for air strikes, or simply was the victim of a manufactured incident serving the same purpose, Tonkin Gulf shows the quantum jump one may be making in threatening to sink a ship of a power like the United States.

It also might be recalled that an American aircraft carrier was scheduled to pass through the Suez Canal from the Mediterranean Sea on its way to Southeast Asia, just after the Egyptians had ousted the U.N.E.F. and announced the closing of the straits of Tiran, but prior to the outbreak of fighting between Israel and Egypt in 1967.[5] The carrier hesitated under orders from Washington, but then passed through the Canal without incident. One wonders whether either Israel or Egypt could have dared commencing hostilities while the huge American naval vessel was in the Canal; could the United States have remained as uninvolved if the same fate had befallen a carrier as befell the merchant ships which did become trapped in the Canal?

Submarine Warfare

Some attention must also be paid to underwater ships of the various navies, ships which can similarly be evaluated for their symbolic as opposed to functional uses. Careful distinction must be drawn between tactical submarines and those which fire nuclear-warheaded missiles at cities of the opposing side; the kinds of games one could play with the ordinary submarine, armed only with torpedoes, would be vastly more hazardous if attempted with submarines of the Polaris type.

Submarines of any sort are of course less visible, and

therefore commit less of nations' prestige by their presence. Operating in three dimensions, they do not normally occupy part of the scarce and crowded surface of the sea, getting in other ships' way, or being gotten in the way of.

Yet some symbolic games can be played whenever the submarine's invisibility is compromised. In terms of symbolism, it may be possible for the surface ships of another power to follow and hound the submarine, simply with a view to being present when it must come to the surface, thus as a humiliating demonstration of that submarine's vulnerability. If a submarine has not been clearly identified, moreover, another nation might even go so far as to attempt to sink it by use of depth charges; even in ordinary peacetime, such an act may not seem so untoward or threatening of World War III, if a state claims simply to be defending its territorial waters. The submarine is normally not as large as a surface ship, and if it is sunk, the facts of the sinking will be far less certain or humiliating than even with a destroyer escort of similar displacement. The Swedish Navy thus would not dare sink a Russian surface vessel, for fear that Moscow could not bear such an obvious affront without some serious countermove; but it could drop depth charges on a (presumably Soviet) submarine which appreared near maneuvers within Sweden's territorial waters; accounts differ on whether the mysterious submarine suffered any damage, or indeed survived.[6]

The functional role of tactical submarines is clearly more limited than that of surface ships. Submarines cannot participate effectively in the land battles of this age, except perhaps by delivering supplies or crucial leaders to insurgencies in the Philippines, etc. In a limited war situation, such submarines might also attempt to harass commerce and supply ships of the enemy as during World War II. Yet the very nature of such torpedo attacks has all the risks of escalation noted earlier in any sinking of sizable surface ships. Because navies are so symbolic, as well as functional, submarines probably will be unable to fulfill their functional role, since so little of it extends into the land area where combat is more tolerable.

It thus comes as no surprise that submarines have not conducted any offensive operations since World War II. Russian and Chinese submarines did not intervene during the Korean War, and have played no role in the Vietnam conflict. Russian submarines have been increasingly present in the Mediterranean since the 1967 war between Israel and the Arab states, and were symbolically deployed along the supply routes to Cuba during the 1962 Cuban missile crisis, but made no further move. The symbolic "counterattack" on such submarines by United States naval vessels in 1962 indeed consisted simply of a continuous pursuit until the submarines involved, diesel-powered rather than nuclear-powered, had to rise to the surface.[7] Since a number of the submarines involved experienced breakdowns and operating difficulties, the U.S. Navy gleefully could bring back its photographs of these ships being taken ignominiously in tow by Russian surface ships.

A very different kind of submarine is involved once one has introduced ballistic or cruise missiles with nuclear warheads, capable of striking at the home cities of the major powers. At first glance, one might feel it imperative that such submarines be kept far from any active, or even potentially active, theater of conventional naval operations. It would be equally imperative to equip such submarines with every modern feature that could contribute to their immunity from detection. If such a submarine were to be harassed, or sunk, or involved in a collision, or even were cut off entirely from communications with its home base, the ensuing risks of an accidental launching of World War III might seem unbearable. Stategic-missile-firing submarines after all are not merely trip wires; they are the nuclear "gun" itself.

Yet as with the other games of chicken outlined above, precisely such considerations might lead one or both navies to bring its Polaris-type submarines "visibly" into a sensitive area, on the expectation that this would force the other side to back off. Such confrontations could also bring competing surface fleets into the cruising space of the missile-firing submarines, perhaps to deploy anti-submarine warfare (A.S.W.) gear. Investment in missile-carrying surface ships, either clearly labelled as warships or configured to resemble freighters, has, moreover, been under consideration at least as long as the Multi-Lateral Force (M.L.F.) proposal. Such ships might reinforce the assured second-strike deterrent of either side, but would obviously increase the likelihood of a symbolic game of "chicken" between nuclear navies trying to elbow each other out of an ocean area.

If the two super-powers were to place strategic stability and the prevention of World War III ahead of all other goals, they would never play such games with Polaris-equipped submarines or surface ships. They would also presumably avoid extensive research in A.S.W. detection techniques, and perhaps would guarantee each other sanctuary zones within which missile-firing submarines might be securely deployed. But with this high a priority for peace and stability, the two super-powers would probably also not have been playing "chicken" with conventional surface vessels in recent years.

Yet the symbolic game will most presumably not be as extensively played with strategic or other submarines, if only because of the continuing relative invisibility of submarines, rather than any prudential caution in Washington or Moscow. Invisible ships simply do not lend themselves as much to symbolic actions of interposition. Questions of political symbolism mesh here with payoffs for arms control. For purposes of the overall strategic balance, it is highly fortunate that strategic-missile submarines remain undetectable; this avoids the risk of preemptive strikes, and of preemptive logic, the kind of logic that could produce a World War III no one wanted. For purposes of avoiding "naval engagements" short of World War III, it will similarly be fortunate if the submarine remains invisible, neither a vehicle nor a target for symbolic challenge. Invisibility has always been an important combat attribute for the submarine, while it has been quite unimportant for the battleship or cruiser or aircraft carrier. At times, this invisibility has been compromised by break-throughs in A.S.W. techniques; yet at other points the march of technology has served to reinforce this invisibility once again.

There continues to be some ambivalence in American thinking with reference to Soviet investment in submarine-based missiles systems. In terms of arms control principles, such investments might long have been acceptable or even welcome in Washington, not meriting any challenge by A.S.W., because the assured deterrent thus provided the Russian leaders should presumably ease tensions and reduce risks of stampedes into preemptive war. Yet each expansion of the Soviet missile-submarine force also has produced expressions of alarm in the U.S. Navy and in Congress. The U.S.S.R. has been warned away from the use of Cuban bases to refuel such submarines and to extend their time on station in the Atlantic.

For a time it seemed that the U.S.S.R. was moving quite slowly into such submarine deployments, even when the United States was procuring 41 of such submarines carrying 16 missiles each. The latter 1960s saw the U.S.S.R. expanding its land-based missile force, while still lagging in the submarine category. Only in the last four years did the U.S.S.R. then finally place emphasis on the submarine-based strategic force, ending with 62 submarines with a total of 950 missiles, under the freeze on offensive missiles specified in the 1972 Strategic Arms Limitation (S.A.L.T.) agreements.

The world may take interest in the relative strengths of these two naval forces, in terms of numbers of submarines or of missiles, and draw some real or false conclusions on whether the Russians are now "ahead." Yet if this is part of the "naval arms race," it is not fully a part, because the two forces of missile submarines are hardly likely to confront, block, or bump each other in the manner of surface navies, or even to get into competition on how many port visits they can generate.

For these submarines to become a real part of our "naval arms race," a great breakthrough would have to be made on each side in anti-submarine warfare techniques, sufficient to make the location of these ships detectable, with an investment in "killer submarines" or surface A.S.W. ships to threaten their destruction. There is reason to hope that this can be avoided.

Perhaps nature will be so kind as always to provide more ways to conceal a submarine than ways to detect its location. Perhaps nature will not be so kind, but a conscious self-discipline can be imposed on the two military-industrial complexes involved, so that the research carried forward on undersea warfare would stress the protection and conceal- ment of submarines, rather than the detection and destruc- tion implicit in the initials A.S.W., *anti*-submarine warfare. Could not the watchword on naval research, as well as naval deployments, be: "What protects the submarine is good for peace, what threatens the submarine is bad"? Yet such self-discipline may be more easily spoken than implemented.

How does one instruct trained scientists to explore undersea warfare, but only to do research on possibilities which would protect missile-carrying submarines rather than endanger them? Any good physicist would respond that a true researcher could not function in such an intellectual straightjacket. The response would further elaborate that possible anti-submarine techniques have to be explored, if only to assure one's self that they will not succeed, or to establish the new submarine-protecting techniques that have to be developed in order to counter such threats. Unless we do all we can to develop anti-submarine weapons, the argument goes, we cannot be sure that we are doing all we can to develop pro-submarine weapons.

As an aside, it is interesting to note that similar philosophi- cal paradoxes have been presented for the detection of unauthorized diversions of plutonium from peaceful nuclear projects to bomb production. The technology of monitoring here confronts an obverse technology of concealment and dissimulation. German physicists were entrusted by their government with the task of devising foolproof and automated techniques for monitoring plutonium flows, techniques which would not have to disrupt the operations of nuclear reactors producing electricity. In the process of the exercise, the same scientists took turns playing "hiders" and "finders," in the process developing a host of new techniques for concealing the diversion of plutonium, and (hopefully) another host of techniques for detecting diversions.

There is something to be said for exploring both ends of the technological race, to be sure that one is accomplishing something on the side of augmenting the defense. Yet all of what has just been said might simply become a rationalization among scientists for blindly pursuing whatever avenues technology will offer. Surely this is the most personally interesting approach to research on any technology, including military technology. It is also the most profitable, generating the most employment. Yet if nature is so perverse as to offer more breakthroughs for offensive than for defensive techniques, peace will not be secure.

Some hopeful possibilities remain. It is possible that the most effective modes of submarine detection will have to depend on "active" rather than "passive" systems, i.e. systems which send out large quantities of sound somehow to be reflected off submarines to betray their positions. If the major powers wished to steer clear of these systems, it then might be relatively easier to police agreements that such A.S.W. equipment not be tested, installed, or operated, since the other side could surely detect the sounds of any such A.S.W. system. When each side can assure itself of the compliance of the other, agreements are always easier to negotiate and to maintain. When this is not the case, troubles can arise.

It may also be that some of our alarm about the likely success of A.S.W. research is premature. Much of such research is intended for the protection of merchant ships against such submarine attacks as those of German U-boats in

World War II, rather than for preemptive attacks against Soviet missile-carrying submarines. While breakthroughs on one A.S.W. function are potentially applicable to the others, the difficulty of the task is obviously far greater in the case of missile-carrying submarines, which try as much as possible to conceal their position. In the case of a convoy of merchantmen, the enemy submarine betrays its general location in the process of commencing its attack, and thus substantially narrows the portion of ocean in which the A.S.W. effort must be conducted.

Submarines in general will thus continue to lend themselves less to sea confrontations than do surface ships, and therefore figure less in the Soviet-U.S. naval "race." They will appear symbolically mainly when they elect to compromise their own visibility, as when shadowing a convoy, or as in the Cuban case, attempting to be seen as an escort for a convoy. Strategic missile submarines may elect to eschew even this much visibility, this much of a symbolic role. If the two super-powers do not make a fetish of compromising the security of each other's submarine-based missile forces, this exemption of missile-carrying submarines from the navy vs. navy confrontation may be easy enough to maintain.

Merchant Fleets

Apart from expansions of the Soviet Navy, considerable concern has been expressed in the West about the growth of the Soviet Merchant Marine. As with other commercial enterprises in the U.S.S.R., the merchant fleet is hardly a "private-sector" venture, but clearly interpretable as an arm of Soviet state policy.[8]

In sheer tonnage, the Russian merchant fleet has grown from about 2 million tons in 1950 and 3.4 million in 1960, to almost 15 million tons in 1970, comparable to a U.S. merchant fleet nominally today at about 19 million. As is the case with the Soviet Navy, having begun later, the Russian merchant marine is equipped with speedier and more modern vessels, while a certain fraction of western merchant shipping must always verge on the obsolete.

Soviet shipping services have hardly been constricted to intercoastal Soviet domestic shipping, or even to commerce with satellites. Rather the Soviet merchant force has begun to offer its services on a number of the classic trade routes of the non-Communist world, and often at rates substantially lower than those set by the "Conferences" which govern most of the free world shippers on such routes.

The sheer tonnages figures can be misleading if seen simply in a U.S.-Soviet comparison, of course. A fair amount of American-owned shipping is registered under the "flags of convenience" of Panama and Liberia. The national tonnages of Japan, Great Britain and Norway, formal treaty allies of the United States, each exceed the figures for either the United States or the Soviet Union. American Admirals perhaps like to cite the specific U.S.-Russian comparison for its impact in shocking their public. Yet the relevant issue is obviously not parity in shipping tonnage, but the very genuinely remarkable expansion of the Soviet figure. The Soviet expansion of more than 300% since 1960 is rivalled only by the growth in Japanese merchant shipping over the same time.

How much should the free world feel threatened by a Soviet venture into what is clearly a useful and peaceful pursuit on the high seas? If goods need to be delivered, how can a believer in free trade and competition be concerned about one more competitor entering the fray?

There are military fears, of course. Each Russian merchant vessel will presumably be at the disposal of the Russian navy, and could be used as a supply vessel to keep warships on the high seas for longer periods of time. As has been historically demonstrated in the American experience, such vessels can be used also to carry troops on their way to amphibious invasions. It is even conceivable that merchantmen can be equipped with guns or surface-to-surface rockets to serve as commerce raiders or *bona fide* warships in the event of hostilities. Lacking even the most rudimentary armor, however, it is questionable how long such ships could hold up as participants in some large-scale but limited sea war.

A little away from the realm of military operations, the Soviet merchant fleet can "show the flag" in the same way as the Soviet Navy. A visible commercial presence can well amount to a more effective political presence; if "courtesy calls" have long been seen as a way to impress local rulers or citizenries favorably, the appearance of sleek modern cargo ships can do the same. On all such trade questions, the hope has been expressed on each side again and again that full commercial exchanges will lead to better understanding and closer relations between countries. Yet on each side a parallel fear has also been expressed that trade will ease hostility unevenly, perhaps reducing vigilance on our side, but not on theirs. Such fears, for example, were voiced in Poland when the first contacts with West German industrialists were opened. The same fear inhibits China from leaping to seek trade benefits. And in this case, it causes Western concern at the appearance of Soviet merchant vessels.

Such fears are not totally unreasonable. In effect, the country that gets to play the role of merchant shipper gets to enter the other's home ports, while keeping such alien influences away from its own ports. Goods shipped from Australia to Russia might thus well be lured into Soviet freighters, to achieve a symbolic impact in Australian ports, and to avoid such impact in Soviet ports. Yet one can easily exaggerate how much difference this makes. We have become accustomed to the existence of Aeroflot offices in New York and London; once the novelty of such presence is behind us, the political impact becomes secondary.

Moving away from symbolism, one might express a more real fear that repeated use of cheaper Soviet shipping services within the free world will cause Western shipping capabilities to atrophy, with the result that the Soviet might suddenly deny such services during a crisis, imposing serious pressures on the Western position. The mere knowledge that a loss of regular shipping services will follow from the worsening of a crisis may inhibit Western leaderships from being resolute in such a period.

Yet the "dependence effect" in the growth of a Soviet merchant capability may not be as one-sided as suggested above. In the event of an all-out war, the Russians surely would not mind the loss of foreign-currency income in having to withdraw their freighters from routes and patronage that had been developed. Yet for more limited war, any prolonged cutoff of such revenues, after the Soviet economy has grown accustomed to them, will seem like a substantial sacrifice. If Australians come to depend on Russian freighter services, the Russians may have a dependency in reverse.

Some of the new Russian carrying capacity, moreover, tends to get tied up by Soviet political decisions to extend logistics support to distant enclaves of the Socialist bloc. The delivery of essential goods to Cuba has thus committed a considerable part of the expansion of Soviet capacity. Similar commitments have been entailed by the delivery of war material to Haiphong in support of North Vietnam and the insurrection in South Vietnam. If Chile were to become more dependent on aid from, and trade with, the Soviet Union (one of the principal fears of the free world leadership at the moment), it will at least have the incidental effect of forcing the Russians to tie up some more of their tonnage in one more new "lifeline."

This kind of reasonsing can be too optimistic from the Western point of view. Losing Chile or South Vietnam or Cuba to the socialist camp is a real loss from a free world calculus. Yet a few of such losses may be inevitable. The above argument is meant merely to remind us that few clouds are totally lacking in silver linings. The Russians cannot have their cake and eat it; if they become enmeshed in trying to support and hold ideological outposts far across the seas, their merchant marine may be taxed at close to its capacity.

One might thus be tempted to see no political effect at all

in any increases in Soviet merchant tonnage, as long as the increases are consumed in overseas support of Soviet political causes. Yet there are some important effects even if the net of available and surplus Russian tonnage stays about the same. The more the Russians sail the seas, whether doing the free world's work or the socialist bloc's work, the more the U.S.S.R. accumulates a vested interest in keeping the seas peaceful. At the very least, the investment in freighted tonnage puts a significant slice of Soviet assets into a very fragile form; ships can easily be sunk if wars break out, even if limited wars break out, unless rules are written and enforced to protect this kind of investment.

It has long been assumed that the U.S.S.R. would have a vested interest in submarine warfare in the future, even under some conditions of large-scale limited war. Perhaps the entire operation might yet be conducted clandestinely and anonymously, as various submarines and their crews "volunteer" for duty in the Mediterranean or the Indian Ocean, or in the South China Sea; this could come on the pattern of Russian volunteers who fly jets in Nigeria or Egypt, or the Chinese volunteers who fought in Korea.

As noted, this form of war has not occurred in the past, even when unescorted merchant ships have carried U.S. war materials to Korea and Vietnam. The explanation of this in earlier periods may have been that the U.S. was in exchange offering non-symmetrical restraints on its own armed forces, for example, no bombings of Manchuria. More recently, the exchange counter might rather have been the safe passage of Polish and Russian ships to Haiphong, just as undisturbed as U.S. ships going to Saigon. Limited wars are thus all the more likely to stay limited as the potential zones of escalation become populated with fragile assets of all the sides. The more merchant ships at sea under Communist flag, up to a point, the less likely again is any escalation of warfare from land out to the sea.

One must ask at the end how much of this argument is supported or disproven by President Nixon's decision in 1972 to bomb the docks of Haiphong, and then to place mines in the harbor to prevent merchant ships from reaching North Vietnam. Does this not show that each side is less afraid of escalation in warfare at sea than has been indicated? Has the United States since 1965 perhaps learned how to sink Russian ships in ways which do not risk a war which would wipe out the world?

To begin, one should note that Nixon's action did indeed cause a great deal of domestic criticism as to its riskiness. While the stepped-up bombing of North Vietnam was incomparably more destructive to life, it was the interference with sea-lanes that fixated American news commentators, leading them to draw comparisons with the Cuban missile crisis, and its implicit risk of general war. Yet Nixon, by using a minefield, had indeed chosen the one form of naval warfare that was much less likely to pose risks of escalation in tests of resolve. The "last clear chance" of avoiding sinkings was thus left to the Russians, who elected not to lose their merchant ships. The minefield thus resembles the blocking function as much as the shooting function of navies. Speculation was advanced on whether the Soviet Navy would send mine-sweepers (in some ways the most innocuous of naval ships) to try to open Haiphong, and on what the U.S. response would be. "Background" leaks hinted that the U.S. would again not sink the Soviet vessels, but merely drop more mines to replace those the Russians had removed. Again this pays off the side with the most ships, but by the rules of diplomacy more than by the rules of Trafalgar or the Coral Sea.

Indeed, one should note how long Haiphong's docks went unbombed, and wonder whether this would have persisted if there had ever been a week in which no Soviet merchant ships were at dockside. Apart from the demands of logistic schedules, it would have been folly for Hanoi or Moscow to have ever left Haiphong empty of Russian ships in the years of aerial bombing by either the Johnson or Nixon administrations.

The Likelihood of War

What, therefore, are the prospects of war at sea? It has been contended here that we will see a complete exemption of the sea from warfare much more often than we have thought. The sea, in effect, may become everyman's sanctuary, even as one in 1967 almost ludicrously saw Communist merchant ships sailing past American aircraft carriers off the Vietnam coast, carriers that a few weeks later would be launching air-strikes directed at the very supplies the merchantmen had brought in.

Should World War III occur, of course, the seas by a certain definition would become very "active," as Polaris missile submarines of the U.S. Navy, and their opposite numbers, fired off missiles to retaliate against the cities of the two major powers.

Is there much prospect of any war in between, a World War II duplicate greater in scale than today's limited war, in which navies really are protected, but less than the all-out missile exchanges of World War III? The navies of the world obviously take such a scenario seriously enough so that it cannot be discounted. Yet the above arguments are meant to suggest that this scenario has now become a symbolic contruct not to be actualized, but to be exploited for the real political and strategic uses of navies.

In both warships and merchant ships, the Russians have thus entered the race. There is indeed a race, in that great superiorities for the U.S.S.R. in either category, even if only within a particular region, can alter the political results around the shores of that body of water. Yet Russian entry into the race has done more than make it more interesting for the spectators; in an important way, it has changed the rules, with the result that the entire exercise probably will be modified.

The bolstering of the Russian fleet therefore does not "check" the U.S. Navy in any ordinary sense of the term, for the American fleet was already checked by the importance both sides attach to avoiding World War III. Except for very unusual circumstances, Soviet warships and merchant ships have been able to deliver military equipment where they pleased.

NOTES

1. Apart from official statements of this sort by Admiral Zumwalt and other senior officers of the U.S. Navy, one can find an alarmed position expressed in various nongovernmental publications, for example, Norman Polmar, *Soviet Naval Power: Challenge for the 1970's* (New York, National Strategy Information Center, Inc., 1972), Robert G. Weinland, *The Changing Mission Structure of the Soviet Navy* (Arlington, Center for Naval Analyses, 1971); and Ernest M. Eller, *The Soviet Sea Challenge* (Chicago, Cowles, 1971).

2. See W. H. Honan, "Russian and American Pilots Play 'Chicken' " *The New York Times Magazine*, November 22, 1970, p. 25.

3. An analysis in depth of the naval aspects of the 1958 Quemoy crisis can be found in Jonathan Trumbull Howe, *Multicrises: Sea Power and Global Politics in the Missile Age* (Cambridge, MIT Press, 1971).

4. See Anthony Austin, *The President's War* (Philadelphia, Lippincott, 1971) for an extended reconstruction of the Tonkin Gulf incidents.

5. *The New York Times*, June 1, 1967, p. 1; June 2, 1967, p. 1.

6. *The New York Times*, October 6, 1966, p. 1; October 7, 1966, p. 3.

7. Elie Abel, *The Missile Crisis* (Philadelphia, Lippincott, 1966), p. 155.

8. A great deal of information on the non-military aspects of Soviet sea strength is to be found in Chapters 5 through 9 of David Fairhall, *Russian Sea Power* (Boston, Gambit, 1971).

3 Where Does the Navy Go from Here?

Arnold M. Kuzmack

It is not generally realized, least of all by the Navy itself, but the Navy has been doing fantastically well in the annual competition for budget dollars. At a time when the total defense budget has been going down, particularly after allowing for inflation and pay raises, the Navy budget has been increasing.[1]

Let us look at the figures. Consider, first, the period when the Vietnam war was building up to its peak, say, from Fiscal Year 1965 through Fiscal Year 1969. During this period, of course, the defense budget and the budgets of all the services rose substantially. However, when we remove those costs that would not have been incurred without the war (the "incremental cost" of the war) and consider only the non-Vietnam portions of the service budgets, an interesting pattern develops.

Table 1 shows these calculations, based on official Defense Department estimates of the incremental cost of the war in Vietnam. The figure shows that the Navy's outlays, excluding the Marine Corps, for its non-Vietnam forces increased 36 percent from Fiscal Year 1965 to Fiscal Year 1969, substantially more than the other services and substantially more than inflation and pay raises would account for (which would be about 19 percent). Thus, it is not true that spending for the Navy's non-Vietnam programs was reduced

43

below prewar levels during the Vietnam buildup. In fact, in real terms, it increased about 13 percent.

Table 1. Changes in Non-Vietnam Outlays by Service, Fiscal Years 1965-69 (in billions of current dollars)

	Fiscal Year 1965	Fiscal Year 1969		
		Vietnam	Non-Vietnam	Percent Change, Non-Vietnam
Army	$ 11.6	$ 11.3	$ 13.8	+19
Navy (Excluding	13.4	4.5	18.0	+34
Marine Corps)	(12.3)	(3.1)	(16.7)	(+36
Air Force	18.2	5.6	20.3	+12
Other	3.0	0.1	4.4	
Total	$ 46.2	$ 21.5	$ 56.5	+22

Looking at the period of "winding down" the war in Vietnam we find an equally striking pattern. Table 2 compares the total service budgets for Fiscal Years 1969 and 1973. Since we do not have official estimates of the cost of the war in Fiscal Year 1973, we cannot determine the non-Vietnam portion of the budget as we did for the earlier period. We do know, however, that the Navy has been ahead of the other services in Vietnamizing its operations in Vietnam, so the remaining incremental war costs in the Navy's Fiscal Year 1973 budget are quite small, probably less than one billion dollars.

Table 2 shows that, as the Navy's involvement in the Vietnam war has decreased, its total budget, excluding the Marine Corps, has increased 21 percent, while the budgets of the other services have decreased by substantial amounts. In his March 1971 testimony before the Senate Armed Services Committee, the Chief of Naval Operations, Admiral Elmo R.

Zumwalt, Jr., stated that the Navy's total obligational authority, not counting the Marine Corps, has increased 16 percent in real terms, after allowing for pay and price increases, between Fiscal Years 1964 and 1972. This figure understates the increase in the Navy budget for general purpose forces since funding for Navy strategic nuclear forces in Fiscal Year 1964 was very high because of the Polaris buildup.

Another conclusion can be drawn from this budget data. Since the budget for non-Vietnam naval forces increased, in real terms, during both the Vietnam war buildup and its winding down, there is no evidence, contrary to popular opinion, that the non-Vietnam portion of the Navy budget was reduced below prewar levels during the war.

In spite of the Navy's success in recent years in increasing its budget, there are several large clouds on the horizon. First, chances are that the Navy budget will not continue to increase, in real terms, as it has in the past. Continuing demands for new domestic programs make it likely that future defense budgets will be roughly constant in actual purchasing power. Admiral Zumwalt, in the testimony cited above, refers to "the austere outlook for the future" and emphasizes the need for reducing costs and increasing efficiency.

Table 2. Changes in Total Obligational Authority by Service, Fiscal Years 1969–73 (in millions of current dollars)[2]

	Fiscal Year 1969	Fiscal Year 1973 a/	Percent Change
Army	$ 26,180	$ 22,131	−15
Navy (excluding Marine Corps)	21,795 (19,120)	25,197 (23,096)	+16 (+21)
Air Force	26,126	23,549	−10
Other	4,642	8,769	
Total	$ 78,743	$ 79,646	+ 1

Second, a constant, or even moderately increased, real budget level will exacerbate the Navy's problems in trying to maintain its force levels and, at the same time, to modernize with highly sophisticated and expensive ships and aircraft. Consider, for example, the F-14 fighter. These aircraft will probably end up costing close to $20 million each, compared to $4 million (in today's prices) for the F-4s they are designed to replace.

Moreover, much the same story could be told about carriers, destroyers, submarines, antisubmarine warfare aircraft, and even support ships. Something will have to give—force levels, the rate of modernization, or the level of sophistication of new weapons systems. An omen for the future may be seen in the fact that the total planned buy of F-14s has been cut by more than half because of budget pressures.

Third, although the budget for general purpose naval forces has been going up, force levels have been going down. Between Fiscal Years 1964 and 1972, the number of active ships in the Navy has dropped from 917 to 658. During the same period, the number of aircraft carriers (CVA and CVS) decreased from 24 to 16, and the number of tactical air wings from 15 to 11.

Fourth, it is almost certain that carrier force levels will be reduced further over the next decade. The Navy now recognizes that it will be able to operate no more than twelve aircraft carriers by 1980 or so.

Navy Policy Problems

Since the Navy will be facing many hard choices over the next several years, a review of some of the basic assumptions of naval force planning seems to be in order. The discussion which follows will center around the role of the aircraft carrier since so much of the Navy's operations and its budget revolve around the carriers, their aircraft, and the forces and activities needed to defend and supply them.

Some historical perspective may be helpful. During World War II, we discovered that the aircraft carrier, rather than the battleship, was the key to defeating the enemy's surface fleet. In the aftermath of the war, the Navy found itself in the position where no potential enemy had a surface fleet close to ours in size or capability. The Navy, and particularly the aircraft carriers, had lost their principal mission. What was left was attack of land targets, and it required great effort for the Navy to establish this as one of its roles and missions. This change has substantial implications for our present subject. Most important, it makes carrier-based aircraft much more directly competitive with land-based tactical aircraft.

Aircraft Carrier Vulnerability

In the period since World War II, carriers have seen extensive combat in Korea and Vietnam. They have also been used on numerous occasions to "show the flag," provide air cover for evacuation of U.S. civilians, and the like. In none of these situations have the carriers been attacked by enemy submarines, aircraft, or surface ships. Although our experience has been in more limited wars, U.S. defense planning continues to be dominated, and rightfully so, by large-scale conventional wars in which the Soviet Union is heavily involved. It is, therefore, crucial that we evaluate the vulnerability of aircraft carriers in such wars, both in absolute terms and relative to land-based tactical aircraft which perform many of the same missions.

Perhaps the most important disadvantage of the aircraft carrier is its greater vulnerability to air and submarine attack than the land-based air wing. On the one hand, we have learned, in recent years, how to build aircraft shelters, how to protect fuel and maintenance facilities, and how to repair runways rapidly so that losses of aircraft on the ground to air attack using conventional weapons can be reduced to very low levels and disruption of operations can be minimized.

On the other hand, technology and other developments have made the aircraft carriers more, rather than less, vulnerable. First, the development by the Soviet Union of large air-to-surface missiles with conventional warheads and terminal guidance has made it possible to launch the equivalent of World War II *kamikaze* attacks without sacrificing pilots and aircraft.

Second, the development of satellite and long-range aircraft reconnaissance has radically reduced the ability of naval task forces to hide in the broad expanses of the oceans. Further, because the carriers will generally be involved in strikes against land targets, they will have to remain in the same general area for long periods of time to have much effect.

Third, these developments, as well as more sensitive submarine sonars and higher speed submarines, make it much easier for submarines to find and attack the carriers. Finally, both antiair and antisubmarine defense, while they can exact high attrition over a long period of time, remain so unreliable in any particular engagement that they cannot guarantee that no more than a few attackers will penetrate. As a result of these developments, a strong case can be made that the carriers could not remain on station in any situation where the Soviets could concentrate their land-based aircraft or their submarines against them.

Although it is difficult to sink an aircraft carrier—and no modern carrier (Essex class or later) was sunk in World War II—it is much easier to damage it enough that flight operations are impossible and to force it to return to port for an extended period of time for repairs. Particularly in the context of current planning for a conventional war with the Soviets lasting not much longer than 90 days, forcing the carrier out of action for three months or more is almost as good, from the enemy's point of view, as sinking it.

Table 3 summarizes the results of *kamikaze* attacks on U.S. carriers (CV's) in World War II. We can see that 40 percent of those taking one hit by a *kamikaze*, and all those taking more than one hit, were forced to return to port for repairs and that the improved damage control features of the Essex class and later carriers did not improve these figures.

Based on this evidence and making ample allowance for improvements in damage control since World War II, it appears that four or five hits by Soviet air-to-surface missiles would be enough to force a carrier to retire. Similarly, four or five hits on the carrier's screws by submarine-launched acoustic homing torpedoes can reasonably be expected to cause enough loss of propulsion power to make normal flight operations impossible and to reduce greatly the carriers's ability to avoid further damage.

Because there would only be a small number of carriers deployed, perhaps 10 or 12, and because only a few hits on each, whether by air-to-surface missiles or torpedoes, are needed to force it to retire, it seems unlikely that the carriers could be successfully defended against a concentrated attack by sophisticated land-based aircraft or submarines, regardless of foreseeable technological advances and regardless of the funds, within reasonable limits, devoted to defenses.

No feasible defense will be able to prevent four or five air-to-surface missiles or torpedoes from getting through and hitting the carrier. In fact, both air defenses and antisubmarine defenses typically have a low probability of success on any given engagement, so that, if the enemy needs only a few successful penetrations to accomplish his objective, he will be able to do so.

Some purely illustrative calculations using a simplified model will elucidate the structure of the problem. Suppose the Soviets are willing to lose 25 bombers, each capable of carrying one air-to-surface missile, and perhaps their fighter escorts, to disable a carrier. This is not unreasonable since the Soviets have some 300 air-to-surface missile-capable bombers in their naval aviation force. We assume the air-to-surface missiles have 80-percent reliability and, optimistically, that our fighter defense would have a 40-percent chance of shooting down a given bomber in a single engagement, that all of the bomber losses occur prior to air-to-surface missile launch, and that our surface-to-air missile systems have an 80-percent probability of shooting down an incoming air-to-surface missile.

With these assumptions, the bombers would get six hits on the carrier, more than enough to force it to retire.[3]

Table 3. Results of World War II Kamikaze Attacks on U.S. Aircraft Carriers[4]

Number of Hits	Number of Cases	Number Forced to Return to Port
All carriers[a]		
1	14	6
2 or more	4	4
Essex-class and later carriers only		
1	12	5
2 or more	3	3[5]

If we are less optimistic and assume that the fighters have a 20-percent kill probability and the missile defenses a 60-percent kill probability, then the expected number of hits would be 32, and a much smaller bomber force would be enough. Thus, even with optimistic assumptions, the carrier cannot be successfully defended against air attack. If the performance of defensive systems does not reach these high expectations, then the level of damage increases rapidly.

Of course, it is possible that some kind of electronic countermeasure—jamming, decoys, or others—will make the enemy air-to-surface missiles largely ineffective. While it appears sensible to devote substantial resources to developing and testing such devices, there is no way of knowing in advance of their use in actual combat whether the enemy has a successful counter-countermeasure. Electronic countermeasure devices, therefore, do not significantly increase our level of confidence that we could defend the carrier. Similar arguments to the above apply to defense of the carrier against concentrated submarine attack.

The conclusion of the above arguments is that we should not plan to use our aircraft carriers for strikes against land targets in situations where the Soviets can concentrate their land-based aircraft or their submarines against them. Thus, any use of the aircraft carriers for strikes against land targets, where they would be constrained by aircraft range to operate in a restricted area, seems unsustainable in any war in which the Soviets are fully involved.

On the other hand, the Soviets are the only potential enemy with the large and sophisticated air and submarine forces needed to mount an intensive attack on the aircraft carriers. China does not have such forces, nor do the smaller powers against whom we might intervene. Against such smaller forces, it should be possible to defend adequately the carriers although the possibility of substantial damage even here cannot be ruled out. Of course, there are many contingencies in which the carriers would be able to operate from sanctuaries.

Other Considerations

There is also a spectrum of other issues which have implications for carrier force levels. These deal with the particular advantages and disadvantages of putting larger or smaller portions of our tactical air forces on sea bases (carriers) rather than land bases and with the unique characteristics of each. The particular advantages of sea basing include the ability to provide a U.S. presence without commitment, to operate where land bases are not available, and to attack surface ships at sea beyond the range of land-based aircraft. Its disadvantages include greater cost and greater vulnerability than a comparable land-based air wing.

Unique Capabilities

Aircraft carriers, and naval forces more generally, have the unique and the useful property that they can be deployed to a crisis area and held offshore in international waters, thus signaling our ability and perhaps intention to intervene, without actually committing us and without the need for political clearances to land troops or even for overflight rights. Neither Army nor Air Force units can do this. Similarly, continuous deployment of naval forces in potential crisis areas provides continuous evidence of our ability to intervene.

The second unique capability of aircraft carriers is their ability to operate without the use of nearby land bases. Of course, this does not have much significance in areas like central Europe where we have numerous prepared bases, but, in other areas, it could be extremely important.

During a crisis, or the resulting fighting, we cannot count on being able to use existing nearby airbases if the host country is not directly involved and if it wishes to remain neutral. For example, existing land bases in Greece and Turkey would probably be available in case of a war in NATO Europe, but probably not in case of U.S. involvement in an Arab-Israeli conflict. Similarly, if we decided to intervene in an area where we had not previously made plans for it, the carriers would be able to begin flight operations as soon as they reach the area.

The Air Force has developed a "bare-base kit" which is designed to enable land-based aircraft to deploy to an unprepared airport—of which there appears to be an ample number—and begin operations in a short time. However, this is as yet an unproved capability and adds considerably to required airlift forces. In addition, in some situations, the necessary airfields might have been overrun by enemy ground troops. Thus, deployability without prepared land bases remains a substantial advantage of the sea-based tactical air forces.

Aircraft carriers can also attack enemy surface ships that are farther from shore than the range of land-based tactical aircraft—for instance, 600 nautical miles or more. This was, in fact, the major use of attack aircraft carriers during World War II. A further discussion of this mission is deferred until the threat of the Soviet surface fleet is considered.

Disadvantages

Among the disadvantages of aircraft carriers, we consider, in addition to vulnerability, greater cost than a comparable land-based air wing. A valid cost comparison is difficult to construct since it is not obvious just what costs should be charged against the two alternatives, which costs are fixed and which are variable, and how to define comparable air wings. No such cost comparison is available in detail on the public record. Nevertheless, it would be surprising if the sea-based air wing did not pay a premium for its mobility and relative freedom from land bases, for its expensive movable airbase, for its sea-based logistic support, and for its need for protection against submarines.

A rough attempt to judge the size of the premium is shown in Table 4, which compares the average cost per air wing for the Navy and Air Force in Fiscal Years 1963-65 as derived by the author from published analyses of their budgets by mission. It is necessary to go back that far in time to eliminate the distorting effect of the war in Vietnam. The figure indicates that the average sea-based wing, which is about the same size as the land-based wing, costs about 20 to 25 percent more.

We also know that classified studies by analysts in the Office of the Secretary of Defense derived a premium of 40

Table 4

Comparison of Annual Cost of Average Navy and
Air Force Air Wings, Fiscal Year 1963-65
(Total Obligational Authority in Millions of Current Dollars)

	Fiscal Year 1963	*Fiscal Year 1964*	*Fiscal Year 1965*
Navy			
Carriers and Aircraft[1]	$3,070	$2,620	$3,030
Antiair Warfare Escort Ships	790	890	610
60 Percent of Antisubmarine Warfare Escort Ships[2]	900	1,050	1,180
70 Percent of Logistic and Support Ships[2]	630	670	850
Total	$5,390	$5,230	$5,670
Number of Air Wings	15	15 .	15
Average Cost Per Air Wing	$ 360	$ 350	$ 380
Air Force			
Tactical Air Costs	$4,400	$4,200	$5,000
Additional Overhead Allocations[3]	1,470	1,600	1,980
Total	$5,870	$5,800	$6,980
Number of Air Wings	20	21	22
Average Cost Per Air Wing	$ 290	$ 280	$ 317

[1] Excludes Marine Corps costs.

[2] Percentages are those associated with carriers in Admiral Thomas H. Morrer's statement.

[3] Air Force mission breakout did not allocate all overhead.

Sources: "Abstract, Analysis of the Relative Cost of Sea-Based and Land-Based Tactical Air" in *CVAN-70 Aircraft Carrier*, Joint Hearings Before the Joint Senate-House Armed Services Subcommittee of the Senate and House Armed Services Committee on *CVAN-70* Aircraft Carrier, 91st Congress, Second Session, 1970, pp. 41-46; Statement of Admiral Thomas H. Moorer in *Authorization for Military Procurement, Research and Development, Fiscal Year 1970,* and *Reserve Strength,* Hearings Before the Senate Armed Services Committee, 91st Congress, First Session, 1969, p. 667.

percent for the sea-based wing.[6] This premium might be well worth paying, but it is substantial, so that we should tend to emphasize land-based tactical aircraft except in cases where the particular advantages of the carriers, as discussed above, seem to be controlling.

The Soviet Surface Fleet

Until recently, the Soviet Fleet of surface warships did not play a large role in U.S. defense planning. Their surface fleet was much smaller than ours and did not have any aircraft carriers, so it was assumed that it could easily be destroyed by carrier-based aircraft. However, after the sinking of an Israeli destroyer in 1967 by an Egyptian Soviet-built patrol boat with surface-to-surface cruise missiles, the realization has spread that these ships with their surface-to-surface cruise missiles could pose a substantial offensive threat to the U.S. Fleet.

The Soviets have some 24 cruisers and destroyers, 150 patrol boats, and 66 submarines which can fire surface-to-surface cruise missiles, and have given substantial numbers of the surface-to-surface cruise missile patrol boats to their allies.

When we consider ways in which the Soviet surface fleet might be used against the U.S. Fleet, and particularly the aircraft carrier task forces, one of the first that comes to mind is a situation in which the United States and Soviet Fleets are in continuous contact during a crisis leading to war, as they would be in the Mediterranean, for example. If the Soviets struck first, they could launch a coordinated volley of surface-to-surface cruise missiles with no tactical warning. By assumption, we would not be able to take any action against the enemy launching platforms—the ships— until their missiles had already been launched.

The Navy is working on several programs and tactics to improve its ability to deal with this situation, including development of its own surface-to-surface cruise missile

(Harpoon), helicopters to improve warning, and increased emphasis on jamming and other electronic countermeasures to deflect the incoming missiles.[7] However, none of these can prevent the initial volley of missiles from being launched, and only a handful of missiles for a large, coordinated attack need penetrate the defenses to do a great deal of damage. Therefore, the threat of a Soviet first strike against the U.S. Fleet is not likely to be eliminated in the foreseeable future.

If the U.S. carrier task forces survive the initial attack, or if the war develops in such a way that such an attack does not occur, then the outcome depends strongly on whether the Soviet surface ships have land-based air cover. If the Soviets do not have air cover, then the U.S. aircraft carriers could remain outside missile range of the Soviet surface fleet and still attack it with carrier-based aircraft. Although some U.S. aircraft would be lost, there is little doubt that most of the Soviet surface ships would be sunk.

On the other hand, if the battle occurs in an area where the Soviet surface fleet does have air cover, then the situation is quite different. The Soviet land-based aircraft could be used in two ways: to provide an area defense for their ships or to attack the carriers directly. As we have seen above, if they attack the aircraft carriers directly, they can probably force them to retire from the battle area although they might have to expend a substantial number of aircraft to do so.

From our point of view, we would not be able to operate our carriers in these areas if the Soviets were directly involved, even without their surface fleet because of the air and submarine threat. In this sense, their surface fleet is not, in this situation, an additional threat.

The Soviet surface fleet might also be used against merchant ship convoys carrying logistic support for our armies overseas and economic goods required by our allies' economics. The surface ships involved would be their cruisers and destroyers since their surface-to-surface cruise missile patrol boats would not have the range, endurance, and sea-keeping ability to engage in these operations.

In such operations, the Soviet surface ships would be operating outside land-based air cover and would, therefore, be vulnerable to strikes by carrier-based aircraft, while the carriers themselves remained outside missile range. The carriers would face Soviet submarine opposition, but would be less vulnerable than when launching strikes against land targets—the situation described earlier—since they would not be constrained to operate in a restricted area. They could, therefore, use their speed and mobility to limit the ability of enemy submarines to get close enough to attack.

The carriers would have a reasonable chance of being able to carry out this mission. If not, we could stop shipping, while antisubmarine warfare aircraft wear down the deployed enemy submarine force or use our own attack submarines against the Soviet surface ships. The implications of this mission for aircraft carrier force levels will be discussed later.

In summary, the Soviet surface fleet reinforces their ability to deny us the use of our aircraft carriers for strikes against land targets in any war in which they are heavily involved, but they would be able to do so even without it. They could use their surface fleet against merchant ship convoys, but this use could be countered.

Adequacy of Antisubmarine Warfare Forces

An evaluation of the ability of planned antisubmarine warfare forces to defeat the Soviet submarine force would be subject to considerable uncertainty. Nevertheless, some important qualitative observations can be made.

First, if we accept the arguments above that aircraft carriers used against land targets cannot be adequately protected against concentrations of Soviet submarines at reasonable cost, then the need for antisubmarine warfare forces is greatly reduced. It is inherently harder to protect a small number of high-value targets than a large number of low-value targets, as in the protection of merchant shipping.

If one or two submarines penetrate a carrier's defenses and get, say, five hits on the carrier's screws, they will disable the task force. The same submarines penetrating a convoy would damage perhaps five to 10 merchant ships. In order to have an effect on the land war by sinking merchant ships, the Soviet submarines must sink a large number of them which is easier to prevent than the small number of successful attacks necessary to force aircraft carriers to withdraw.

Second, we have a substantial investment in antisubmarine warfare platforms—ships, aircraft, and submarines—which are expensive to procure and operate. There would appear to be a much greater payoff for measures which would improve the performance of existing forces than for increases in force levels. Such measures would include not only development of new and more effective sensors—such as sonars and sonobuoys—and weapons—such as torpedoes and mines—but also improvements in the operator proficiency and maintenance provided in the operating forces. Similarly, at a time when budgets are being reduced, these measures should be protected at the expense, if need be, of force levels.

Alternative Approaches

In considering the implications of these arguments for force levels, we take, as a starting point, the validity of the argument that aircraft carriers are useful for providing a presence during peacetime or during a crisis. The requirements for this function set a minimum for carrier force levels. This minimum level is taken here as nine carriers.

Assuming that the Navy implements its plan to homeport two carrier task forces overseas, one in the Mediterranean and one in the Western Pacific, a force level of nine carriers would be enough to maintain a continuous deployment of four carriers overseas. Two carrier task forces could be maintained continuously in the Mediterranean and two in the Western Pacific (compared with the current pattern of two and three, respectively). In each area, the deployed carriers could be reinforced during a crisis by one or two more, making possible a display of willingness to commit ourselves. Such a posture should be adequate to satisfy our needs for an overseas presence and for crisis control.

In addition, Secretary of Defense Melvin R. Laird has stated that, if we again become involved in a war as large as Vietnam, we would have to rely on mobilization and a callup of the Reserves; this suggests that wartime rotation policies should be assumed. In that case, and with overseas homeporting, a force of nine aircraft carriers could provide three to five on station for the war—particularly during the early period when land-based aircraft might not be fully operational—and also one to three on station elsewhere for presence and crisis control. Thus, a force level of nine aircraft carriers appears adequate for limited wars in which the Soviet Union is not directly involved.

The question is, then, how many additional carriers, over and above these nine, we should have. Here, three alternative answers are outlined.

The first alternative takes, at face value, the arguments that the carriers would be vulnerable in any war with the Soviets if used for strikes against land targets. Therefore, no carriers are bought for this purpose, and land-based aircraft are relied on for our tactical air needs in such wars.

In a major war in Asia with the Chinese, but not the Soviets involved, carriers would be used in addition to land-based aircraft, but the nine provided should be adequate for this purpose. Since these nine would not be used against land targets in a war with the Soviets, they would be available for use against the Soviet surface fleet or the Soviet naval bomber force, should these be used against merchant shipping in the open ocean. Considering the small number of surface-to-surface missile cruisers and destroyers that the Soviets have and the difficulties they would face in bringing their naval bombers to bear against shipping, the nine carriers should be enough to handle these threats.

Substantial antisubmarine warfare forces would have to be maintained under this alternative, but sizable reductions could be made because we no longer attempt to use the aircraft carriers under the conditions where they would be most vulnerable.

Efforts to improve the performance of existing antisubmarine warfare forces would be maintained with high priority. The new F-14 fighter is designed to protect the carriers from an advanced Soviet air threat and would lose its *raison d'etre*. A replacement for the existing F-4 fighter, probably a much less expensive design than the F-14, might still be needed. The air and cruise missile defenses we provide the carriers should be designed for high reliability against a threat of low or medium sophistication which would be presented by potential enemies other than the Soviets.

A variation of this approach may be attractive over the long term. An aircraft carrier task force designed for more limited wars would probably have a much lighter escort ship screen. The carrier itself might be smaller and less expensive, and its aircraft might be designed against a less sophisticated threat and more with a close air-support mission in mind.

If these changes are made, the cost advantage of land-based aircraft would be greatly reduced, if not eliminated, and additional carriers might be attractive to meet our needs for tactical air in situations where the Soviets are not involved, including a Chinese and North Korean attack on the Republic of Korea.

The second alternative approach might be characterized as a partial acceptance of the argument on carrier vulnerability. It neither counts on the carriers for airstrikes in a major war with the Soviets nor writes them off in this situation. It recognizes that it may well be impossible to maintain carriers in the eastern Mediterranean during such a war, but it argues that some combination of improved defenses, successful electronic countermeasures, enemy mistakes, and luck may make the survival of the carriers sufficiently likely that it is worth gambling on. We would, therefore, be willing to operate a greater number of aircraft carriers than the minimum of nine.

At the same time, they would be less attractive than we had previously thought, so a reduction, perhaps to about 12, from the force level of 15 maintained in recent years would seem to be in order. Because of the need to defend the aircraft carriers against enemy submarines, any reduction in antisubmarine warfare forces would be small at most. Measures for defense against cruise missiles would be emphasized, including electronic countermeasures, the new Harpoon antiship missile, and helicopter-borne early warning sensors.

According to this view, the Soviet surface fleet is a disturbing threat to our carriers and might make a crucial difference in our ability to maintain them on station, in contrast to the first approach which saw the Soviet surface fleet as simply reinforcing the Soviets' ability to deny us such use of our carriers. Actions to counter it are particularly important in the second approach.

The third approach described here rejects the arguments concerning carrier vulnerability and cost. With respect to vulnerability, this view was expressed by Admiral Thomas H. Moorer, then Chief of Naval Operations and now Chairman of the Joint Chiefs of Staff, as follows:

> I certainly don't accept the allegations that the carrier is vulnerable to the degree that often has been mentioned . . . I don't believe surface ships are vulnerable. I believe in the next war we will perhaps suffer greater losses than we have in the past, but I am confident that we can stay out there and operate.[8]

This approach would essentially continue the force levels maintained in Fiscal Year 1971. The current relative priorities in and among tactical air, antisubmarine warfare, and other forces would also be maintained. In particular, defense against the Soviet surface fleet would be considered important, but it would not have the same degree of urgency as under the second approach.

The Navy would do well to confront the issues raised here and to sort them out collectively and come to some tentative conclusions about them. There is a bureaucratic incentive to do so since the issues have been and will continue to be raised by many outside the Navy. Congressional opposition to construction of new aircraft carriers has been successful, for example. More important, however, national security is best served by realistic estimates of our military capabilities. If the arguments presented here are anywhere near the mark, our reliance on aircraft carriers must be reevaluated in the light of the changed conditions we now face.

Writing of such changes, and of our reluctance to recognize them, Admiral Alfred T. Mahan observed:

> It can be remedied only by a candid recognition of each change, by careful study of the powers and limitations of the new ship or weapon, and by a consequent adaptation of the method of using it to the qualities it possesses, which will constitute its tactics. History shows that it is vain to hope that military men generally will be at pains to do this, but that[9] the one who does, will go into battle with a great advantage. . . .

Efforts to overcome this tendency now seem to be required.

NOTES

1. The interpretations and conclusions in this paper are those of the author alone and do not necessarily reflect the views of the staff, officers, or trustees of the Brookings Institution or of organizations that support its research.

2. Reflects President's FY 1973 budget, as presented in January, 1972. Excludes January, 1972 and January, 1973 pay raises. Figure 2 presents the budget in terms of total obligational authority (TOA), rather than actual outlays. TOA represents, roughly speaking, the rate at which the Government commits itself to additional expenditures, even though the money may not actually be paid out for several years and is, therefore, a better measure of the size of our effort. Figure 1 shows outlays because the data on incremental war costs are presented in those terms.

3. Using whole numbers, if the enemy launches 63 bomber sorties, he will lose 25 bombers to fighters, and 38 air-to-surface missiles will be launched, of which 30 will be reliable and 6 will penetrate the surface-to-air missile defenses.

4. Does not include light carriers (CVLs).

5. Samuel Eliot Morison, *History of United States Naval Operations in World War II* (Boston, Little, Brown, 1958-62), Vols. 12-15; Table, "Summary of Battle Damage to U.S. Carriers, World War II, Including Cause and Effect of Damage," in testimony of VADM H. G. Rickover in *Naval Nuclear Propulsion Program—1970*, Hearings before the Joint Committee on Atomic Energy, 91st Cong. 2 sess. (1970), pp. 61-62. The table includes 4 cases listed by Rickover but not by Morison (probably because they resulted in only minor damage and did not affect the larger battle), it also includes three cases attributed to bomb damage by Rickover, although Morison's narrative indicates Kamikaze attacks were involved.

6. CVAN-70 *Aircraft Carrier*, Joint Hearings Before the Joint Senate-House Armed Services Subcommittee of the Senate and House Armed Services Committees on CVAN-70 Aircraft Carrier, 91st Cong., 2 sess. (1970), p. 630.

7. "CNO Zumwalt Presses to Retain 15 Carriers, Plans to Reorder Navy Mission Priorities," *Armed Forces Journal*, December 7, 1970, pp. 26-27; Brooke Nihart, "Harpoon: Navy's Answer to Soviet Missile Boats," *Armed Forces Journal*, November 16, 1970, pp. 22-23.

8. *Authorization for Military Procurement, Research and Development, Fiscal Year 1971, and Reserve Strength*, Hearings Before the Senate Armed Services Committee, 91st Cong., 2 sess., part 2 (1970) p. 1308.

9. Admiral Alfred T. Mahan, *The Influence of Seapower Upon History* (New York, Hill & Wang), p. 8.

4 The Evolution of the Soviet Navy

Barry M. Blechman

The Soviet Union, being a nation with finite resources just as any other, faces difficult choices with regard to the amount of funds and manpower to be allocated to its Navy, and with regard to the distribution of resources within the Navy itself. These choices, which reflect Soviet conceptions of the utility of naval power, are indicated by the size of building programs and force levels, by the types and characteristics of ships, aircraft, and equipment deployed, and by the activity of those forces once they are operational. While the multi-functionality of most naval vessels makes indicators of mission priorities somewhat ambiguous, it is possible by examining patterns in naval shipbuilding, weapons procurement, deployments, and exercises, and by relating those factors to pertinent writings on military doctrine and strategy, to infer the assumptions regarding the utility of various forms of naval endeavor upon which such decisions are founded.[1]

There is, however, a considerable time lag between decisions regarding the types of missions which should be undertaken and the weapons which should be obtained to carry them out, and the actual appearance of these forces. The size and composition of the Soviet Navy today are fundamentally the result of decisions regarding military doctrine and strategy reached by Stalin's successors in the aftermath of his death. At that time, drastic alterations were made to the massive naval rebuilding program instituted by Stalin in 1945-46. Force level objectives were cut back dramatically, some shipbuilding programs were cancelled altogether, new development programs were initiated and others given greater priority than they previously had been accorded. Subsequent events caused further modifications to the naval program laid out in 1953-54 (1957-58 and 1961-62 are said to be particularly important decision periods), but the basic outline of priorities in naval power remained unaltered.[2]

There is, however, increasing evidence that the Soviets may be in the process of re-evaluating their naval strategy once again. Our purposes in this paper, therefore, are twofold.

First, we wish to illuminate the present-day mission priorities and capabilities of the Soviet fleets. To accomplish this task, the Soviet Navy in 1972 is compared to the Soviet Navy in 1958. This year is representative of the condition of the Soviet Navy just before the impact of the post-Stalin decisions began to be made manifest. It marks the initial appearance of several radically new naval weapons and vessels; for example, nuclear-powered submarines and warships armed with cruise (air-breathing) surface-to-surface missiles. Nineteen fifty-eight also marks a point just before the Soviets began to retire large numbers of older and less effective vessels. We assume that the number, type, and characteristics of naval units deployed (and retired) during the interval between 1958 and 1972 reflect the evolution of Soviet thought regarding the utility of seapower. These comparative force structure data are supplemented with information regarding the operations, exercises, and deployment patterns of Soviet naval forces.

Our second purpose is to speculate regarding possible future directions of Soviet naval development. Key indicators of decisions in this regard will be described.

Components of the Soviet Navy

The Soviet Navy has changed a great deal since 1958. It is a far more modern military force and, consequently, far more capable in many respects. It is impressive in the scope of its modernization; in the performance of its new weapons, sensors, and electronic equipment; in its seamanship; and in its now global deployments. At the same time, it is a smaller force than the 1958 Soviet Navy—smaller in manpower, in aircraft, and in submarines. The contrast between the diminished size but increasing quality and prominence of the Soviet Navy has not gone unnoticed. Admiral Zumwalt, for example, remarked on this:

> ... I have not asserted that _total_ Soviet naval inventories have been growing in number. Rather ... that the essential composition and employment policies of the Soviet Navy have been changing in ways which make it a significantly more capable and challenging force.[3]

In order to understand the ways in which the Soviet Navy has been changing, we will examine several types of forces individually.

Submarines.—The submarine force (Table 1) has experienced the largest decline in number of units. Excluding ballistic missile submarines, the force dropped more than 25 percent between 1958 and 1972. Furthermore, it can be expected to decline to a greater extent in the near future. The Soviets face a block obsolescence problem involving "W" class submarines, which comprise more than 40 percent of the 1972 force listed in the table. These submarines, built between 1950 and 1957, are rapidly being retired and are not being replaced on a one-for-one basis. Admiral Zumwalt has already listed the Soviet attack and cruise missile submarine force level as 288, more than 50 fewer than the number in

Table 1. The Soviet Submarine Force

Torpedo Attack and Cruise Missile Submarines*

Characteristics	Diesel-Powered		Nuclear-Powered	
	1958	1972	1958	1972
Number of units	474	286	(3)[c]	61
Mean tonnage[a]	0.8	1.3	3.5	4.4
Mean range[b]	9.5	14.5	0 0	0 0
Mean complement	43.7	61.6	88	95
Total number of torpedo tubes	2,478	1,808	18	400
Total number of cruise missile tubes (rails)	—	98	—	304

Strategic (Ballistic Missile) Submarines

Characteristics	Diesel-Powered		Nuclear-Powered	
	1958	1972	1958	1972
Number of units	7[d]	25	—	34
Total number of missile tubes	14	72	—	427
Mean tonnage[a]	2.1	2.6	—	6.9
Mean range[b]	20.0	23.1	—	0 0

*Sources: Force level data are taken from Raymond V. B. Blackman (ed.), *Jane's Fighting Ships* (London, 1958/59, 1972/73). Data pertaining to the characteristics of naval vessels is taken from *Jane's* and Siegfried Breyer, *Guide to the Soviet Navy*, trans. by Lt. Cdr. M. W. Henley (Annapolis, U.S. Naval Institute, 1970).

[a]Maximum surface displacement in thousand tons.
[b]At cruising speed, in thousand nautical miles.
[c]Three nuclear units were under construction in 1958.
[d]This data was derived from subsequent issues of *Jane's*.

our table.[4] Given current construction rates and the composition of the fleet in 1972, one would expect Soviet attack and cruise missile submarine force levels to stabilize between 200 and 250 by 1980.

While considerably smaller than in 1958, the Soviet submarine force is more capable in many respects. Nuclear-propelled units, first appearing in 1958, now total 83 of the strategic, cruise missile, and torpedo attack varieties. The force is likely to be almost exclusively nuclear-powered by

1980. The diesel-powered force in 1972 is also more capable than its 1958 counterpart. The increase in their mean range reflects the halt in the construction of coastal and medium-range units resulting from the 1954 and 1957 decisions, and the retirement of many short range submarines of pre-war design or construction. Aggregate submarine tonnage has grown by' 50 percent despite the decline in force levels, implying increased capabilities for individual units. Similarly, the decline in the total number of torpedo tubes has not been proportional to the decline in force levels, as newer submarines incorporate more tubes per boat.

Two improvements in Soviet submarine capabilities deserve particular mention. First, deployment of "Yankee" class strategic submarines gives the Soviet Union a credible, sea-based strategic missile force for the first time. Twenty-five units were operational in January 1972, and the initiation of construction of the forty-second "Yankee" (or a modified version) has been reported.[5] Second, the deployment of submarines equipped with cruise missiles gives the Soviets an impressive capability against surface vessels. Some 65 submarines are now equipped with these weapons.[6]

Major surface warships. —A different trend has been experienced in the Soviet force of major surface warships (Table 2). In this case, force levels have remained fairly stable, but mean tonnage has diminished, reflecting a shift in the relative building rates between escorts and larger cruisers and destroyers. The Soviets have retained a surprisingly large number of older gun cruisers.

A block obsolescence problem will also confront the Soviets in surface warships, similar to, but of a lesser scale than, that in submarines. Skoryi class destroyers, built between 1949 and 1953, comprise nearly 20 percent of the force described in Table 2 and are becoming increasingly obsolescent. "Kotlin" class destroyers, comprising an additional 10 percent of the force, were built between 1954 and 1957. The eventual retirement of these vessels should counteract the effect of new construction on total force levels, and result in slightly decreasing force levels in the future.[7]

The Soviet surface fleet, like its submarine force, is more capable than in 1958, even if no larger. Individual units, despite their smaller mean size, pack greater firepower on more diversified systems, are speedier, and carry more elaborate and sophisticated electronic systems. The Soviets have apparently made major advances in surface ship design and engineering efficiency. Ton for ton, the newest Soviet destroyer—the Krivak—is said to be the most powerful warship ever built.[8] Fifty percent of the cruisers, 40 percent of the destroyers, and 50 percent of the escorts have become operational since 1958. These new ships incorporate advanced capabilities in propulsion, detection, communication, and weapon systems. Surface-to-surface and surface-to-air missiles have become fairly common. Anti-submarine capabilities have been improved with the introduction of new sonars and torpedoes, ship-borne helicopters, and large numbers of anti-submarine rockets. Only mine capacity seems to have declined substantially.

A particularly important change has become apparent with regard to the deployment patterns of Soviet surface warships, and of other components of their Navy as well. Within the past 15 years, and particularly since 1967, the Soviets have greatly expanded the geographic scope of their naval operations, and have established a peacetime naval presence in regions of traditional Western naval dominance. This trend has been marked, for example, by a sharp increase in the number of port calls by Soviet vessels in various regions. Soviet naval visits outside the Black and Baltic Seas were infrequent until 1957. Similarly, the Soviets have extended the areas in which they carry out naval exercises. Until 1956, naval maneuvers were held only within the Black, Baltic, and Barents Seas. In the Atlantic, exercise areas were extended

Table 2. Soviet Major Surface Warships*

	Cruisers[a]		Destroyers[b]		Escorts[c]		All Major Combatants	
	1958	1972	1958	1972	1958	1972	1958	1972
Number of units	31	29	146	101	66	124	243	255
Mean tonnage[d]	12.4	10.4	2.3	2.9	1.3	1.2	3.3	2.9
Mean complement[e]	9?2	760	260	299	168	124	321	265
Number of surface-surface missile rails	–	72	–	16	–	–	–	88
Number of surface-air missile rails	–	46	–	86	–	–	–	132
No. of torpedo tubes[f]	216	218	1,318	831	198	657	1,732	1,706
No. of anti-submarine rockets[g]	–	396	832	1,636	1,152	4,552	1,984	6,584
Helo capacity[b]	–	50	22	20	–	–	22	70
Mine capacity[e]	5,140	2,980	11,270	5,260	2,700	3,930	19,110	12,170

*Sources: Force level data are taken from Raymond V. B. Blackman (ed.), *Jane's Fighting Ships* (London, 1958/59, 1972/73). Data pertaining to the characteristics of naval vessels is taken from *Jane's* and Siegfried Breyer, *Guide to the Soviet Navy*, trans. by Lt. Cdr. M. W. Henley (Annapolis, U.S. Naval Institute, 1970).

[a]Includes two "Moskva" class helicopter cruisers in 1972.

[b]As defined by *Jane's*.

[c]Ocean-going escorts larger than 1,000 tons.

[d]Standard displacement in 1,000 tons.

[e]Maximum listed.

[f]The comparison of torpedo tubes is not really meaningful. The 1958 torpedoes were anti-surface ship weapons. The 1972 torpedoes are designed for anti-submarine warfare.

[g]Number of launcher barrels; if ship may be configured with depth charges or rockets, I assume the latter.

[h]On-board maintenance, maximum capacity.

slowly through the Norwegian Sea and into the North Atlantic over a period of twelve years. In 1970, the Soviets held their first naval exercise of global dimensions— "Okean."[9]

The increase in "out-of-area" operations can best be seen in Soviet deployments to the Mediterranean and the Indian

Ocean (Table 3). A continuous Soviet warship presence in the Mediterranean did not originate until after 1964 and did not grow significantly until mid-1967. Total Soviet ship operating days in the Mediterranean doubled between 1965 and 1967, doubled once again by 1970, and have continued to increase, albeit at a more gradual pace, since then.[10] Soviet combat units began to deploy to the Indian Ocean regularly in 1968. This presence grew rapidly for two years but then levelled off.

Elsewhere, surface warship sorties into the Pacific did not originate until 1963-64, and into the Caribbean until 1969. An even more recent development has been the initiation of a near continuous presence in the South Atlantic, off the West African coast, in late 1970.[11] The implications of these deployment changes will be discussed subsequently.

Table 3. Soviet Ship Operating Days in the Mediterranean Sea and Indian Ocean[a]

Year	Mediterranean Sea[b]	Indian Ocean[c]
1965	4,000	d
1966	4,500	d
1967	8,500	d
1968	12,000	1,800
1969	14,000	2,800
1970	17,500	3,200
1971	19,000	3,400

[a]Estimated from a chart appearing in Admiral Elmo R. Zumwalt, "Statement Before the Committee on Armed Services, United States Senate, Concerning FY 1973 Military Posture and Budget of the United States Navy" (Processed: no date).
[b]Rounded to nearest 500.
[c]Rounded to nearest 200.
[d]Indicates a total less than 100.

Other Naval forces—Comparative data for other components of the Soviet Navy are found in Table 4. It will be noted that overall the size of the Soviet Navy, as indexed by manpower, has declined by one third. These figures are only representative, however, as they are rough estimates from Western sources, and should not be taken too seriously. Perhaps greater significance can be attributed to the 1967 reduction in the Navy term of conscription from four to three years. Assuming no increase in total manpower, such a move would have a significant effect on the number of men available for operational forces.

Coastal escorts and other patrol vessels have nearly doubled in number but decreased in tonnage since 1958. Three-fourths of the ships of this type have been built since 1958. Although the newer ships are smaller than their predecessors, their on-board weapon suits are relatively more impressive.

There has been a considerable decline in the number of torpedo boats and gunboats. Introduction of missile-equipped patrol vessels has been a compensating trend, however. The Nanuchka, a missile corvette, is an important recent addition to the missile patrol boat grouping.

Growth has been experienced in both force levels and tonnage in the amphibious and mine warfare categories. It should be added though, that amphibious warfare is one area which the Soviets have sorely neglected. The largest ship in the Soviet amphibious warfare force, the "Alligator" class, displaces only 4,000 tons and resembles nothing so much as a large landing ship (tank), one of the smaller U.S. vessels used for such purposes. It is doubtful if the unloaded displacement of the entire Soviet amphibious force exceeds 125,000 tons. For comparison, the amphibious force built by the United States since 1960 alone will displace (unloaded) more than 700,000 tons. Moreover, the Soviets have no assault ships capable of helicopter operations, and a naval infantry (equivalent to the U.S. Marines) of 15,000. Since 1960, the U.S. has built seven helicopter assault ships ("Iwo Jima" class), and initiated construction of five much larger vessels for these purposes ("Tarawa" class). The U.S. Marine Corps consists of roughly 200,000 men and women. The Soviets do have the capability to sealift several divisions utilizing their merchant marine, but this is quite different than an assault landing force.[12]

Table 4. Other Soviet Naval Forces*

General	1958	1972
Number of personnel	750,000	500,000
Coastal escorts and other patrol vessels[a]		
Number of units	133	258
Mean tonnage[b]	361	287
No. of surface-to-air missile rails	—	16
No. of torpedo tubes	75	632
No. of anti-submarine rockets (barrels)	—	3,728
Mine capacity[c]	2,690	3,000
Missile Patrol Boats		
Number of units	—	151
Number of surface-to-surface missile rails	—	566
Motor torpedo/gun boats		
Number of units[d]	500	225
Amphibious warfare vessels[e]		
Number of units	120	200
Mean tonnage[b]	350	800
Minesweepers		
Ocean-going, number of units	149	189
Coastal & inshore, number of units	161	130
Naval aviation		
Number of aircraft	3,000	1,200

*Sources: Force level data are taken from Raymond V. B. Blackman (ed.), *Jane's Fighting Ships* (London, 1958/59, 1972/73). Data pertaining to the characteristics of naval vessels is taken from *Jane's* and Siegfried Breyer, *Guide to the Soviet Navy*, trans. by Lt. Cdr. M. W. Henley (Annapolis, U.S. Naval Institute, 1970).

[a]All surface combatants other than those already listed, including coastal escorts, patrol vessels, and submarine chasers.

[b]Standard displacement in tons.

[c]Maximum capacity if normally carried.

[d]Excluding river craft.

[e]Including amphibious craft.

The Soviets have also neglected the development of support ships, a category for which publicly available data is too spotty to present quantitative measures. Generally, they have made support forces do with civilian ships converted for naval use.[13] What new construction there has been in the support area has tended to focus on the support of submarines. The Soviet Navy today has no real equivalent to the U.S. Navy's underway replenishment groups, and "is only beginning to develop a sizable at-sea logistic capability."[14]

Finally, Soviet naval aviation is very different from that seen in 1958. The older force was composed in large part of land-based interceptor squadrons, to be used for the defense of ports, bases, and fleet areas from air attacks. These units have been phased out or transferred to other branches of the Soviet military. In 1972, the much smaller naval air arm consists of (a) medium-range strike aircraft, some equipped with cruise missiles, cast in an anti-ship role; and (b) helicopters and fixed-wing aircraft designed for anti-submarine warfare. The naval air force of 1,200 aircraft continues to be land-based; only a limited number of helicopters fly from Soviet cruisers and destroyers.[15]

Soviet Naval Priorities

As we have noted, naval vessels are multi-functional; they potentially may be used to accomplish a variety of missions. To actuate such possibilities, however, an assortment of tasks must be undertaken: suitable equipment procured, tactics developed, personnel trained, deployments made, and various procedures rehearsed. By observing these sorts of things, it is possible to infer the priorities which are accorded to various missions. This section summarizes the apparent Soviet view of the utility of various forms of naval activity, as evidenced by the composition of their fleets and by the sorts of behavior mentioned above. Many of these appraisals are contentious and, in these cases, alternative points of view are presented.

1. Strategic offense.—A major feature of the evolution of

Soviet naval capabilities has been the appearance of a credible, sea-based strategic missile force. The construction rate of strategic submarines in recent years alone, 8-9 per year, indicates the high priority accorded to this mission by Soviet planners. The "Yankee" class submarine, equipped with 16 SS-N-6 missiles, is the first such Soviet weapon system deserving serious concern in the West. Moreover, a longer range sea-based missile has been tested (SS-N-8) and will be deployed, 12 per boat in a modified version of the "Yankee."[16]

Under the terms of the arms limitation agreement signed in May 1972, the Soviets will be permitted to deploy 740 ballistic missile launchers at sea, plus an additional 210 launchers if they retire an equal number of older land-based systems.[17] This will give them an edge in number of launchers over the United States, and a force of 46 to 62 strategic submarines depending upon the eventual mix of 12 and 16 tube units and whether they avail themselves of the option regarding the replacement of land-based systems.

In range and perhaps accuracy, the Soviet Yankee/SS-N-6 system is roughly equivalent to the Polaris/A-1 system fully deployed by the United States by the mid-1960s. The SS-N-8 missile will be more comparable to later U.S. weapons, but not to its most modern systems. In two important respects, the Soviet sea-based strategic missile force remains markedly inferior: (a) the U.S.S.R. has not developed the technology necessary to deploy multiple independently targetable re-entry vehicles (MIRV) on their missiles as yet, such as the U.S. Poseidon system, and are unlikely to do so for several years; (b) U.S. submarines are quieter and, consequently, less susceptible to detection than their Soviet counterparts.[18]

2. Strategic defense.—Nearly all analysts agree that the primary mission of the Soviet Navy is to deter and, if necessary, to blunt any attack on the Soviet homeland from sea-based weapon systems. Two major tasks are involved in strategic defense, each requiring quite distinct types of naval forces.

First, the U.S.S.R. must maintain the capability to engage and prevent the launch of aircraft from U.S. attack carriers operating in regions within strike range of Soviet territory— particularly, the Eastern Mediterranean and the Norwegian Sea. A substantial increase in the range of carrier-based strike aircraft in the mid-1950s is said to have prompted the Soviet naval procurement decisions made in 1957-58, and to have been the original impetus for extensions in the Soviet Navy's operating areas.[19]

Soviet naval doctrine stresses coordinated operations involving a variety of platforms carrying nuclear-armed missiles for the anti-carrier mission, and a large portion of their force seems to be directed toward this end. As has been noted, a growing portion of the Soviet submarine force is equipped with cruise missiles; in 1972 there were 65 such boats, of the "E," "J," "W conversion," and "C" classes. The most recent class, the "C," represents a change in tactics as its missiles are of short range, but capable of underwater launch. This combination permits the submarine to close its target, and obviates the requirement posed by earlier classes with longer range but surface-launched missiles, for the supply of target-location data from an external source, for example, from a reconnaissance aircraft. Additionally, Soviet naval aviation includes about 300 medium-range strike aircraft carrying the AS-2 and AS-5 missiles, designed primarily for anti-carrier operations. Also, a "significant portion" of the U.S.S.R.'s "Long Range Aviation" (the equivalent of the United States' Strategic Air Command) is assigned to naval targets.[20] Finally, missile-equipped major surface combatants are also tasked with anti-carrier missions in regions within strike range of the Soviet homeland.

While the importance of the anti-carrier mission has been downgraded somewhat due to development of the U.S. ballistic missile submarine threat, it retains a prominent role in Soviet naval planning. Anti-carrier operations are accorded a central role in all major Soviet naval exercises, including the highly publicized exercise "Okean." In his introduction to a

Russian-language book describing "Okean," Defense Minister Grechko noted:

> Today aggressive blocs are dominated by imperialist states with large naval forces at their command. These forces are built around groups of fleet ballistic missile submarines (nuclear propulsion) *and attack aircraft carriers with aircraft armed with nuclear weapons.*
> . . . (The Okean maneuvers) demonstrated to the entire world . . . our fleet's preparedness to repel any aggression against our country from the sea and inflict decisive blows on the enemy.[21]

The second and more difficult task of strategic defense involves the detection and successful engagement of deployed Polaris/Poseidon submarines. While there is no evidence suggesting that the Soviets have obtained such a capability, it does seem clear that the development of some types of vessels and aircraft has been motivated primarily by a desire to do *something* about the threat posed by strategic submarines. Decisions reached during the 1961/62 period are particularly important in this regard. These forces are unlikely to be effective, however, unless more capable sensors and weapons are developed.

Two broad approaches are generally considered for the anti-strategic submarine mission; each requires different types of naval forces. One, area defense, focuses on systems capable of detecting submarines over large ocean areas, identifying those that are detected, and sinking them near simultaneously when ordered to do so. The deployment of anti-submarine helicopter cruisers, the "Moskva" class, has been a step in this direction. Similarly, deployment of land-based IL-18 ("May") aircraft also could be designed for these purposes. Some 30 such aircraft were said to be operational in 1972, some reportedly based in Egypt.[22]

The second approach attempts to maintain a continual track on strategic submarines throughout their patrol. In this case, a hunter/killer submarine would pick up a strategic submarine as it left its base, or while transiting a narrow strait on the way to its launch area and, utilizing passive sonars, trail the quarry throughout its period on station. Such a pursuer, if successful, likely would be in a position to attack the strategic submarine quickly, should a conflict erupt. The new "Victor" class nuclear attack submarine could be used in this sort of role, but the even newer "Alpha" class, which has not entered serial production as yet, is an even more likely candidate. This is due to the long lead times previously mentioned; at the time the decision to develop the "Victor" would have been made, it was unlikely that the degree of threat posed by U.S. strategic submarines would have been foreseen.

3. Missions supporting foreign policy objectives.—Naval vessels can be used to further the foreign policy goals of their owners in a manner only indirectly related to the war-fighting capabilities of the ships. The movement of warships, their activity while on patrol, and their ports of call can be used to signal a state's intentions in various situations, as a means of commitment, as a threat, and so forth. Additionally, naval forces can perform various acts which, while certainly hostile, incorporate only limited and measured degrees of force; blockade and interposition fall into this category. In these situations, naval activity is designed to impact upon the expectations of the nations directly involved, and upon those which might consider becoming involved. As such, naval activity is generally accompanied by diplomatic or other forms of verbal activity, and serves as a signal of the seriousness with which verbal undertakings should be understood. The West has long employed naval forces for such purposes in a form of behavior generally referred to as "gunboat diplomacy."

Most generally, of course, the mere presence of a naval force in any region serves a political function, regardless of its composition, its missions, or its behavior, and even in the absence of any diplomatic activity consciously directed to its part. The existence of the force automatically causes the states of the region to weigh a new factor in their calculation of the balance of power, and in their expectations of the likely behavior of other states in various contingencies. In the long run, many believe, such phenomena might contribute to the possible realignment of international allegiances. A particularly strong impact along these lines might be felt in areas such as the Mediterranean, where the Soviet presence has grown sharply while the U.S. fleet has diminished somewhat. Specific manifestations of this sort of effect are difficult to identify, however. In more concrete terms, four roles in which the Soviet Navy has served immediate diplomatic/ political purposes can be described.

First, the U.S.S.R. has employed its Navy to try to constrain the United States' ability to intervene in crises in the Middle East and South Asia. This mission frequently is cited by Soviet leaders as justification for their naval presence in the Mediterranean. For example, at a time of considerable tension in the Mediterranean, Admiral Gorshkov said:

> Ships of the Soviet Navy are systematically present in the ocean, including the areas of the presence of shock navies (naval strike forces—BB) of NATO. The presence of our ships in these areas binds the hands of the imperialists, deprives them of a possibility to interfere unhindered into internal affairs of the peoples.[23]

There have been reports indicating that unusually large numbers of Soviet combatant vessels were maintained in the general area of the fighting during the June War (1967), the Jordanian Civil War (1970), and the 1971 India-Pakistan War.[24] Presumably, these deployments were made in response to (or in anticipation of) U.S. activity, with the purpose of deterring the unilateral exercise of Western naval power, such as was the case during the Lebanese Civil War (1958).

Second, the Soviet Navy has been employed in actions designed to protect Soviet client regimes from threats mounted by their enemies, domestic and foreign. Increasing Soviet involvement in the third world implies greater Soviet commitments to local regimes. On occasion, the U.S.S.R. has utilized its naval resources to demonstrate and implement those commitments.

(a) In the Fall of 1967 Soviet combatants visited Port Said following the sinking of the destroyer Eilat, in an obvious attempt to deter Israeli reprisals;[25]

(b) In the Spring of 1970 prolonged port calls were made to Mogadiscio, Somali Republic, seemingly as a means of demonstrating support to the incumbent regime threatened by domestic instability;[26]

(c) In December, 1970 Soviet units established a naval patrol off the coast of Guinea, apparently to deter further Portuguese incursions such as had been staged the previous month.[27]

Third, on at least one occasion the U.S.S.R. seems to have employed naval vessels to coerce a second nation, in defense of Soviet maritime resources. In this little-known case, the best example to date of Soviet recourse to traditional gunboat diplomacy, combatants were deployed off the coast of Ghana in February/March, 1969 in conjunction with diplomatic efforts to secure the release of Soviet fishing trawlers. The fishing boats had been impounded the previous October because of their alleged involvement in arms smuggling. Following the failure of diplomatic and economic activity to secure their release, the Soviets made an unprecedented deployment of three warships to the Gulf of Guinea. Their presence off the Ghanaian coast coincided with release of the trawlers.[28]

Finally, ships of the Soviet Navy have made increasing use of local port facilities in recent years. While most port visits are primarily designed to meet operational requirements generated by the maintenance of a permanent naval presence in distant waters, they also can be used to create goodwill between the host nation and the Soviet Union. Moreover, certain situations lend themselves to the use of port visits for more immediate and direct political ends. For example, in May, 1971 Soviet warship visits to Sierra Leone seem to have been used to help legitimize a new and shaky regime.[29]

There exists some controversy regarding the importance of these missions to the Soviet Navy, and the degree to which a desire to have such capabilities may have impacted on their shipbuilding programs. Some analysts trace adoption of political and diplomatic roles by the Soviet Navy to the Cuban missile crisis. The United States' ability to challenge the Soviets at sea, and to blockade Cuba and credibly threaten an invasion is said to have: (a) demonstrated to the Soviets the value of naval forces for such purposes; and (b) caused them to resolve not to be placed in such a position of military inferiority again. Most significantly, the Cuban missile crisis is said to have convinced the Soviets that strategic nuclear power was not a sufficient basis for attainment of their foreign policy goals; that it also would be necessary to develop general purpose forces capable of defending their foreign interests. Consequently, this viewpoint traces much of the evolution of Soviet naval capabilities, particularly their development of new surface warships to this event.

Other analysts, however, downplay the significance of the missile crisis. They point out that the Soviet and Tsarist Navies had undertaken political missions long before 1962, and that the necessarily long lead times between decisions and new ship deployments would indicate that development of the new classes of warships which made their appearance in the late 1960s was probably initiated before the crisis.[31] Most analysts would agree that present deployment patterns partially can be attributed to political missions.[32]

4. Interdiction of sea-lanes of communication.—U.S. Navy spokesmen maintain that the main thrust of Soviet naval development has been "to counter our naval forces and deny us the use of the seas to support our allies and our overseas forces."[33] This mission, which is generally referred to as "interdiction," incorporates two separable contingencies. One foresees the possibility of a major conflict in Europe or elsewhere, and use of Soviet submarines and naval aviation to disrupt U.S. efforts to deploy and supply military forces in the combat theatre. The other contingency, which has been termed "commerce war of attrition," considers the possibility of submarine and air interdiction of civilian merchant shipping, either in conjunction with a protracted land war or independently, as a form of limited war. Recently, the possibility has been raised that the latter type of conflict might focus on U.S. and allied oil imports from the Persian Gulf.[34]

The importance of these missions to the Soviet Navy and the degree to which they impact on Soviet naval planning are contentious points, particularly so for "commerce wars of attrition." Those who believe the Soviets place a high priority on interdiction missions emphasize the importance of secure sea-lanes of communication to the West, particularly in the context of a protracted land war in Europe. Contrapuntally, they stress the large numbers of torpedo attack and cruise missile submarines deployed by the Soviets, particularly those assigned to the Northern Fleet, which is responsible for the Atlantic. This school also notes that Soviet submarines and naval strike aircraft, regardless of their original purpose, would be capable of interdiction missions should major East-West conflict develop.

The contrary viewpoint argues that Soviet military doctrine and the composition and structure of Soviet ground forces indicate a low priority for interdiction missions. It has been stated that the U.S.S.R. makes little or no provision for protracted warfare in Europe, and that its armies are designed, equipped, and deployed so as to win "a short war based on shock power." These arguments pay particular attention to the relative weakness of the Soviets' logistical system; their relatively high combat to support troop ratio; their use of a unit, rather than an individual personnel replacement system; and their military writings and exercises.[35] In a short war, military and civilian resupply would be of lesser importance than in protracted conflict.

This viewpoint considers the force levels and characteristics of Soviet submarines and naval aircraft to be more dependent upon their perceived requirements for "strategic defense," particularly the anti-carrier mission. It notes the large decline in the number of torpedo attack submarines, the weapon system likely to be primary in any interdiction campaign. It also points to the lack of evidence of Soviet naval exercises involving co-ordinated interdiction campaigns. It should be added, however, that a portion of the decline in submarines is compensated for by the increased capabilities of individual units. Also, it must be admitted that Soviet forces which survived engagements with carrier task forces, if these were their primary target, would be then available for interdiction roles.

5. *Projection of land and air power overseas.*—This mission has consumed the major portion of U.S. naval resources during the past decade. Perhaps because of the common tendency to see ourselves in others, American commentators tend to stress potential Soviet interests in similar pursuits. Much has been made of the U.S.S.R.'s reactivation of naval infantry (i.e., Marines) in 1963, and the alleged potentiality of "Moskva" class anti-submarine helicopter cruisers to serve as assault ships, or to accommodate vertical or short takeoff and landing (V/STOL) aircraft.[36] In point of fact, however, the projection capability of the Soviet Navy is modest in the extreme.

It has been pointed out previously that the amphibious assault force of the Soviet Navy is relatively small, that they have not deployed amphibious warfare ships capable of helicopter operations, and that the Naval Infantry consists of only 15,000 men. To the best of this writer's information, neither the "Moskva" nor its sister ship have been seen in other than anti-submarine operations. Furthermore, the

Soviet Navy presently has no capability to deploy fixed-wing aircraft on naval vessels and thus could not supply air cover for an amphibious landing, nor provide air power based at sea to client regimes.[37]

Under such conditions, it seems likely that the only projection missions envisioned by Soviet planners at present are: (a) those which can be undertaken under peacetime conditions, such as the Egypt case; and (b) those in regions contiguous to the Soviet Union and within range of Soviet land-based aircraft. The latter is generally thought of as means of securing access by the Soviet fleets to and from their confined home waters, in conjunction with a more general conflict. Of greatest priority in this regard would be seizure of the Turkish Straits and, secondarily, the northern coast of Norway.

6. Sustained combat at sea.—The failure of the Soviet Navy to deploy sea-based airpower also limits its ability to maintain surface forces at sea in hostile environments. This limitation is further aggravated by three additional factors:

(a) Support forces—It has been noted that the Soviet Navy has neglected the construction of support forces and is only beginning to develop afloat logistical capabilities. While they still have been able to maintain substantial continuous deployments in distant areas, making use of civilian ships and local port facilities for support, such a logistical system presumes a peacetime environment. In wartime, such an arrangement would be considered neither practical nor secure.

(b) Ship Design—Observers have marvelled at the relatively small size of Soviet warships. New Soviet destroyers are roughly only half the size of their American counterparts for example, yet demonstrate considerable advantage in some areas, such as firepower. While part of this difference may be attributed to greater Soviet advances in ship design, clearly they have had to sacrifice some capabilities in order to achieve smaller size and its consequent lesser cost. These sacrifices strongly affect Soviet capability for sustained combat at sea. They include crew habitability, range, endurance, and weapons reload capacity. [38]

(c) Overseas bases—The consequences of both the above factors are aggravated by the U.S.S.R.'s reluctance to make use of bases overseas. While of necessity the Soviet Navy has utilized certain facilities in Egypt and Syria since the events of July, 1972, development of a Soviet shore establishment has not kept pace with their rapidly growing deployments. Whether for ideological reasons, because of their observation of U.S. experience, or because of lack of opportunities, the Soviet Navy's support infrastructure in foreign countries is relatively limited. Although much has been made of arrangements with various states for the use of ports and airfields for the support of merchant, fishing, and in some cases, naval vessels, such arrangements are quite different from the attainment of less transitory and more exclusive naval "bases." [39] Although the use of foreign facilities is helpful in maintaining a standing peacetime presence in distant areas, they are unlikely to be of much use in conflict situations; or at least Soviet decision makers cannot count on their availability. As the U.S. has learned during various Mediterranean contingencies, even the use of naval "bases" is often constrained by host governments.

Future Directions

In the twenty years since the re-evaluation of Soviet naval strategy and force structure which followed Stalin's demise, the Soviet Union has developed a modern "blue-water" Navy of major proportions; a force fully capable of attaining many of the specific objectives which have been set out for it. The Soviets have developed and deployed a fleet of ballistic missile submarines with capabilities comparable, if still qualitatively inferior to their U.S. counterparts. They have built a relatively small number of major surface warships of ultramodern design; ships that have dazzled the West in their design efficiency, in their firepower, and in their propulsion and electronic systems. They have built a much larger force of smaller surface vessels, and have deployed substantial numbers of land-based aircraft for the defense of waters contiguous to the U.S.S.R. They are constructing a large force of nuclear-powered torpedo attack and cruise missile submarines which would present severe problems to U.S. naval task forces and to U.S. and allied merchant shipping in the event of open hostilities. Finally, the Soviets have become increasingly prone to deploy their Navy to regions relatively distant from their home waters, and to maintain standing naval forces in regions of traditional Western maritime dominance.

All this should not, however, obscure the fact that Soviet naval capabilities have developed not as a result of increasing force levels, but rather as a consequence of improvements in individual unit capabilities and an expansion in the scope of the navy's peacetime role. Moreover, capabilities have been improved selectively, with some missions greatly emphasized and others largely neglected. Generally, and with the exception of strategic submarines, the Soviet Navy does not appear to be designed to project the Soviet Union's power far from its own shores, but to defend the security and interests of the U.S.S.R. by preventing attacks on its homeland, and by deterring the United States from intervening in regions close to Soviet borders. The Soviet Navy's past building programs, its exercises, its peacetime deployments, and Soviet military doctrine all support the assessment that the primary emphasis in Soviet naval evolution has been, and is likely to remain, defensively oriented.

Additionally, several weaknesses in the Soviet Navy will limit the degree to which more worrisome missions may be undertaken. It lacks a capability of any magnitude for intervening overseas in the face of military opposition, having neither fixed-wing aircraft based at sea nor sizable amphibious lift capability. It would have difficulty supporting sustained operations on the high seas in wartime as it lacks an overseas infrastructure, has only limited support forces, and apparently has not designed its combat vessels for protracted war at sea. Despite its best efforts and the deployment of relatively large numbers of anti-submarine systems, its capabilities against modern quiet-running submarines still appear to be quite limited.

This is not to say that the Soviet Navy is useless for more offensive operations, nor that the relative emphasis on defense might not be modified somewhat in the future. Indeed, there are some indications that such changes may be in the cards for the not too distant future. The Soviet Navy seems to be approaching a turning point in its evolution. Many programs that were long under development are now completed or have resulted in series production of various types of units. Forces have been deployed which seem to be capable of successfully carrying out certain long sought after missions, although others (such as the anti-strategic submarine mission) remain far from complete.

The Commander-in-Chief of the Soviet Navy, Admiral S.G. Gorshkov, is nearing twenty years in office and soon may be ready to step down. Speculation as to the Admiral's possible retirement, and as to the existence of a new internal Soviet debate on naval force structure and missions, has been fueled by publication of a series of articles in 1972, authored by Admiral Gorshkov, in the Soviet Navy journal, *Morskoy Sbornik*.[40] This series, ostensibly a history of the Russian and Soviet navies, appears to be, in fact, a remarkably open discussion of conflicting approaches to the navy's role, couched in historical terms. In these articles, the Admiral argues for a larger navy, even at the expense of other components of the Soviet military, primarily because of the unique value of naval forces in peacetime. Additionally, he reminds the reader of historical examples when the Russians were ill-prepared for conflict because of their neglect of naval forces. He cleverly notes, "There is widespread propaganda produced by American ideologists asserting that the Soviet state does not need a powerful Navy,"[41] thus placing those who oppose naval expansion in the imperialist camp.

Basically, the choice facing the Soviets is this. They can continue to concentrate on defensive capabilities, maintaining the size and composition of the navy essentially as they appear today except for the forthcoming reductions in torpedo attack submarines and destroyers mentioned in the first part of this paper. If such a choice is made there would be, no doubt, continued modernization as improved weapons, sensors, and other equipment are made available by technological development. These measures would, however, continue to concentrate on strategic defense and on countering Western interventionary capabilities in regions close to Soviet shores. Within such a focus, the Soviet Navy could carry out political missions of the sort described previously, but only in situations not involving a sizable risk of conflict with the United States in distant waters.

Alternatively, the Soviet Union could begin to develop the forces necessary to project its power far from its own shores. Prerequisites for such a capability would include: (a) development of new classes of surface warships; (b) acquisition of a sea-based fixed-wing aircraft capability; (c) construction of larger and more capable assault forces; (d) expansion of the navy's land-based infrastructure; and (e) development of logistics forces capable of providing afloat support in hostile environments. These measures would be quite costly, and would result in a marked increase in the amount of resources expended by the Soviet Navy. Many would argue that in view of this expense, and because of other pressing civilian and military demands upon the Soviet Union's limited resources, adoption of such a course of action would be quite unlikely. Nonetheless, several factors lead one to reserve judgment as to the eventual outcome of the debate.

First, the public prominence of the Soviet Navy and its utilization in various political roles are fairly recent phenomena; 1967 being a good point of reference for the renewed emphasis placed on such activity. The Soviet Union has enjoyed, no doubt, the prestige accorded to it because of this prominence and has reaped more specific benefits in India, Somalia, Guinea, and elsewhere. While the 1972 downturn in Soviet fortunes in their Egyptian "adventure" will bolster those who argue to the contrary, these other successes may well spur the Soviets to obtain the projection capabilities necessary to achieve similar outcomes in less marginal situations—those involving greater risk of conflict with the United States.

Second, in 1972 the first ship of a new class of guided missile cruisers, the "Kara," made her initial appearance. One or two other ships of this class were reported to be under construction. The vessel is important as it is considerably larger than other modern Soviet cruisers (9,000 tons versus 6,000 for the "Kresta II"), and thus is probably intended as a replacement for the larger but older "Sverdlov" gun cruisers, built between 1951 and 1956. The relatively large size of the "Kara" should make ships of this class well-suited for sustained operations at sea. The added space could be used to improve endurance and reload capacity, and to equip the vessels as flagships with additional communications gear and accommodations for flag staffs.[42] The importance of the "Kara" as an indicator of Soviet intentions should not be exaggerated, however, insofar as a replacement for the "Sverdlov's" obviously was necessary and because the decision to build the "Kara" was probably made some time ago. Nonetheless, the class is an important improvement to Soviet capabilities for sustained operations on the high seas.

Third, and more significant, are reports of the construction of a much larger vessel, one expected to be some sort of aircraft carrier, in the Nikolaev shipyard on the Black Sea. In the past Soviet spokesmen have disparaged the efficacy of aircraft carriers. Recently, however, Admiral Zumwalt noted:

. . . we now have evidence that the Soviet Navy . . . is reevaluating its requirements and is planning to take tactical aircraft to sea. We project that the Soviet's first carrier will, in fact, appear within the next few years.[43]

Estimates of the new vessel's size range between 25,000 and 35,000 tons. It is said to be capable of aircraft operations, having a full flight deck roughly 800 feet long.[44]

The significance of the vessel will depend upon its actual size, the types of aircraft which are operated from it, and its function. One would suspect that current size estimates are exaggerated somewhat, as they report leaks from U.S. Navy sources whose forecasts are likely to be conservative. Initial public estimates of the size of the "Moskva," which did not appear until after the ship had begun its sea trials (a point one to two years away for the new ship), overestimated that vessel's size by more than 25 percent.[45]

The new ship does not appear likely to be capable of operating modern fixed-wing jet aircraft. Its size is much smaller than that of newer U.S. carriers used for such purposes (60-80,000 tons). Nor is there any evidence in the public domain as yet, that the new ship will feature characteristics desirable for such operations—angled flight deck, catapults, arresting gear. Navy sources have speculated, however, that the ship might be planned to operate vertical or short take-off and landing (V/STOL) aircraft. These reports are based on the size of the vessel, particularly the apparent length of its flight deck, which could be considered excessive if only helicopter operations were envisioned. It also has been noted that the Soviet Navy recently began flight testing V/STOL aircraft.[46] Alternatively, the ship could be used solely for helicopter operations, such as has been the case for the "Moskva" class. Several important deficiencies in V/STOL technology argue for such an outcome.

Speculation as to possible functions of the new ship encompass a wide variety of possibilities. On the one hand, some believe that it may be simply a follow-on to the

"Moskva," carrying helicopters designed for anti-submarine operations. Others, who also rule out V/STOL deployments, argue that the new ship will more likely be intended for, and carry, helicopters designed for assault operations. Similar variations can be considered within the school which believes that the ship will carry V/STOL aircraft. These aircraft could be designed for anti-submarine warfare, for close-in air defense of Soviet surface vessels, or for air strike operations. Still another theory speculates that the new vessel is probably a support ship, equipped with a flight deck so as to permit on-board delivery of supplies and repair parts.

The new ship's function is not solely a question of the type of aircraft which is deployed to it. Design characteristics of the vessel itself will determine such possibilities, in part. For example, if the ship is intended as an assault vessel, it will incorporate cargo storage facilities for tanks and other large items of equipment; it will have troop accommodations, and so forth. Unfortunately, information presently available regarding these characteristics is far too scanty to permit reasoned judgments as to which of the above possibilities are more probable.

The appearance of a true aircraft carrier would be a momentous event in the evolution of Soviet naval power. Assuming it were not simply a case of wanting to imitate the United States and building a large ship for prestige and other non-mission oriented purposes, its appearance could well presage an upgrading of the priority accorded to the projection mission, and to other forms of surface operations. Such a decision will not be taken lightly by the Soviets, however, as it would imply enormous costs, both in investment and operating expenses. Not only will the carriers themselves have to be bought, but their specialized equipment (e.g., arresting gear and catapults) developed. Moreover, carrier operations require aircraft with special characteristics (e.g., folding wings, strengthened undercarriage), which would have to be designed and procured. Finally, a larger number of Soviet seamen and pilots would have to be trained in skills very different from those currently employed in Soviet naval operations.

As has been noted, the mystery ship at Nikolaev is unlikely to be a true aircraft carrier, in the sense the term is applied to modern U.S. carriers. Nonetheless, if it is designed for other than helicopter-borne anti-submarine operations, it would indicate continuing evolution of Soviet capabilities toward such an end. This would imply a new direction in Soviet conceptions of the utility of sea power, and that the internal debate in the Soviet Union had been resolved, at least for the time being, in the direction of those who viewed the advantages of providing their surface naval forces with sea-based air power as well worth the incremental cost.

NOTES

1. The views expressed in this paper are those of the author. They should not, necessarily, be attributed to the trustees, officers, or staff of the Brookings Institution. I would like to acknowledge my indebtedness to Michael K. MccGwire (Dalhousie University), whose articles and comments on an earlier version have been of major assistance throughout the paper. I am solely responsible for any errors, however.

2. One informed observer has estimated that the following time-lags are pertinent to various types of Soviet decisions: (a) those which add equipment to existing vessels but do not require design changes: 2-3 years; (b) those to modify equipment which requires modest design changes: 5-6 years; (c) those requiring new ship designs, but utilizing many items already available: 8 years; and (d) those requiring complete redesign from the ground up: 10-12 years. Source: Michael MccGwire, at a seminar on "Soviet Naval Development," Halifax, Nova Scotia, October 25, 1972.

The pioneer and most complete study of the development of Soviet naval thought is Robert W. Herrick, *Soviet Naval Strategy: Fifty Years of Theory and Practice* (Annapolis, U.S. Naval Institute, 1968).

Additional information, particularly regarding decision periods in Soviet naval procurement, can be seen in: Michael MccGwire, *Soviet Naval Capabilities and Intentions*, paper presented at the R.U.S.I. conference, "The Soviet Union in Europe and the Near East" (Milford-on-Sea, 1970) (As reprinted in the *Congressional Record* (July 1, 1971), pp. 6850-58); also, Michael MccGwire, *Soviet Naval Procurement*, reprinted as above.

3. Letter from Admiral E. R. Zumwalt, Jr. to Senator William Proxmire (June 8, 1972); reprinted in the *Congressional Record* (June 12, 1972), pp. S-9193-95. (Hereafter: Zumwalt letter of June 8).

4. Letter from Admiral E. R. Zumwalt, Jr. to Senator William Proxmire (June 2, 1972); reprinted in the *Congressional Record* (June 12, 1972), pp. S-9186-92. (Hereafter: Zumwalt letter of June 2). The force level data in the tables are drawn exclusively from Raymond V. B. Blackman (ed.), *Jane's Fighting Ships* (London, 1958/59 and 1972/73). This annual publication is generally understood to be the most authoritative, comprehensive, and detailed unclassified source. Also, exclusive dependence on *Jane's Fighting Ships* permitted a more systematic comparison of the two years than would have been possible if many sources had been utilized.

The data in *Jane's Fighting Ships*, however, is generally not the most recent available. The 1972/73 *Jane's Fighting Ships*, for example, which appeared in summer of 1972, reflects estimates of the Soviet order of battle around the beginning of the year. There is also a tendency to err on the conservative side regarding the possible retirement of older vessels. Consequently, the tables are supplemented with more recent information where pertinent.

5. Admiral Thomas H. Moorer, "Statement Before the Senate Armed Services Committee," (Processed: February 15, 1972), p. 11; Secretary of Defense Melvin R. Laird, "Statement Before the Senate Armed Services Committee on the FY 1973 Defense Budget and FY 1973-1977 Program," (Processed: February 15, 1972), p. 39.

6. Zumwalt letter of June 2, p. 7.

7. Admiral Zumwalt's letter of June 2, lists 25 gun destroyers fewer than the number incorporated in Table 2. It should be noted that a number of the Skoryi destroyers were retrofitted with more modern SSW weapons between 1958 and 1961.

8. Zumwalt letter of June 2, p. 6.

9. See MccGwire, *Soviet Naval Capabilities, loc. cit.*, pp. E6853-55; also, Admiral Ephraim P. Holmes, "The Soviet Presence in the Atlantic: NATO *Letter*, XVIII (September 1970), pp. 6-11. Prominent exceptions to the rule on naval port calls were two visits to Britain—one in 1953 in connection with the coronation naval review, one in 1955 in conjunction with Khruschev's visit—and a 1955 visit to China.

10. A good discussion of the development of Soviet Mediterranean

deployments can be seen in Robert G. Weinland, *Soviet Transits of the Turkish Straits* (Professional Paper No. 94; Arlington, Center for Naval Analyses, 1972).

11. Robert G. Weinland, *The Changing Mission Structure of the Soviet Navy* (Professional Paper No. 80; Arlington, Center for Naval Analyses, 1971), pp. 11-12; MccGwire, *Soviet Naval Capabilities, loc. cit.*, pp. E6853-55.

12. Data in this paragraph have been derived from *Jane's Fighting Ships 1972/73*.

13. Breyer, *loc. cit.*, pp. 129-34.

14. Zumwalt letter of June 2, p. 2

15. *Jane's Fighting Ships 1972/73*, p. 577.

16. *Washington Post* (May 13, 1972), p. 12; a more recent article indicated that the first modified "Yankee" may be already operational: *New York Times* (October 1, 1972).

17. "Protocol—To the Interim Agreement Between the United States of America and The Union of Soviet Socialist Republics on Certain Measures With Respect to Limitation of Strategic Offensive Arms."

18. "Interview With Defense Secretary Laird," *U.S. News and World Report* (March 27, 1972), p. 44; Zumwalt letter of June 8, p. 5.

19. MccGwire, *The Soviet Union in Europe and the Near East, loc. cit.*, provides the best arguments along these lines; a counter position is provided by Weinland, *The Changing Mission Structure of the Soviet Navy, loc. cit.*

20. Zumwalt letter of June 2, p. 2.

21. Shablikov et al., *Okean. Maneuvers of the U.S.S.R. Navy Conducted in April-May 1970*, translated by the Joint Publications Research Service (Processed: April 19, 1971), p. 6 (Italics added).

22. *Jane's Fighting Ships 1971/72*, p. 577.

23. TASS, International Service (July 25, 1970); as reported by *FBIS, Daily Report: Soviet Union* (July 27, 1971), p. E-1.

24. *New York Times* (May 31, 1967); *New York Times* (October 8, 1970); *Philadelphia Inquirer* (December 17, 1971); and Zumwalt, *loc. cit.*, p. 5.

25. Lt. Cdr. David R. Cox, "Seapower and Soviet Foreign Policy," *U.S. Naval Institute Proceedings*, XCV (June, 1969), pp. 42-43.

26. James M. McConnell, *The Soviet Navy in the Indian Ocean* (Professional Paper No. 77; Arlington, Center for Naval Analyses, 1971), p. 11.

27. Weinland, *The Changing Mission Structure of the Soviet Navy, loc. cit.*, p. 11; *Washington Post* (February 9, 1972), p. A-9.

28. Weinland, *The Changing Mission Structure of the Soviet Navy, loc. cit.*, p. 11.

29. *Ibid.*, p. 12.

30. See: Zumwalt, *loc. cit.*, p. 7; Cox, *loc. cit.*, pp. 35-36; Thomas W. Wolfe, *The Soviet Quest for More Globally Mobile Military Power* (RAND Memo RM-554-PR; Santa Monica, 1967).

31. For persuasive arrangements in this regard, see: Michael K. MccGwire, "Soviet Maritime Strategy, Capabilities, and Intentions in the Caribbean," in J. D. Theberge (ed.), *Soviet Seapower in the Caribbean* (New York, Praeger, 1972), pp. 39-54.

32. Weinland, *The Changing Mission Structure of the Soviet Navy*, *loc. cit.*

33. U. S. House of Representatives, *Hearings on Military Posture* (Washington, GPO, 1971), p. 2762.

34. Zumwalt, *loc. cit.*, p. 3.

35. Steven L. Canby, *NATO Military Policy: The Constraints Imposed By An Inappropriate Military Structure* (Santa Monica, Processed, 1972), p. 15. Also see: John Erickson, *Soviet Military Power* (London, R.U.S.I., 1971); James M. McConnell, "Ideology and Soviet Military Strategy," in Richard F. Starr (ed.), *Aspects of Modern Communism* (Columbia, University of South Carolina Press, 1968); Malcolm MacIntosh, *The Role of Flexible Response in Soviet Strategic Thinking*, paper presented at the first "Symposium on Soviet Affairs" (Garmish-Parten Kirchen, Germany, 1967); XXX, "The Adaptation of Soviet Ground Forces to Nuclear War," *Military Review*, XLVI (September, 1966), pp. 11-17.

36. For example, J. T. Howe, *Multicrises: Seapower and Global Politics in the Missile Age* (Cambridge, MIT Press, 1971), pp. 305-7.

37. It is possible, of course, to fly in air cover or to transport it with merchant shipping, if the seas remain sanctuary, such as the Soviets demonstrated in Egypt in 1969. Such a capability is quite different from that required to undertake opposed operations, however, and is not as flexible nor as quickly reactive as sea-based air power.

38. Zumwalt letter of June 2, p. 4. Zumwalt letter of June 8, p. 7.

39. In a statement which presaged his expulsion of much of the Soviet military presence in Egypt, President Sadat carefully distinguished between "facilities" and "bases." *Radio Cairo Domestic Service*, May 1, 1972.

40. Admiral S. G. Gorshkov, "Navies in War and in Peace," *Morskoy Sbornik*. February 1972. I am indebted to Robert W. Herrick for his assistance in understanding these articles.

41. Gorshkov, "Russia's Difficult Road to the Sea," *Morskoy Sbornik*, No. 3 (March 1972), p. 21.

42. *Jane's Fighting Ships 1972/73*, pp. 80, 612; *New York Times* (October 17, 1972), p. 15.

43. Zumwalt letter of June 2, p. 5.

44. *Time* (January 21, 1972); *New York Times* (October 17, 1972), p. 15; *Jane's Fighting Ships 1972/73*, pp. 79-80, 576.

45. An estimated 23-25,000 tons vs. 18,000 actual full-load displacement. *New York Times* (October 23, 1967), p. 1; *New York Times* (February 14, 1968), p. 10. The much earlier reporting date for the new ship could indicate either improvements in U.S. intelligence capabilities or the greater importance of the Soviet Navy for budget-related politics in the U.S.

46. *New York Times* (October 17, 1972), p. 15.

5 Naval Armaments in the Mediterranean

Curt Gasteyger

Naval armaments—like any other kind of armament—gain or lose their relevance according to the strategic importance and the political situation of their environment, i.e., the context within which they are deployed. This is, of course, a commonplace. But in order to judge the present nature and future evolution of naval armaments in the Mediterranean it seems appropriate to remind ourselves briefly of the general political situation in, and the changing strategic function of, this area.[1]

The Changing Political Climate

A number of recent events—the abortive *coup d'état* in Morocco, the "agonizing reappraisal" of the French-Algerian relationship, internal unrest in Turkey, potential external pressure against Yugoslavia, social turmoil in Italy (though, as the last elections show, a surprising degree of political continuity), uncertainty about the political future of Tunisia and Spain once President Bourguiba and General Franco will have left the scene, rumors about dissensions within the inscrutable Libyan leadership, shifts in Maltese politics and a rather unexpected flare-up of the Cyprus crisis—could suggest

that the Mediterranean area might be once more on the verge
of new tensions and conflicts. Also, there are the continuous
ups and downs in the relationship between the oil-producing
(mainly Arab) and the oil-consuming (mainly Western)
countries (or oil companies) which have become an ever-pres-
ent element of friction. And there is, last but not least, the
still unsolved Arab-Israeli conflict which casts its shadow over
the entire Eastern Mediterranean and beyond. On the other
hand, the Mediterranean has always been an area of constant
change, crisis and rivalry. It would be rather difficult to prove
that the present period is more tormented and volatile than,
say, the thirties or fifties.

There is little doubt that the emergence of the Soviet
Union as a second great power and challenger of American
strategic predominance has introduced new uncertainties and
contributed to widen the spectrum of political outlooks,
alignments and nonalignments. In our own view the expansion of the Soviet-American rivalry into the Mediterranean
has given a number of countries the opportunity to extricate
themselves from an all too one-sided relationship with, or
dependence on, one of the superpowers and to take a more
independent, "balanced" or even occasionally "neutralistic"
stand.

As was to be expected this process of partial disengagement affected more the position of the quasi omnipresent
United States than of the newcomer Soviet Union. One need
not, however, be a prophet to predict that sooner or later the
latter will go through similar disillusioning experiences.
Already today the visitor runs frequently into people on the
Southern shores who, like the *"apprenti sorcier,"* first
welcomed Moscow's appearance on the scene but are now
finding it increasingly cumbersome.

The recent *eclat* in Soviet-Egyptian relations has abruptly
brought into the open Egypt's growing uneasiness about her
almost total dependence on Soviet aid and benevolence; at
the same time it confirms that she has been groping—or at
least hoping—for a cautious rapprochement with the United

States and a more active role with Western Europe. Algeria in her turn has re-established relations with Britain and the Federal Republic of Germany (though not yet, in a formal sense, with the United States). In a number of recent meetings Presidents Bourguiba, Boumediene, El Ghadhafi and, though with visible reluctance, Sadat came out with a clear condemnation of "spheres of influence," "bases" and "imperialism," leaving it ambiguously open whether they were thinking of the United States alone or the "other" super-powers as well. Their rediscovery of the advantages of "neutralism" would point that way. Even Libya, whose revolutionary zeal makes it difficult to predict her future political orientation, made it quite clear that she not only wants to keep the Soviet Union at arm's length herself but also encourages neighboring countries, including Malta, to do so as well.

On the Western and Northern shores we find that the Mediterranean members of the Atlantic Alliance—from France to Turkey—as well as Spain have (like their Central and North European partners) adopted a more flexible attitude toward the Soviet Union and the other Communist countries. While remaining loyal allies of NATO, Italy, Turkey and even the Greece of the Colonels pursue a policy which corresponds better to the more complex political and strategic situation that has evolved since the end of the "Cold War." Equally, both Morocco and Spain have gradually improved or expanded their relations with the Communist world. Malta under Prime Minister Mintoff backed up by a strange combination of Libyan support, Soviet interest and Chinese encouragement, could wrench from the British and NATO a much higher price for the future use (or better, Soviet non-use) of Maltese base facilities. Archbishop Makarios in turn seems to have rather skilfully exploited Moscow's desire to counteract the expansion of American base facilities in Greece (Piraeus) for his own quarrel with the Greek regime: the arrival of "Czech weapons" in Cypriot ports did not only evoke unpleasant memories of a similar incident in

Egypt 17 years ago. It could also indicate that henceforth the Soviet Union will not remain indifferent to changes in the politico-strategic status of that region—and Cyprus in particular—and that she has now the means to demonstrate this quite clearly. It is in fact the first time since her emergence as a naval power in the Mediterranean that she has actively interfered in an issue unconnected with the Arab-Israeli conflict and until now within the exclusive domain of NATO.

Special Characteristics of the Mediterranean

This then is the highly complex and potentially explosive political and social framework within which the various powers and their navies operate in the Mediterranean. Like any other area it has therefore a number of special characteristics. They determine, influence and limit the naval policies of the various countries involved. Six of them seem to be of particular relevance in the case of the Mediterranean:

First, it is the area with the highest concentration of merchant and war ships in the world, with naval forces of at least fifteen countries, including three external powers (the United States, the Soviet Union, and Great Britain).

Second, this considerable naval deployment is all the more conspicuous as the Mediterranean is small in size but has a relatively high number of open or latent conflicts.

Third, the Mediterranean as an inland sea has only three accesses on sea: two of them are narrow straits (Gibraltar and the Turkish Straits), the third, the Suez Canal, still being closed for an indefinite future. Movements in and out of the Mediterranean are therefore particularly vulnerable to outside interference, and easily controllable—a disadvantage it shares only with the Baltic and the Black Sea.

Fourth, this specific geographic situation is all the more important to those external powers for whom the Mediterranean is still of considerable politico-strategic significance. The credibility and impact of their naval deployment depends therefore more than anywhere else on permanent access, high mobility and adequate air cover.

Fifth, a number of the Mediterranean countries such as Greece, Italy, Israel and to some lesser degree Turkey, Albania, and Yugoslavia depend for their trade essentially on sea communications and so does Western Europe as a whole with about 80 percent of its oil supply coming from the Middle East, plus Libya and Algeria; at present much of the oil is being transported, at considerable expense, via the Cape of Good Hope.

Sixth and finally, the Mediterranean encompasses, within a relatively small area, about every conceivable variation of political regimes, ideologies and stages of economic development. It is here that the "North-South" conflict between the industrialized and the developing world could and does make itself felt because distances are short and communications dense and the manifold historical and commercial links between North and South, East and West get more and more interwoven with a mounting flow of trade and aid, foreign labor moving northwards, tourists and capital moving southwards. The result is an ever-growing interdependence of interests but also a shared vulnerability to economic recession and political crises.

Naval forces

The naval forces in the Mediterranean can be divided into four categories:

First, those navies whose primary or only purpose is *policing and coastal protection*. Under this category fall the naval forces of Morocco, Tunisia, Malta, the Lebanon and Cyprus. They consist—with the exception of Cyprus which owns some Soviet-built motor torpedo-boats (flying the Greek flag!)—mainly of some patrolcraft for coastal guard duties, fishery protection and against smuggling. None of these coastguard navies has any fighting value.

The second category encompasses *small coastal defense forces* whose bulk consists of motor torpedo-boats, rocket-firing boats, and minecraft, occasionally some submarines and/or a few larger surface vessels like destroyers, gunboats and escorts, together with some landing craft.

The following countries belong to this category:

Algeria, whose navy is almost exclusively equipped with Soviet-built warships;

Libya, with entirely British-built vessels, many of which are inoperative due to insufficient maintenance and lack of qualified engineers;

Syria, with mainly Soviet-built ships;

Israel, whose navy mainly consists of 12 modern French-built boats armed with Israeli-made rockets. Two submarines are reported to be under construction in Britain. The Israeli shipbuilding industry is now being expanded. It can, therefore, be expected that the navy will soon receive locally built fighting ships.

Albania has only a small coastal defense force, mostly of Soviet and Chinese origin. Information according to which China delivered some Chinese-made spare parts for the former Soviet warships, especially the submarines (taken over by Albania after her break with the Soviet Union in 1961), has been confirmed; also the presence of Chinese specialists aboard several vessels of the Albanian Navy. There is, however, no evidence that Chinese warships operate from Albanian ports.

Yugoslavia's coast defense consists mainly of three old destroyers, about half a dozen submarines and, since 1966, a number of Soviet-built small ships, some of them equipped with Styx-SSM rockets. Yugoslavia's expanding shipbuilding industry should soon be able to build almost all types of vessels needed for coastal defense.

Finally, the **U.A.R.**, whose naval forces are numerically so strong that they should be counted among the following category of large coastal and escort forces. Their fighting capacity is, however, still low. The navy consists of mainly

Soviet-built submarines, destroyers and patrolboats equipped with Styx-SSM. The U.A.R. is one of the few Arab countries which, some years ago, attempted to build warships. It has, however, discontinued this costly programme since Soviet warships became available. A Soviet-Egyptian treaty opened in February 1972 envisages substantial Soviet help for the build-up of a merchant ship construction programme in the U.A.R.

The third category comprises *large coastal defense and escort forces*. The navies falling under this category include a certain number of submarines and destroyers which can be used for offensive operations outside coastal waters. They also have escort forces which can protect the seaborne supply routes at least within the Mediterranean basin.

To this category belong the navies of Spain, Greece, Turkey, and Italy, i.e., all of them either members of NATO or, in the case of Spain, linked to the U.S. by a bilateral treaty.

Spain's navy consists mainly of 1 helicopter-carrier, 4-5 submarines, 17 ASW destroyers, 3 destroyers and 8 frigates. Four submarines are being built in France and five frigates are under construction in Spain. About two thirds of the navy is deployed in the Mediterranean. The Spanish naval bases near Cadix, Cartagena and Port Mahon in the Baleares serve for surveillance in the Western Mediterranean.

Greece has one of the few navies in the Mediterranean which today owns more warships than in 1940. However, most of the ships are old and of all the NATO forces in the Mediterranean it is the weakest.

Turkey's navy resembles that of Greece. It also consists mostly of former American and British warships built during World War II. It is reported that it was offered recently (in Spring, 1972) one destroyer and two diesel submarines by the United States. Four modern submarines are under construction with German help, also two escorts. The bulk of the Turkish Navy is usually deployed in the Black Sea or around Istanbul and in the Marmara Sea. In surface-firepower the navies of Greece and Turkey, however, are today inferior to those of Algeria and the U.A.R., which possess the Soviet-built Styx missiles.

Italy has the most modern conventional navy of all Mediterranean countries. Her modern ships, such as the three light helicopter-carrying cruisers, are of excellent quality. Still about one third of the navy is over thirty years old. Given her geographic situation and strategic importance, Italy would need some sort of task-force equipped with ship-to-ship missiles and a strong naval air arm.

This leaves us with the fourth category, the *long-distance strike and nuclear-armed navies*, i.e., those of the four major powers, the United States, the Soviet Union, France and Britain.

The Place of Britain and France

Taking them in reverse order, one realizes immediately that there is very little left of Britain's former naval presence in the Mediterranean. Only a very small number of ships is permanently stationed there, generally some frigates, escorts and auxiliaries, from time to time also a commando-carrier or a submarine. Thus, the Mediterranean has profited little from Britain's "coming home" from "East of Suez" as the bulk of the former Eastern fleet was deployed in the Atlantic. Unless the "Europe of the Nine" is going to develop a more active and coherent politico-military presence in the Mediterranean in which Britain would play an important part, there is little prospect of any substantial come-back to this formerly central area of British naval activities.

France's navy is relatively small but modern. Following a decision by President de Gaulle its major part has, however, been transferred from the Mediterranean to the Atlantic and the Channel (with Brest instead of Toulon as headquarters). It is only in recent years that, along with a reactivation of French Mediterranean policy, one can observe a cautious and modest "re-engagement" in that area. Thus a French carrier took part in NATO manoeuvers there in Fall 1971 but returned to its home base at Brest afterwards. The French squadron in the Mediterranean consists normally of 14 escorts and frigates, 11 submarines, one helicopter-carrier and some mine-sweepers.

According to the new "White Book" on France's defense, policy has three major and interrelated objectives: first, to assure the security of the French territory proper; second, to contribute to the security of Europe and the adjacent areas, *in particular the Mediterranean*; and third, to protect overseas territories associated in one way or another with France.

It is evident that the two latter objectives cannot be reached without a substantial naval capability and an appropriate naval presence in the Mediterranean (and the Atlantic). Hence not only the continuing build-up of the strategic nuclear forces (in particular five nuclear armed submarines until 1975) but also the promise of strengthening and modernizing the "conventional" navy (e.g., construction of several escorts, and a new helicopter-carrier by the mid-seventies). Given France's growing economic interests in the Mediterranean and the political role she wants to play there—either as a non-aligned "third force" or as a forerunner of a common European policy—it can be expected that her naval presence there is likely to grow rather than diminish. Again, much depends on what the policy and objectives of an enlarged European Community in the Mediterranean are going to be.

Towards a European Naval Force?

The Mediterranean may in fact become the first region towards which, in the wake of, or parallel with, the numerous treaties of association the enlarged EEC might develop something like a common "foreign policy." Here is an area which remains a major commercial thoroughfare on which so important EEC members as France and Italy vitally depend, which supplies industrialized Europe with literally millions of foreign workers, which delivers the bulk of oil, where tourism has become a huge source of investment and income and where sooner or later environmental problems will call for joint action.

While it is unlikely that this "Europe of the Nine" will, in the foreseeable future, become anything like a "third politico-military giant," it is already today the strongest economic power in the area. As such it will have to take, whether it likes it or not, an active part contributing to the orderly development of its commercial partners and the preservation of peace and stability in the Mediterranean: for its own prosperity it depends on both.

This will hardly lead—certainly not in the short run—to a noticeable strengthening of West Europe's military, or even naval, presence in the Mediterranean. It may, however, persuade the Europeans to maintain and further develop a naval capability that is sufficiently strong to prevent the Soviet Union from establishing the kind of deployment which could seriously threaten European economic, political and security interests. While Europe's efforts should be, or already are, concentrated on promoting economic development and, at least indirectly, political stability, they cannot entirely neglect the military-strategic aspects. Thus the idea of a European naval force would have several attractions: "It would be one of the easiest first steps to realize in a prospective European defense collaboration. It would demonstrate to the Americans that the Europeans are doing their part. It would allow a more wholehearted French participation while detracting little from the now NATO supported but largely self-contained Sixth Fleet."[2]

What such a force would mean in terms of hardware is difficult to say. It would surely be a function of political and economic considerations as well as strategic requirements. Its size and structure would probably not enable it to adopt an active strategy in the pursuit of political and military influence—an instrument of political power and military intervention so to speak. It would rather have to serve a merely defensive or "negative" strategy of denial. In other words it would have to manifest Europe's determination to prevent the Soviet Union or any other adversary power from doing certain things in which Europe has a vital interest (e.g., free access to a re-opened Suez canal).

If so perceived this strategy will influence or even determine the nature of Europe's naval armaments in the future. It is likely to concentrate on small and fast ships for interception and anti-submarine warfare, on submarines and planes again mainly for ASW, on improving naval and air surveillance as well as naval (surface-to-surface and surface-to-air) missiles, and with an increased emphasis on (shore-based) planes, which, given the geographic situation of the European and other NATO countries and the relatively small size of the Mediterranean, can reach the entire basin from the ground.

The Superpowers

This leaves us with the naval forces of the two superpowers, the United States and the Soviet Union. Like Britain they are not contiguous to the Mediterranean. They are, therefore, to a different degree, vulnerable as regards access routes and dependent on local base and port facilities.

The U.S. Sixth Fleet consists of some 50 ships, including two aircraft carriers (with some 200 aircraft) and one to two helicopter-carriers as well as a few nuclear submarines. The American supply lines stretch westwards through the Gibraltar Straits. They are so far relatively immune from Soviet interference. Some U.S. warships carry ship-to-air missiles, but none has as yet a sufficient ship-to-ship missile.

The size of the Soviet Mediterranean "Eskadra" varies between 30 and 60 ships, usually including one helicopter-carrier (mainly for ASW and landing-support purposes) and about eight to ten submarines, some of which are equipped with surface-to-surface missiles.

The major difference between the Sixth Fleet and the Soviet Eskadra (or rather NATO naval forces on the one hand and the Soviet on the other) is that NATO can count on aircraft carriers as well as land-supported air cover. The former provide a powerful tactical air force that can maintain local air supremacy in any area of the Mediterranean. As long as the Soviet Union lacks such air power—particularly in the Western Mediterranean where she cannot use airfields—this Western supremacy seems unchallenged. On the other hand, a number of Soviet ships are equipped with surface-to-surface missiles of the air-breathing type, some of them having a range over 300 miles. So far there is no equivalent to this weapon on the NATO side. Also, the Soviet submarines, which are difficult to trace, are considered to be a potentially serious threat to NATO forces. Finally, the Soviet Union is reported to be building at Nicolaiev in the Black Sea at least one ship of large proportions. Experts disagree as to whether it is going to be an aircraft carrier or an oil supertanker. If it were the former it would confirm the expectations of those observers who believe that the Soviet Union, too, is sooner or later bound to go for aircraft carriers in order to reduce her dependence on foreign bases and to improve both the strategic mobility and the air-cover of her ever-expanding naval forces.

Even in the Mediterranean the position of the Soviet naval forces is tenuous with respect to access, port facilities and air-cover. With the sole exception of the East Adriatic coast (Yugoslavia and Albania), all the ports and airfields in the politically and economically most important countries, from Gibraltar to Turkey, are under Western (mainly NATO) control, and so are the two presently open accesses.

In contrast to this the Warsaw Pact countries do not possess any shore or port in the Mediterranean; the only Communist countries bordering it, Yugoslavia and Albania, are, for the time being, not disposed to offer their ports or airfields to Pact members; their own naval forces are insignificant. Britain is the only external possessing a naval base in the Mediterranean, Gibraltar. She also uses facilities in Malta and Cyprus. The U.S.A. has been granted certain rights to use ports and airfields in Spain (Torrejon, Moron, Valanzuela and Rota); the Sixth Fleet is using ports in Italy and Turkey and is negotiating with Greece the stationing of its crew at Piraeus.

NATO's reaction to the Soviet naval build-up in the Mediterranean has been surprisingly moderate. This is probably due to the fact that in a period of East-West "détente" the member countries were reluctant to respond with a major military effort, and that at the same time they recognized that even with such an effort little could be achieved to counter or neutralize the political impact of this emerging Soviet presence. NATO has thus basically limited its counter-measures to an improvement of coordinated air surveillance (by creating MARAIRMED = Maritime Air Force Mediterranean) and by agreeing to a multinational "on-call" fleet. It consists of three to four destroyers from several nations. In addition, the United States has ostentatiously been sending elements of the Sixth Fleet into the Black Sea and occasionally dispatching an additional aircraft carrier to the Mediterranean; French ships have again taken part in joint manoeuvers.

Soviet Objectives

The recent considerable build-up of Soviet naval forces and long-range capabilities in general has provided Moscow with new and more options for strategic and political action on a wider geographical scale. Soviet naval penetration into the Mediterranean is the most obvious but by no means the only proof of this. So far the main effect of this all too much publicized and frequently overrated Soviet presence has been a psychological one. It now seems almost unthinkable that a major crisis or conflict could occur in the Mediterranean area without the Soviet Union playing some role in it. Prime Minister Mintoff's bold stand against Britain and NATO would hardly have been taken so seriously without a Soviet Union eager to inherit Malta's base facilities.

Moscow's arrival on the Mediterranean scene has, therefore, increased its influence and widened the spectrum of its possible action. It seems to serve four main and interrelated objectives: first, to establish the Soviet Union as a major power in this area. As such it is part of her striving for strategic parity with the United States and a function of her involvement in the Middle East conflict; second, to reduce, wherever possible, Western, above all American, influence by either supporting anti-Western policies or promoting neutralist tendencies (imposing a reduction of Western influence) in countries allied with, or oriented towards, the West; third, to counter or neutralize the Western (U.S.) strategic posture by strengthening and expanding her own forward naval deployment in general, and improving her ASW capability in particular; and finally, to secure better access routes to the open sea, first and foremost to the Atlantic, and hopefully later also to the Persian Gulf and the Indian Ocean via a re-opened Suez Canal.

The Soviet Union thus appears to have a number of specific political and strategic interests in the Mediterranean and, related to it, the Middle East. They are, in sum, more directly relevant to her security than is the case with the interests of the United States in the same area. Economically speaking, the Mediterranean is to Washington a region of minor interest, and the Middle East oil provides so far only a small fraction for American home consumption. However, forecasts show that the continuous growth of this consumption could force the United States to increase imports from the Middle East much beyond the present amount. Equally, pending a more or less durable settlement of the Arab-Israeli conflict, a substantial American naval presence will be maintained. Having said all this, one would nevertheless be unduly optimistic to exclude completely the possibility of its gradual reduction as part of a general re-appraisal of American ground and naval engagements in and around Europe.

Soviet interests in turn are likely to be more permanent and less subject to change. Even a Middle East settlement, while possibly affecting the scope and nature of Soviet naval deployment, will hardly alter its basic objectives mentioned above. As far as her naval expansion goes the Soviet Union is still in an "acquisitive" stage. One of her primary aims (on whose achievement greatly depend the long-range objectives) must be to overcome or at least reduce what T.B. Millar very appropriately calls "the insecurity of tenure." Practically speaking this means securing permanent and direct access to those areas where she has major interests and commitments; improving logistics and supply as well as air surveillance and air protection.

The Soviet Union still lacks on a global scale several of these requirements which would make her a fully operative and mobile naval power. This is even still true for the Mediterranean, particularly in its Western part. So far the Soviet "Eskadra" has been using Egyptian ports (at Alexandria and Port Said and possibly already at the new air and naval basis at Marsa Matruh) and airfields; it pays visits to countries like Algeria, reportedly Libya, and is expanding its military assistance to Syria, whose harbour at Lattakia it has been using for several years. It is also anchoring frequently just outside the territorial waters of Tunisia, Spain, Malta and Greece.

Cairo's request for a withdrawal of Soviet military personnel from Egyptian territory shows, however, how fragile and subject to abrupt change this Soviet "tenure" is. A Soviet military withdrawal from the U.A.R. is, leaving the potentially far-reaching political consequences for the Middle East conflict aside, likely to be accompanied by a drastic reduction of the Soviets use of Egyptian ports and airfields.

Under these circumstances it seems only natural that the Soviet Union should try to improve her still incomplete and one-sided reliance on ports which belong exclusively to Arab countries, situated on the Eastern and Southern shores of the Mediterranean, by diversifying the number and locations of port or base facilities wherever the opportunity presents itself. In this context we would not be surprised if, possibly in the wake of President Tito's departure, possibly even before, Moscow would be granted permission to use Yugoslav ports.

The Western powers who in terms of bases find themselves still in a much better (though by no means "foolproof") situation have of course an interest in preventing precisely such a further diversification and expansion of Soviet naval deployment. The recent haggling over the future use of Malta's bases provided a lively illustration of this Soviet strategy of "expanding by opportunity" and of Western "policy of denial." Cyprus may well become another illustration of it.

In spite of, or perhaps just because of, the spirally changing political and military situation the Mediterranean could become the first area in which a new pattern of "maritime coexistence" might evolve, that is an area in which the temptation to seek political influence or project military (naval) power is likely to be restrained by the simultaneous presence of not just the two super powers but a relatively great number of smaller but nevertheless rather important powers. One may rightly argue about the usefulness of big and costly navies in times of relative peace. The case of the Mediterranean shows however that their presence can have a restraining and hopefully even stabilizing influence in an area of great political fluidity and growing economic interdependence.

NOTES

1. See also "Europe and the Maghreb," *Atlantic Paper* No. 1, 1972.
2. cf. Wolfgang Hager, "A Mediterranean Policy for the Enlarged Community," contribution to the seminar "European Policies in the Arab-Israeli Conflict," Oslo, April 10-14, 1972.

6 Naval Armaments in the Indian Ocean

Jack Spence

In recent years the Indian Ocean has become a subject of considerable discussion in political and strategic terms. In particular, two developments which occurred in the middle and late 1960s did much to stimulate this discussion: the announcement by the British Labour government in January, 1968 that it intended a progressive and ultimately complete reduction of its commitments east of Suez and the appearance three months later of Soviet warships in the Indian Ocean. The debate that followed these events was further stimulated by the newly elected Conservative government's formal announcement in June, 1970 that Britain was considering a partial reversal of the ban on supplies of arms to the Republic of South Africa, instituted by its Labour predecessor on coming to office in October, 1964.[1]

Any analysis of the present and potential role of naval armanents in the Indian Ocean must clearly take into account the political and economic interests of the major powers concerned, as well as the regional aspirations of the litoral states. In some respects this is a daunting task in view of the variety and number of states involved and—more important—the conflicting interpretations that can be placed on the policies of some of the principal actors and in particular those of the Soviet Union. One difficulty confronting the analyst relates to the fact that—unlike the Mediterranean—there is not at present a major conflict in the Indian Ocean area involving the proxies of the super-powers, requiring the deployment of naval forces on a significant scale, and the presence of which is directly related in both deterrent and defensive terms to the substantial interests that both the Soviet Union and the United States have at stake in the Arab-Israeli dispute.

By contrast, the Indian Ocean does not offer a comparable case study of dramatic involvement by super-powers concerned at one and the same time to restrain mutually antagonistic client states and prevent each other from acquiring a dominant position in the region as a whole. It might be thought that recent events on the Asian subcontinent suggest a contrary interpretation. Yet, while it is true that the United States and the Soviet Union found themselves on opposite sides in the recent war between India and Pakistan, it is still too early to forecast with any certainty that this trend will harden into the fixed positions which both the super-powers appear to have adopted vis-a-vis the conflict in the Middle East and which has been associated with massive deployment of naval capability.

The point of this comparison between these two areas of current and perhaps potential great power concern respectively is simply to demonstrate that, in the Mediterranean, the Arab-Israeli conflict has absorbed the attention of the major powers—presumably on the grounds that a decisive and lasting change in the balance of power in the Middle East would have critically important implications for the Mediterranean as a whole and indeed the entire structure of super-power relations. At present none of the local rivalries in the Indian Ocean area appears to engage the energies of outside powers to anything like the same degree and this is reflected in the relatively low level of naval armaments deployed there. Moreover, no one of the litoral states can dominate the Indian Ocean in terms of naval power. It is this factor, together with the existence of a series of regional conflicts, which gives the area at least the potential for great power naval penetration leading perhaps in the long run to tension and rivalry for hegemony. This in part, as far as the Soviet Union is concerned, depends on the opening of the Suez Canal, reference to which should remind us that there is inevitably an element of artificiality in any treatment of the Indian and Mediterranean Oceans as discrete areas for strategic analysis—however justified this may be in terms of a division of academic labor.

The Economic Significance of the Indian Ocean

The relative indifference shown by the Western powers (with the exceptions of South Africa and Australia) to the strategic consequences of British withdrawal from its military commitments east of Suez contrasts markedly with the high value placed on this Ocean as an area of considerable commercial importance to the operations of their economics. There is relatively little trade within the region between the litoral states, most of which maintain the economic links forged in the pre-independence period with Western metropoles or alternatively more recent ones forged with specific powers such as Japan and Australia.

Oil is the most obvious example of the persistence of extra regional trading patterns: the oil-producing countries of the Persian Gulf contain over sixty percent of the world's proven oil reserves, Western Europe (50 percent), Australia (65 percent), Japan (90 percent) and Africa (83 percent) are all heavily dependent on this area for their oil requirements.[2] The Indian Ocean is also important as an economic artery for the supply of Western European needs in foodstuffs and raw materials such as wheat, cotton, and jute. Australia, for example, has important commercial interests in Indian Ocean trade: forty-six percent of its exports and thirty-six of its imports use the trade routes across it, while Japan's economic expansion in the postwar period has meant the import of a wide range of raw materials from abroad, not least from the Middle East, Australia and Southern Africa.

The closure of the Suez Canal in 1967 must also be taken into account in this context. In effect, the result has been a considerable shift in the importance of the route around the Cape, a development which was beginning to take place even before 1967 as super-tankers of one hundred thousand tons and more began to come into operation. Oil in some quantity was already being carried by these giant tankers from the Persian Gulf to Western Europe via the Cape and this process was accelerated after 1967. By 1970 there were some one hundred ships of over two hundred thousand tons already in service. This increase in super-tanker tonnage is regarded as having both economic and political advantages: the cost of transporting oil by this means via the Cape, as compared with the use of smaller tankers taking the Suez Canal route, is certainly competitive,[3] while the oil companies need no longer rely on a route which has been so prone to political disruption in the past.[4] Thus even if the Canal were to be reopened to the world's trade, it seems improbable that it would ever recover its former significance—at least in terms of oil transportation—unless it were widened and deepened and this at a cost which might prove prohibitively expensive.

For some products such as minerals from Southern Africa, the Cape route retains its traditional significance and this would apply even in the case of Zambian copper using Mozambique and East African ports as points of outlet. Moreover, while it is true that the journey from Melbourne is some nine hundred miles longer via the Cape, the cost to Australian wheat exporters is not apparently markedly higher. On the other hand, the longer route does make a difference to the export of raw materials from India and Pakistan and imports to these countries from Western Europe. This trade is, however, a relatively small proportion of total Western trade with the countries in the Indian Ocean area.

The closure of the Canal does, however, affect the Soviet Union's links with the Far East. Lacking super-tankers, the task of exporting oil from the Black Sea region to North Vietnam, for example, involves the much longer journey round the Cape. Reopening of the Canal would, therefore, be of some advantage to the Russians in terms of a shorter trade route to the Far East, although we must be wary of exaggerating its commercial importance to the Russians who before 1967 made little use of the Canal in this way. Thus Soviet attempts to get the Canal reopened must rather be seen in the context of the current aspiration to project Russian naval power into the area as a whole.

The importance of the Cape route is indicated by the fact that in the first eighteen months after the Canal's closure in 1967, more than ten thousand ships were diverted round the Cape. According to an official South African source

... the volume of shipping increases by four and a half percent per annum at the Cape. It went from 6,067 in 1954 to the present figure of 8,659. Diverted ships calling at South African ports come through at the rate of approximately 3,500 a year ... a fair estimate indicates some 14,000 pass without calling ... the countries of origin of the normal callers is as follows, NATO 60%, of which 21% is U.K. .... diverted callers: NATO 71%, of which 21% is U.K. ....[5]

Thus the great bulk of the trade carried across the Indian Ocean is extra-regional, involving powers as far afield as Britain and Japan, South Africa and the Soviet Union. Its importance as a waterway is not in dispute, particularly in view of the dependence of many highly industrialized societies on the oil resources of the Persian Gulf, the rubber and tin of Malaysia and, in the case of Britain, foodstuffs from Australia. Yet while the pattern of economic interest and trade relations can be clearly discerned and their importance to Western economies be assessed in qualitative terms, it is less easy to devise a comparable framework for analysis in political and strategic terms and within which one could account for the military and political roles of all the powers concerned in neat and relatively straightforward terms.

This would have been a relatively simple exercise in the days of imperial rule when Britain by virtue of the Indian army, bases at Singapore and in the Canal zone, and a substantial naval presence could dominate the region. Today, however, with those powerful assets liquidated there is no obvious replacement for Britain. Indeed, it is doubtful whether any one power, however strong in military terms, could now play a similar role given the emergence of Asian and African nationalisms increasingly sensitive on neo-colonial grounds to any suggestion that the imperial presence be reactivated. One does not have to agree wholeheartedly with Michael Howard's view that

British supremacy depended neither on the Royal Navy nor on scattered imperial garrisons, but on the skill with which administrators asserted authority over simple cultures or cooperated with existing elites and on the absence of any major external threat . . .[6],

but there is enough substance in his argument to suggest the very real obstacles that would confront any power wishing to emulate the British role and having to operate in an environment compounded of domestic instability and regional conflict between self-assertive local powers.

Whatever explanation of British predominance one subscribes to—whether Howard's version of 'legitimacy' or the more orthodox interpretation of gun-boat diplomacy (and the two were not always mutually exclusive)—the fact remains, as Lawrence Martin has pointed out, that the burden of British commitments "could not be picked up in the form in which Britain is laying it down, for it had developed from historical circumstances peculiarly her own."[7] And it is as well to remember that at least since 1945, "British military efforts east of Suez have not really had much to do with the

Indian Ocean as such. Sail and fly across it the British have, but only to go about their business at its extemities."[8]

Implicit in this argument is the assumption that British involvement east of Suez in the postwar period was not so much based on a coherent strategic doctrine treating the Indian Ocean as a systemic whole, but rather represented a series of responses to specific areas of tension such as the Middle East, South-East Asia, or the East coast of Africa. Simply to list a number of the situations with which Britain felt obliged to deal in this period illustrates this point: the Malayan counter-insurgency of the late 1940s, the intervention in Kuwait in 1961, the despatch of British forces to East Africa in 1964 to quell army mutinies, and the establishment of the Beira patrol to cope with sanction breakers in the Rhodesian crisis, are all good examples of the variety of responses which the British presence east of Suez made possible. It would, however, be misleading to see these instances as forming part of some predetermined grand design to contain Communism in the Indian Ocean region.

Thus given the above interpretation of British policy in the period before contraction of military commitments began in 1968,[9] it is unhelpful to talk of the consequences of British departure in terms of 'power vacuums' and the like. As T. B. Millar has remarked, "We can only discuss *bits* of it"[10] and only in terms of the specific interests that particular powers perceive to be at stake. The fact remains that the Indian Ocean as a whole has not so far become a major arena of competition and confrontation in orthodox cold war terms, although there are areas within it where local conflict might conceivably escalate to involve deployment of naval forces by one or more of the extra regional powers. That this has so far not happened on any significant scale should not blind us to the general interest of the world's major trading powers in the security of the shipping lanes crossing the Indian Ocean—an interest which nevertheless there has been little effort to protect by orthodox military means.[11] It is significant that it is at the entrances to the Ocean—the North West approaches, the exit from the Persian Gulf, the Cape of Good Hope, and the Malacca straits—that varying degrees of tension between local protagonists (together with Russian attempts to expand influence) appear to threaten either specific Western economic interests such as oil supplies or, in more general terms—as revealed by the recent debate over the strategic value of the Republic of South Africa—the security of the shipping lanes across the Ocean.

The Role of the Soviet Union in the Indian Ocean

Space will not permit an exhaustive survey of the complexities of regional conflict in the Indian Ocean area. The relevance of such conflicts to the theme of this paper turns first, on the capacity and, more important, the degree of intention on the part of the Soviet Union to profit from such conflicts to the disadvantage of the West. Secondly, the extent to which the deployment of Russian naval power—albeit on a modest scale at this stage—will enable it to do so. This is a complicated task as estimates of Soviet intentions—as distinct from capacity—vary widely and much current discussion in the literature on the subject is inevitably speculative involving the positing of alternative hypotheses in the light of one's particular reading of the general thrust of Soviet foreign policy since World War II.

To begin with, it might be helpful to describe current Soviet capability in the Indian Ocean and at the same time indicate those areas where the Russians have acquired a degree of political influence. The first manifestation of a Soviet naval presence in the Indian Ocean occurred shortly after the British Government's announcement in January 1968 that it proposed running down its military forces between Aden and Singapore, although whether there was a direct causal connection in the timing of these two developments is a matter of dispute between experts on this subject. This first venture into the Indian Ocean involved a twenty-five-thousand-mile voyage by a squadron of three warships 'showing the flag' in a variety of Indian Ocean ports. Since 1968 Soviet naval units have in fact visited Madras, Bombay, Columbo, Basra, Aden, Mogadishu, Mombasa and Dar-es-Salaam. The number of ships stationed by the Soviets at any one time in the Indian Ocean has varied between five and twenty during this period and this often includes a missile cruiser, two destroyers and a number of auxiliary ships.[12] There is evidence suggesting that some part of this naval activity is concerned with scientific work such as rocket tests and space satellite tracking. Mooring buoys have been laid off the Seychelles, Mauritius and the Malagasay Republic, although opinion differs as to whether these are connected with the provision of satellite tracking and fuelling facilities or have a more orthodox strategic purpose.[13] In addition, according to Juke's calculations, approximately a hundred Soviet merchant ships can be found in the Indian Ocean at any one time; approximately ten ships a day pass the Cape in transit, including trawlers which fish off the west coast of South Africa and in the Indian Ocean in considerable numbers. The Cape route is particularly important for Soviet trade with India and North Vietnam and in 1970 altogether some three thousand nine hundred transits were made round the Cape by Soviet ships, including fishing vessels.

It is in the North-West approaches to the Indian Ocean that an extension of Soviet interest and influence has been most clearly observed. Refuelling and repair facilities have been obtained at a number of points in this area including Suez (U.A.R.), Hodeida (Yemen), Aden (South Yemen), Berbera and Mogadishu (Somalia), and there has been considerable speculation about the scope of Russian naval activity on the South Yemini island of Socotra which controls the eastern entry into the Gulf of Aden.[14] Southern Yemen now has the status of a client state of Moscow, although Russian ambitions in the neighbouring state of Yemen and support for the republican rebels there were checked by the long-drawn-out and continuing resistance of the royalist faction in that state.

As far as Somalia is concerned, economic and military assistance has been provided by the Russians. The significance of Russian influence in this area relates in part to the claims made by the Somali government to territories currently under Ethiopian and French Somaliland jurisdiction, respectively. The latter contains the important port of Djibouti which the continuation of French rule has so far denied to the Russians. Also important in this context from a Western point of view is the American communication center at Asmara in Ethiopia. Thus the Soviets and the United States find themselves on opposite sides in the Ethiopian/Somalia conflict, but both super-powers have been cautious in their relations with each other on this particular issue and a degree of balance seems to have been struck between them.

One must be careful not to confuse access to the various facilities outlined above with the possession of bases as this term was commonly understood in the colonial era. As T. B. Millar has concluded:

> The Russians have thus not replaced the British in any formal sense. Their presence is more precarious; they are invited guests, resident or non-resident protectors, money-lenders: they have no constitutional authority or power. This makes them less an object of nationalist antagonism but equally makes their tenure less secure. They have nevertheless replaced the British to this extent, especially due to their assured access to Egyptian air and naval bases; they have become the predominant eternal power from Port Said to Aden and Somalia.[15]

This insecurity of tenure to which Millar refers as characteristic of external powers seeking influence in particular regions has recently been given dramatic emphatic confirmation by the Egyptian refusal to allow the Soviet Union two bases in the Mediterranean and the Red Sea area respectively. According to the *London Times*, ". . . both were to be completely under the control of the Soviet Navy" and it was for this reason that President Sadat has apparently refused to entertain the Russian proposal for the time being.[16]

As far as the Persian Gulf is concerned, there have been a number of Russian naval visits to Gulf ports. Russia at this stage has little economic interest in the area as her oil requirements are met from other sources, but some commentators have seen the complexities of Gulf politics as providing excellent opportunities for Soviet interference with the precarious stability of the area, especially now that the process of British withdrawal is complete.[17] Yet in the last analysis any Russian initiatives in this area must surely wait on the reopening of the Suez Canal and indeed the possibility of better access to the Gulf may well be one of the chief reasons for the Russian interest in having the Canal restored as a major international highway.

With regard to the Indian subcontinent, the Soviet Union has become the chief supplier of military equipment to the Indian government and in a naval context this has included submarines, torpedo and patrol boats; in addition Russia has undertaken the task of refurbishing and expanding the base at Visokhapatham on the east coast. Russian military involvement with India increased dramatically after the successful mediation of the 1965 conflict between India and Pakistan and relations between the two governments reached new heights of cooperation during and after the recent struggle in East Pakistan. There have been rumors that the Soviets have been offered bases in Bombay, Goa, Cochin, but these are not confirmed, although Soviet vessels have enjoyed repair facilities in Indian dockyards.[18]

Russian advances in the Southern Asian region also merit some attention. Good diplomatic and economic relations exist with Malaysia and Singapore and there exist a cluster of agreements relating to trade, shipping and airlines.[19] Soviet ships have the right to use Singapore's ship-repair yards, but so far permission has not been granted to build separate facilities. In this area the Malacca Straits are an important passage for Russian ships bound for ports on the Pacific coast of the Soviet Union as well as the ports of North Vietnam. Finally, an agreement was signed with Mauritius in 1969 which allows Soviet fishing boats to use Port Louis for "loading and unloading and replacement of crews brought in by the Soviet airline Aeroflot."[20]

What conclusions can be drawn about Soviet intentions from this cluster of interests in the Indian Ocean region and the concomitant intrusion of a naval presence? Clearly in one sense the deployment of Soviet naval units into both the Mediterranean and the Indian Ocean reflects a general aspiration to promote Soviet State interest in keeping with its status as a super-power with global interests to promote. It is plausible—although difficult to prove conclusively—that Soviet leaders, observing the capacity of the NATO powers to intervene militarily in distant areas when their interests there were threatened, have drawn the conclusion that a radical redefinition of the role of sea power in Soviet military doctrine was required if they were to match Western expertise as revealed in operations such as those involving intervention in, for example, the Lebanon (1958), Kuwait (1961), and the Cuban missile crisis of 1962.[21] In this context the 1963 statement of Admiral Gorshkov, the Commander in Chief of the Soviet Navy, is revealing: the ". . . flag of the Soviet Navy now proudly flies over the oceans of the world. Sooner or later, the United States will have to understand that it no longer has mastery of the seas."[22]

In more specific terms it has been argued that Soviet naval expansion into both the Mediterranean and Indian Ocean has been prompted by strategic imperatives and in particular the need to overcome American predominance in strategic nuclear capacity.[23] According to this view, what particularly disturbed the Russians in the Mediterranean context was the deployment of American Polaris submarines which in the course of the early 1960s were successively equipped with Polaris A2 (sixteen-hundred-mile range) and A3 (two-

thousand-five-hundred-mile   range)   missiles   capable   of
reaching   targets   in   Soviet   Central   Asia   from   the   Eastern
Mediterranean.[24]   Geoffrey   Jukes   claims   that   Russian   fears
were   further   stimulated   by   the   1963   agreement   between
Spain   and   the   United   States   to   base   Polaris   submarines   at
Rota,   while   the   Sixth   Fleet   aircraft   carriers   had   by   this   time
been   assigned   aircraft   capable   of   penetrating   Warsaw   Pact
territory with thermonuclear payloads.[25]

The   Russian   counter   to   this   threat   was   to   design   a
Mediterranean   Fleet   equipped   primarily   for   an   ASW   role,
while   at   the   same   time   embarking   on   a   programme   of
building   nuclear-powered   missile-carrying   submarines   to
provide   the   necessary   deterrent   and   defensive   capacity   to
match   in   time   of   peace   and   neutralize   in   time   of   war   the
strength of American seaborne nuclear forces.

If   this   interpretation   of   Soviet   motives   in   the
Mediterranean is acceptable, then the relevance of the parallel
with   the   Indian   Ocean   becomes   clear.   Michael   MccGwire,   for
example,   argues   that   the   "Soviet   navy   moved   reluctantly   into
the   Indian   Ocean   because   it   had   to,   and   in   fact   was
operationally   ill-prepared   for   such   a   move."[26]   From   the
Russian point of view, the Arabian Sea might in time become
an extremely attractive area for the deployment of American
Polaris   submarines   especially   when   longer-range   missiles
become   operational: these   would   give   substantial   target
coverage over China and the Soviet Union. Their fears in this
regard   were   given   further   stimulus   by   the   decision   of   the
British   and   American   governments   to   build   in   1967   a
communications   facility   in   the   British   Indian   Ocean   Territories. Thus, as Jukes argues, "As they (the Russians) would
see it, one of the Indian Ocean's attractions for the United
States is the absence of the Soviet Navy, and this is the only
factor in the situation which is in their power to remedy."[27]
He   rightly   warns   against   exaggerating   this   point   on   the
grounds   that   ASW   techniques   are   still   in   their   infancy,
". . . but all navies live in hopes of a breakthrough in ASW
and it is sensible to acquire operating experience in a likely

deployment area against the hopeful day of the break-through—as was done in the Mediterranean."[28]

Too great an emphasis on the strategic dimension may, however, lead us to minimize the more intangible *political* factors governing Russian conduct. In the Mediterranean, for example, it is plausible to argue that the Russians see a connection between a sizeable naval presence and the need to demonstrate their political commitment to the Arab cause in a tangible way. (This of course is not to deny the value of such a force in the context of a renewal of hostilities between the Arabs and the Israelis as a means of neutralizing any American activity directly in support of the Israelis.) It may be true that this particular role for the Soviet Fleet was a consequence rather than a cause of the initial decision to deploy a portion of the Black Sea Fleet into the Mediterranean in 1963, but this would not necessarily detract from its growing significance as a factor influencing Soviet policy today—especially in the context of the crisis that has existed in the Middle East since 1967. Indeed, given the fundamental changes wrought in the Middle East by the Israeli victory of 1967, the 'political' imperatives governing Soviet deployment probably acquire added significance. And is it altogether too fanciful to suggest that the exclusion of Soviet influence in the Red Sea area has been partly motivated by a desire to make good the loss in prestige incurred indirectly by the defeat of its Egyptian 'client' in the Six Day War? Similarly, in the Indian Ocean political considerations cannot be excluded especially if one accepts the alternative thesis that Soviet entry into the area was motivated less by the need to redress any unfavorable balance in both nuclear and conventional nuclear capacity than by a desire to take political advantage of British withdrawal from the area.

What political advantage may conceivably accrue to the Soviet Union from such deployment in the Indian Ocean? We have already remarked in some detail on the footholds that Russia has gained in the Red Sea, Aden, and Somalia. Their current political predominance in this area would no doubt be enhanced if the Canal were to reopen, although this bald statement requires qualification to the extent that the circumstances attendent upon a reopening of the Canal might not inevitably assure an increase of Russian influence in the Middle East. It is possible that if this were to occur in the context of a general peace settlement between the protagonists, then the Egyptians might feel less inclined to maintain their dependence on their super-power ally. However, if we assume that there will be little alteration in Soviet/Egyptian relations, then equally they would be in a strong position to influence events in the Persian Gulf where Moscow has already made efforts to strengthen its ties with both Iran and Iraq—both of which are in competition with each other for paramountcy in the Gulf.

It is still too early to attempt any prediction of likely Soviet policy in this area. Britain has only recently withdrawn (in December, 1971), and while it is true that the litter of small states in the region and the political and social problems facing their rulers hardly encourage any optimism about their prospects of long-term stability, the Russians might fight shy of too active an involvement in domestic crises, the intensity and open-ended nature of which might challenge the manipulative skills of even the most experienced super-power. And this inhibition might come to apply, regardless of whether the Soviets were initially tempted to emulate the British as guarantor of the region's stability or, alternatively, commit themselves to a policy of fomenting discord and instability. On the other hand, the factor of Chinese competition and its effect on Russian policy in the area cannot be excluded. Thus, it is the degree of uncertainty about ultimate Russian intentions which is perhaps the most serious problem facing the West in the region, although the relatively passive role of the Soviet region in the Gulf to date stands in sharp contrast to the more activist policy pursued along the litoral of the Red Sea and further south.

Yet while the Soviet Union may not at present require Middle Eastern oil in any quantity—and it is this factor which gives some commentators cause for alarm about Russian interest in ultimately making life difficult for the West in the Gulf—this situation may change as the economic advantages become clear of securing supplies from this area for use in the Western regions of Russia, hitherto dependent on the resources of the distant Siberian fields. In terms of this argument, increased naval capacity could be helpful to securing growing Russian economic interests in the Gulf. Alternatively this advantage might be forsworn for the hypothetical gains that might accrue if Moscow were able to deny the oil resources of the region to the West by exclusive naval domination of the sea approaches to the producer countries. As T. B. Millar has summarized, "The diplomatic, strategic and economic leverage which could come from increased Soviet influence over the principal oil producers is not something which the West can rightly concede."[29]

There is also the more general advantage stemming from a position to intervene in the affairs of a litoral State undergoing social upheaval. The East African States and the Trucial Kingdoms seem obvious candidates in this context and there is the further possibility—remote as it may seem at present—of logistic support for liberation struggles in Mozambique and elsewhere in Southern Africa. At a more prosaic level, the possibility of complicating and perhaps neutralizing Western attempts to intervene in these areas might well seem attractive and here the Mediterranean analogy readily comes to mind.[30]

Finally, in this assessment of the political factors involved in Soviet naval strategy in the Indian Ocean, we must take into account Russia's relations with India and Pakistan. These have been governed by the implications of the Sino-Soviet split for Russian policy in Southern Asia. The result in recent years has been an attempt to contain the spread of Chinese influence and the threat of Chinese military intervention by shoring up Indian power through—as was noted earlier—an acceleration of arms deliveries to the Delhi government. Initially this effort was combined with an attempt, following the success at Tashkent in 1965, to stabilize Indo/Pakistan relations and thus prevent the Chinese from taking advantage of the postwar hostility between the two countries. This involved supplying weapons to Pakistan as well in the hope that Pakistan's relations in China would thereby be weakened.

In this particular context political and strategic considerations appear to neatly coincide: on the one hand containment of China became a realizable goal; on the other the Soviets gained access to Indian dockyard facilities for its naval forces in the Indian Ocean.[31] How far the outcome of the 1971 conflict between India and Pakistan will affect Soviet policy in the region is still a matter of speculation. Certainly American prestige in India has suffered as a result of Washington's policy during the war, but a detailed analysis of all the implications of these events must presumably wait, *inter alia*, upon the course of events following President Nixon's visit to China earlier this year.[32]

What can, perhaps, be argued is that India, heartened by its victory, will feel encouraged to aspire to be the dominant naval power in the immediate environment. This might have paradoxical consequences: on the one hand the realization of this aspiration might fit neatly into Russia's ambitions to manage the security of the subcontinent. On the other hand, growing Indian confidence may make its government less willing to countenance too obvious and too close a relationship with the Soviets and this might well have counterproductive influence on Russian ambitions to consolidate and increase its access to Indian port facilities, etc.

In general it seems fair to conclude that the Soviet Union by deploying a modest naval capacity appears to be in the process of achieving a number of limited objectives: (i) it has served notice on the Western powers that Moscow is no longer willing to allow the United States to go unchallenged on the high seas; (ii) it has put itself in a position to have the Russian voice heard on issues of contention in the region involving either of its super-power rivals—the United States or

China; (iii) it has injected an element of uncertainty into any calculation the West might make with regard to countering and responding to this newly created Soviet presence in the Indian Ocean. In the writer's view these political advantages outweigh any of the alleged strategic gains—especially in view of the fact that, as presently constituted, the Soviet presence in the Indian Ocean is hardly in a position to engage in protracted hostile military activity against the interests of the West.

Britain, South Africa and the Defense of the Cape Route.

Acceptance of the arguments listed above need not imply any commitment to a 'grand design' explanation of Soviet policy. It is precisely because at this stage evidence is lacking for such interpretations involving neat single-cause explanations for Soviet policy that awkward choices may be forced upon Western powers. That there is tacit, if not open, disagreement on the military significance to be attached to the Soviet naval presence is clear from the very different views taken by Washington and London on the question of arms sales to the Republic of South Africa.

Even before the Conservatives came to power in June, 1970, several prominent spokesmen in the Party and in particular Sir Alec Douglas Home, the shadow Foreign Secretary, were questioning the validity of maintaining the ban on arms supplies to South Africa.[33] The argument, however, went further than a desire simply to restore the *status quo* that had existed before the advent of the Wilson government in October, 1964. What was now required, argued Sir Alex and others, was some formal arrangement to give the Republic a larger share in Western defense planning involving the extension of the NATO defense perimeter to cover the sea routes round the Cape.[34]

These two issues—arms supplies and the incorporation of South Africa into the structure of Western defense—were related in Conservative thinking to the status of the Simons-town Agreement signed in 1955, providing Britain with the use of that base for facilities in peace and war, whether or not South Africa was a belligerent. The Agreement further provided for joint naval cooperation between the two parties for the protection of the Cape routes, while the British in addition undertook to supply a specified number of naval vessels and spare parts to the South African navy to enable it to contribute to the common external defense of the area round the Cape.

Thus when Conservative leaders spoke of 'reactivating' the Agreement, they had in mind two possibilities: (i) a resumption of the supply of those weapons (in practice ships and aircraft) which would enable the Republic to continue its military role as joint protector with Britain of the security of the sea routes; (ii) a formal treaty arrangement between South Africa and Britain or better still with NATO as a whole. Failing this, the Nationalist government, it was argued, should be encouraged to foster defense cooperation with Southern Hemisphere powers such as the Argentine, Brazil and Portugal.[35]

Yet another possibility that was canvassed in South African public discussion was a degree of defense cooperation between the Republic, Australia and New Zealand. In May, 1968, for example, Mr. Piet Botha, the Minister of Defense, revealed that international discussions at 'service level' had taken place between Southern Hemispheric countries and recommendations made to the governments concerned. There have also been courtesy visits by the South African Navy to Australia and the Argentine in the recent past.[36] Hence the notion of a South Atlantic Treaty Organization (SATO) corresponding in scope and purpose to its equivalent in the Northern Hemisphere.

In defense of this position a variety of arguments have been put forward by both Conservative and South African spokesmen: (i) South Africa is a stable polity, despite the dire predictions of its opponents to the contrary over the last twenty-five years; (ii) it is a highly industrialized society of considerable significance to the West and more especially the United Kingdom; the latter has investments of over one thousand million pounds in the Republic, while the Republic is also an important market for British exports as well as a supplier of foodstuffs, raw materials and especially minerals to the West; (iii) the Republic is likely to remain a reliable partner of the West and is totally committed to an anti-communist posture in external affairs; (iv) since 1960, its armed forces have been considerably modernized and a degree of self-sufficiency in many fields of arms production has been acquired largely because of government foresight in anticipating the effects of the U.N.-sponsored arms embargo of the early 1960s;[37] (v) the Republic is in a crucial geographic position astride an important sector of the world's shipping routes, and this has been enhanced by the closure of the Suez Canal. The growing interest of the Soviet Navy in the Indian Ocean, therefore, makes protection of these routes essential: not to do so would enable the Russians to enhance their support for liberation in 'movements' in South Africa and, worse still, leave vulnerable to Russian harassment a significant proportion of the world's merchant shipping; (vi) finally the Republic's 'outward movement' in foreign policy is succeeding in breaking down the hostility of the African states towards its government's policies. Thus, South Africa deserves Western recognition for its role as the guarantor of stability in South and Central Africa and in its capacity as the one power able to promote a significant measure of economic development for its poorer neighbors.

Two levels of argument must be distinguished in the South African exposition of the case outlined above: the first is ideological in the sense that during the 1960s, the Republic's leaders felt increasingly isolated from the main stream of Western defense planning. Their initial bewilderment at the apparent indifference of the West to what is regarded as a vital area of interest and security for all parties concerned changed to hostility at what seemed to be cavalier treatment by Britain's Labor government of South Africa's claims to be a 'bastion of the free world's' security. Thus the revival of interest in South Africa's potential contribution to Western defense by British Conservatives in the late 1960s was hailed as proof that the Republic's definition of this contribution was at last gaining acceptance. The arms issue, therefore, and its derivatives—revision of the Simonstown Agreement, etc.—must be seen as a deeply felt aspiration to acquire a degree of ideological and political respectability in the eyes of the West.

The second level of argument is couched in specifically strategic terms and relates to the emphasis placed by South Africa's leaders on the dangers that a Russian intrusion into the Indian Ocean poses for Western shipping using the Cape route. Constant reference is made to the military advantages the Republic can offer the NATO powers to deal with this threat and emphasis placed on the role its forces can play in the event of either conventional or nuclear conflict. In the case of the former, the Republic would replay its traditional role as a supplier of valuable raw materials and foodstuffs, while its ports and harbor facilities would enable it to act as a supply center and staging post for operations further afield. In the event of nuclear war, South African naval and air forces would be invaluable in the containment and detection of sea-borne second-strike nuclear capacity. In times of peace, the Republic could act jointly with Britain and other powers to deter hostile states from interfering with Western shipping and generally serve the negative function of 'denying strategic areas to the Soviets.' [38]

South Africa unlike the other litoral powers is firmly committed to the 'grand design' theory of Soviet foreign and military policy. Hence Mr. Botha's warning that

... the communist forces are out to cut Africa from East to West ... and both Russia and China are concentrating their efforts to gain influence among the new African States . . . the failure of Southern Africa to remain a bastion of the free world would lead eventually to the encirclement of Europe and a direct threat to the Atlantic Ocean.[39]

Hence the continued emphasis on what South Africa has to offer the West in terms of strategic advantage and political reliability. In military terms Mr. Botha, for example, recently argued

> . . . we have the only developed naval base (at Simonstown) in South Africa; the Republic has other large, modern harbors where wartime cargoes can be loaded and where merchant vessels can enjoy protection and shelter, and be refueled and repaired; the Republic has modern airfields . . . from which the sea routes can be patrolled and from which air raids against approaching forces can be launched . . .
>
> Owing to our strategic position South Africa is in itself an aircraft carrier from which . . . protection can be afforded; we have the necessary command and communications systems which are indispensable to the control of operations of merchant shipping in the southern oceans . . . we are already engaged in modernizing our maritime communications systems, at considerable expense; and the Republic has the only real maritime defense forces in Southern Africa, which, coupled with the Republic's territorial and air defense forces, comprise a vitally important bastion for the defense of the free world in the Southern Hemisphere.[40]

In the course of the recent debates on the strategic significance of South Africa considerable doubt has been cast on the South African (and the Heath government's reading of the Soviet's presence in the Indian Ocean and, by implication, the Republic's claim to indispensability in countering either this particular threat or any other that might be construed.

Few would dispute the commercial importance of the Cape route to the West; equally, few would contest the argument that deliberate interference with Western shipping by the Soviets would have damaging effects on Western economics. It is difficult, however, to see what *political* objective would be served by Russian action of this kind except perhaps as a prelude to provoking the Western Alliance into a major confrontation—the dimensions of which would spread rapidly beyond the relatively narrow confines of the southern oceans. Thus it could be argued that it is the possibility of escalation to general war—in other words the concept of deterrence—which would restrain the Russians from harassment of this kind.

Then again, assuming the breakdown of deterrence was a risk the Soviets were prepared to indulge, the Indian and South Atlantic areas seem improbable for ventures of this kind—especially when Western shipping could be harassed more effectively from the approaches to Europe and the sea routes round the West Africa bulge. Furthermore, in these circumstances the Soviet's merchant fleet would be vulnerable to Western retaliation.[41]

By the same token it is difficult to see why South African claims should be taken unduly seriously if the real purpose of the Soviet presence in the Indian Ocean is primarily political and geared to gain influence among the litoral states. Given the unacceptability of the Republic on ideological grounds, an attempt to counter Russian influence by devising a naval capability based on a combination of Western and South African forces might well be counterproductive politically. What is not clear from all that has been asserted in this context by South Africa's spokesmen is how a greatly increased measure of Anglo-South African naval co-operation could prevent the Soviet Union from increasing its naval presence in the Indian Ocean or offering military aid to the guerillas based in East Africa. In the Mediterranean, American naval forces have not been able to prevent the incursion of Soviet ships, and it is difficult to see what steps could be taken—short of forceful measures, such as blockades—to cut off Soviet military assistance to East Africa. Thus talk of 'denying strategic areas to the Soviets' is to underestimate the difficulties (and the risks) involved in a situation where the *use* as distinct from the *display* of force can provoke escalation.

It is also worth stressing that South Africa's primary defense interest must still remain the need to maintain capability to cope with insurgency whether within the Republic or further afield in Rhodesia and the Portuguese territories. This confirms the earlier argument that to some extent Pretoria's concern at the spectacle of Russian ships in the Indian Ocean is motivated by ideological considerations and aspirations to greater recognition by the Western Powers.

How far the Conservative government has been influenced by the weight of political and strategic argument opposed to Mr. Heath's initial proposals to resume the supply of arms is not easy to assess. It is interesting—and perhaps significant in the long run—that the only sale so far concluded is the purchase of seven Wasp helicopters for the Republic's navy. The South Africans, on the other hand, might well wish to avoid being exclusively dependent on a supplier, the policies of which appear fickle over the long run. Governments come and go and there can be no guarantee that agreements entered into with the Conservatives will not be abrogated by a Labor successor. In any case there has been no repetition by the Republic of the threat voiced in the late 1960s to alter unilaterally the terms of the Simonstown Agreement or replace Britain with another Western European power. Thus Britain to a degree still contrives to enjoy the best of both worlds: continued access to the facilities and the knowledge that South Africa is in no position to threaten unfaithfulness to its obligations.[42]

Nevertheless, for some a nagging doubt still persists: it relates to the question of whether the supply of ships and aircraft to replace her near obsolete capacity (especially in the former) should be met to enable its forces to play the role laid down originally for them in 1955. This involves making a judgement about the relevance of this kind of defense cooperation for coping with the relatively new factor of a Soviet naval presence. This writer is sceptical about the Republic's claims in this regard and the strategic assumptions on which they are based, but it must be stressed that one's judgement may be weighted by intangible considerations such as the effect of such Anglo-South African cooperation on Commonwealth opinion in Africa and Asia. Here there can be legitimate disagreement over the importance of such opinion and the extent to which it could be translated into action hostile to Western interests by the more militant African states.

For these, the ideological issue of apartheid is paramount in deciding their attitude to the issue of British security in the Indian Ocean. This is indicated by the unwillingness of many Afro-Asian leaders to accept the traditional Conservative distinction between weapons supplied exclusively for external use and those having the capacity to ensure the maintenance of domestic order—and by definition apartheid—in the Republic. (One may, however, doubt the validity of this distinction on the grounds that for a state as peculiarly constituted as the Republic, the problems of external and internal defense are integrally related and not easily susceptible to a clear-cut distinction based on their hypothetical use in time of crisis).

Thus by construing the 'threat' posed by the Soviets in the Indian Ocean in exclusively military terms, the present British government placed itself in an awkward dilemma involving a conflict between the demands of strategy and the political constraints represented by hostile domestic and Commonwealth option. By the same token, opponents of British policy could only discount the need for an increased measure of Anglo/South African military cooperation on both political and strategic grounds by trying to demonstrate that the presence of the Soviet Union in the Indian Ocean represents an insignificant military threat to the interests of the West and, more especially, to the sea route around

Southern Africa. Alternatively, even if the strategic risk were accepted, the Cape route was deemed to be an unlikely area for danger to threaten.

The Residue of British Commitments.

Britain's economic interests are considerable in the Indian Ocean region. Its economic stake in Southern Africa has already been cited; altogether imports from the area amount to about $3 billion with exports standing at a slightly higher figure. Africa as a whole takes ten percent of British exports and this is more or less equally divided between North and South of the Zambezi. Approximately $7 billion is invested in the Gulf, Malaysia and Singapore and in addition there is the substantial British stake in the merchant-shipping tonnage crossing the Ocean. Relatively little remains of the British military investment that was once deemed appropriate to protect this network of economic interests.[43] (We need not analyze in details the reasons why Britain in the late sixties opted for a defense policy which concentrated its resources in Europe and the North Atlantic areas; the political and economic considerations that prompted this switch in priorities will be familiar to students of Western defense).[44]

The major component of the remaining British presence in the Indian Ocean is to consist of five frigates and destroyers on station East of Suez, one army battalion group, a detachment of Nimrod long-range maritime reconnaisance aircraft and several Whirlwind helicopters. These forces are the substance of the British contribution to the Five-Power Agreement which has replaced the Anglo-Malaysian Defense Agreement. Apart from Simonstown, Britain still maintains its right to moor warships in Mombasa harbour and there is a naval communications center at Mauritius together with the right to use airports there. An airfield is available in the Maldives and until earlier this year Britain deployed aircraft from Malagasy in support of the Beira patrol. In addition there are air, naval and communications facilities in the British Indian Ocean Territory.

The naval and air elements presently available to Britain are designed as a signal to the Russians that their aspirations in the Indian Ocean cannot be expected to go unchallenged. Furthermore, a modest naval presence—it is claimed—can still have some role in deomonstrating British interest in the region on a 'showing the flag' basis. On the military plane, these forces must also be seen as providing at least a possibility of deterring the Russians from taking unimpeded advantage of any crisis in the litoral states. At the same time there is provision to keep watch over Russian naval activities for intelligence purposes. Finally British forces in the region are seen as providing an 'early warning' of any hostile act by an enemy power, thus preparing the way for reinforcement from other Western sources of naval strength.

The role of British forces in the Indian Ocean is based on the assumption—as we noted earlier—of a significant and growing Russian military threat. Hence the importance attached to Simonstown which, in view of its excellent facilities, cuts down the need for prolonged maintenance of afloat support. There is the further assumption that capacity of this kind will enable Britain to help friends and allies in the Indian Ocean should these be menaced by external attack. However, the danger is always present that by so doing Britain will find itself drawn into open-ended commitments, particularly in view of the difficulty involved in clearly distinguishing between external and internal subversion. And even if the greater commitment is unacceptable, there is always the problem of reinforcing existing capacity, given commitments to NATO and, for that matter, Northern Ireland at the present time.

Nevertheless in the last analysis it is difficult to believe that the arrangements the Heath government have made really amount to a significant reversal of their predecessor's policy. As Europe beckons enticingly even existing commitments may come in time to seem irrelevant to Britain's future role. Alternatively, we may see some attempt by Britain to persuade its fellow members of the European community of the need to assume more responsibility for the West's defense of economic and political interests in distant waters.[45] This, however, is to speculate beyond any degree of credibility. It is enough for the present to accept the view that the East of Suez policy of the present British government "represents a relatively minor qualification to the otherwise exclusively European thrust of British policy."[46]

American Interests in the Indian Ocean.

The American return on investments in the oil-producing areas of the Arabian Peninsula and the Persian Gulf amounts to approximately $1.5 billion per annum, although only a small fraction of America's oil requirements are met from these areas. Throughout the postwar period, the United States showed little military interest in the Indian Ocean. It has had a token naval presence in the Gulf consisting of what one writer has called "an ancient war vessel" and two destroyers. This force—if so it can be described—is "based on Bahrain and used as the floating HQ of a U.S. Admiral who lives ashore . . . ."[47] The United States has apparently agreed to take responsibility for part of the British naval base recently vacated at Jufiar in Bahrain.

Apart from this very limited capability in the Gulf, the United States has communication centers at Asmara in Ethiopia and North West Cape in Australia, a joint interest in developing space tracking and surveillance facilities in the British Indian Ocean Territories, and satellite monitoring stations in Australia and South Africa.

Stated baldly in this way, American strategic interests in the Indian Ocean would not seem to amount to very much. The question remains as to whether we can expect a more positive response from Washington now that Britain has departed the Persian Gulf and in view of growing Soviet interest in the area generally. What follows in the remainder of this paper is, therefore, inevitably speculative. There are many intangibles involved: the degree, for example, to which the United States may feel constrained to maintain a 'low profile' in the area in view of domestic pressures and the chastening experience of South Vietman—both of which have combined to force a modification of traditional aspirations to play a global peace-keeping role.

It might be argued that expanded programmes of economic aid and technical assistance for those litoral states, in the stability of which the United States has in the past maintained an interest—Ethiopia, Kenya, Pakistan, Saudi Arabia, for example—are a better prescription for promoting regional security than purely military responses based on the need to counter the growth of Russian naval strength in the area. On the other hand, the current mood of the Congress suggests a degree of disillusionment with the economic and social problems of the Third World and a growing realization that post-Vietnam America will require a searching re-examination of existing commitments whether economic or military—let alone any new ones.

Neutralization and the Interests of the Super-Powers.

One option that has been canvassed for American policy-makers is negotiation of a neutralization agreement for the Indian Ocean. Several of the litoral states have voiced their approval for this proposal: Indonesia, Ceylon and India together with those African states which signed the Lusaka Declaration in September, 1970. Their leaders have stressed that the presence of Soviet naval units may well precipitate a naval arms race in the Indian Ocean and that the resulting competition would mean an extension of Cold War rivalry into the area with harmful consequences for the smaller powers. Their dilemma is heightened by the knowledge that even if a naval arms race does not develop, their states may be faced with one naval power enjoying a monopoly position with all that entails for those with a traditional posture of nonalignment.

It is interesting that the Soviet Union expressed interest in the establishment of a nuclear free zone in the Indian Ocean as early as 1964. This might have been connected with the desire to forestall the deployment of American Polaris submarines in the area.[48] The first hint of American interest in this notion came with a press report in April, 1971 that the United States National Security Council was discussing the possibility of agreement with Moscow on neutralization.[49] There was no formal denial by the Pentagon at that time, but the Russians revived the issue when Breshnev stated in June, 1971 that his government was interested in curtailment of "cruises by navies in distant waters."

At first sight an arms control agreement of this kind seems appropriate for the Indian Ocean, especially if we bear in mind Hedley Bull's comment that arms control "is relevant when tension is at a certain point, above which it is impossible and beneath which it is unnecessary."[50] 'Tension' might be too strong a term to describe the relationships of the extra regional powers in the Indian Ocean, but it could be argued that the degree of doubt and distrust that the Soviet and Western powers currently feel about each other's intentions in this area fulfill Bull's criteria for successful arms control negotiation.

There is, however, a major difficulty inherent in these proposals for neutralization which nullified, to a degree, the relevance of Bull's theorem for this particular region. To begin with, there is the assumption that the Indian Ocean is a self-contained region with the interests of the great powers neatly demarcated and susceptible to resolution 'across the board.' Now it is true that arms control, as distinct from comprehensive, mutilateral disarmanent, does not necessarily require, as a prior condition, the successful mediation of outstanding political disputes between the parties involved.

Presumably, what is required is a recognition that the interests at stake are not vital 'core' ones[51] and that agreement in any event will not leave any of the parties worse off than they were before. Alternatively, a belief that the risks involved in not entering an arms control agreement outweigh a continuation of present discontents.

To what extent does neutralization of the Indian Ocean meet these criteria? First, it is doubtful whether any of the major powers perceive their Indian Ocean interests as neatly interconnected with policy responses dictated by sets of coherent politico-strategic objectives. If this were the case—and more important—if it could be demonstrated that such interests were regarded as subject to a modest degree of compromise "across the board" (perhaps on the basis of demarcation of spheres of political and strategic interest) or, alternatively, were not regarded as critically important to the state's general security needs, then a measure of arms control might be possible.

The difficulty lies, however, in discerning such a pattern of interest on the part of the Soviet Union. Nor does one have to leap to the opposite conclusion and posit a 'grand design' interpretation of Soviet foreign and military policy in order to assume that what the Soviets perceive is a cluster of interests, some of which are regarded as crucial, others perhaps less so. Indeed, a clear definition of these interests may well have to wait on the problematical reopening of the Suez Canal. Until this happens, the Russians might well prefer to hope for the possibility of its reopening (with all this would mean in terms of effectively increasing both political influence and naval capability in the Indian Ocean), rather than abandon the game for the sake of an arms control agreement with its major rivals. This would not be inconsistent with a parallel ambition to get agreement to keep the Ocean free of nuclear capability, if only to deny it to the operations of American Polaris submarines. There would still remain the attraction of deploying conventional naval units to promote political influence among litoral states, as well as maintaining a degree of capacity for judicious intervention in their affairs.

It is not unreasonable, therefore, to assume the existence of a variety of interests for the Soviet Union in the Indian Ocean which at this stage are necessarily interrelated in a coherent pattern. There is, to begin with, Soviet influence in the Northwestern area of the Ocean. Further west, there is considerable support for India on a diplomatic, economic and military basis. One might argue that Russian interest in the Red Sea area is related to its general Mediterranean strategy of support for the Arab states as well as designed to acquire a predominant political and military presence south of Suez. Similarly, the Russians may—it is too early to say with any certainty—stand poised to interfere with the precarious stability bequeathed by the departing British in the Gulf. On the other hand, in the context of the Indian subcontinent, Moscow appears interested in pursuing a containment policy to cope with its Chinese rival. Thus the Soviets might well be seeking different objectives in different areas, although their capacity to control all the variables at work in any one or all of these situations should not be exaggerated. Simply to list this variety of Soviet interests and the conflicting assumptions at work behind them indicates the difficulty of getting some agreement on neutralization of the Indian Ocean on an 'across the board' basis. And this is all the more true even if we accept the view that Soviet policy is primarily influenced by the imperatives of the Sino-Soviet dispute and the competition for ideological supremacy in the Communist world. This, it is admitted, might be construed as one plausible variation on the 'grand design' thesis. But if containment of China is the dominant *motif* in Soviet policy, the chances of an arms control agreement appearing attractive seems thinner than ever, given China's reluctance as a developing military power to foreclose any options in the general context of arms limitations and the high level of distrust between the two Communist rivals.

On the Western side of the equation there is the considerable economic interest at stake, including Japanese and Australian concern about the security of the sea routes that increasingly carry on their commerce with the outside world. Yet, as we have seen, Western policy appears to be based on ad hoc commitments to particular 'bits' of the region rather than some general principle of strategic commitment. Neutralization, however, is unlikely to commend itself to the Western powers despite the fact that, apart from the British, their governments and especially the United States at this stage show little willingness to make a military commitment to match that of the Soviet naval presence. (And we must be wary of exaggerating the British commitment.)

To opt for neutralization would be tantamount to denying themselves the possibility of moving into the region subsequently—at a time and place when the deployment of naval forces from other sources of strength might serve a particular purpose such as assistance for a friend or ally under threat from an external source. Thus for the West, as for the Soviet Union, the complexities of the region render it not easily susceptible to a single comprehensive arms control solution in advance of a clear and mutual perception of the issues at stake for all parties concerned.

This account of naval armaments in the Indian Ocean has perhaps devoted a disproportionate amount of attention to the rather modest naval presence deployed by the Soviet Union and the possible interpretations that can be placed upon it. The justification for structuring the paper in this way is simply that this development is the most significant one that has taken place in the region in recent years and it is not clear what response, if any, the United States proposes to make to counter this pressure.

The problem is a complicated one for the Americans, partly because of the growing dependence of associates like Britain, Australia and Japan on the trade routes that cross the Ocean; partly because the pressures for selective 'disengagement' are likely to mount as the Vietnam War nears its end.

American choices might be easier if Washington—like the British and the South Africans—were convinced that Soviet warships constituted a significant military threat to the security of the sea-lanes and the economic interests of its maritime allies. If this were the case, the debate could at least polarize between those who press for a greater naval commitment to protect their interests and those who claim that powers like Japan and Australia must ultimately come to realize that their security needs must be met by a combination of adroit diplomacy and a greater contribution to their own defense—leading, perhaps, to regional collective security arrangements, for the operation of which the stronger littoral states would bear the chief responsibility.

But would this be a satisfactory answer to the American dilemma? Especially if the Soviet threat is to be construed primarily in political terms designed to increase influence among the weaker and less-developed littoral states, the leaders of which in the face of Western indifference—would have little choice but to accept the fact of Soviet hegemony? Locally sponsored collective security arrangements make little sense in areas like East Africa, the Arabian Peninsula and the Persian Gulf if the internal problems of these states continue to mount to threaten the already precarious stability of their regimes. Indeed the spectacle of Russian cruisers off their coastlines might contribute directly to weakening them still further by encouraging radical, dissatisfied elites to revolt.

Nor can the role of China be ignored. It is true that Peking is unlikely to possess significant naval stability for some years to come. Yet its capacity to exert influence without such capability in distant areas is strikingly evident in Tanzania, for example, where the skillful use of economic aid and technical assistance appears to be paying some dividends. The Tanzam railroad is only the most dramatic example of such assistance and we should also note Chinese support for some, although not all, liberation movements involved in the Southern African struggle. (Other examples of Chinese activity in the region can be found in the assistance given by Chinese military instructors to the rebels in the Dhofar province of the Sultanate of Oman.)[52] Thus, if there is to be an extension of the Sino-Soviet competition into the Indian Ocean, would it be prudent for the United States to maintain its present posture of military indifference, especially in areas where we might expect the competition to become acute?

It might be retorted that an insertion of an American naval presence into the region is hardly the most sensible way of promoting the growth of domestic stability in the poorer littoral states which, in the last analysis, some argue, is the primary American interest. As Bruce Larkin claims in a recent book:

... if Africans adopt a Maoist vision, it is not likely to be because Chinese cooperate with African governments or because Africans visit China, but because African governments break down through incapacity or the ravages of war.[53]

This is true no doubt, but Western leaders seem unsure, if not downright sceptical, about just how much nation-building can be achieved by the instruments of external economic aid and technical assistance. In any case the alleged efficacy of such nonmilitary instruments is presumably long-term. On the other hand we should not forget that such influence as the Soviet Union currently enjoys is due to an adroit combination of military, political and economic blandishments together with a posture of general ideological support in certain areas. That this combination has paid off is evident from Russian diplomacy (interpreting this term to cover a variety of activities, both military and nonmilitary) before and during the recent conflict over the status of East Pakistan. As a preliminary first step, perhaps what is required is a definition of American interests in order of priority, based on an appreciation of the strengths and weaknesses of particular candidature for support. This suggestion is offered with considerable diffidence, in full knowledge of the oversimplifications that can result from academic arrogance in the area of policy-making, but the outside observer is struck by the absence of any clear definition of interests in the region as a whole. While this remains so, it may be difficult to decide what role, if any, should be assigned to a naval capacity in the area.

In the short term, there may, nevertheless, be something to be said for the view that what is required is a periodic demonstration of American naval power in areas like the Red Sea and the Persian Gulf to indicate that it has not been written off—either through political indifference or strategic retrenchment. This policy seems preferable to one based on a sudden, massive deployment of American naval capability which at this stage is unnecessary in view of the closure of the Suez Canal and the logistic difficulties the Russians would inevitably face in maintaining a large and credible strike force in the region. It might also be militarily counterproductive and encourage the Russians to increase their efforts at the political, economic and subversive level of operations. The question of how much capability might be maintained, the likelihood or otherwise of bases being available, and the implications of the re-opening of the Suez Canal for all the powers in the region are at this stage matters for speculation to which perhaps we might address outselves in discussion.*

*The writer is aware that he has devoted relatively little attention to Australian defense needs in the Indian Ocean area. Demarcating the salt water in political and strategic terms is not yet an exact science and I have assumed that Australia will figure prominently in Professor Millar's paper on *Naval Armaments in the Pacific*. If there is any rationale behind this apparent neglect of Australia's Indian Ocean needs, it is the assumption—which might be quite mistaken—that Australian naval policy is not and cannot be neatly compartmentalized by rather arbitrary oceanic boundaries. Obviously, the paper is open to revision in the light of our joint discussion of these matters at the Seminar.

NOTES

1. Mr. Heath, the British Prime Minister, was at pains to stress that the lifting of the ban applied only to weapons for use in *external* defense which, in his government's view, Britain was bound to supply in terms of the Simonstown Agreement signed between the two countries in 1955. The implications of this agreement for the theme of this paper will be considered at length later.

2. See T. B. Millar, *The Indian and Pacific Oceans: Some Strategic Considerations* (Adelphi paper, No. 57, London: Institute for Strategic Studies, 1969), p. 6.

3. If not lower, as claimed by Lloyds Bureau Veritas and the American Bureau of Shipping.

4. Of course, this is not to deny the possibility that oil supplies might be cut off at source during a renewal of conflict between Israel and the Arab states.

5. Rear Admiral M. R. Terry-Lloyd, Armed Forces Attaché at the South African Embassy, London, in *The Cape Route*, Report of a Seminar at the Royal United Service Institution, February 25, 1970.

6. Michael Howard, "Britain's Strategic Problem East of Suez," *International Affairs*, vol. 42, No. 2, 1966, p. 179.

7. Lawrence Martin, "The New Power Gap in the Indian Ocean," *Interplay*, vol. 2, No. 6, January, 1969, p. 37.

8. *Ibid.*, p. 37.

9. The process of withdrawal had of course begun as early as 1947 with the decision to grant independence to the states on the Indian subcontinent. The Wilson government's announcement in January, 1968 really amounted to a declaration to accelerate this process and a demonstration that any aspiration to a peace-keeping role could not be sustained in view of domestic, economic and political considerations.

10. Millar, *op. cit.*, p. 3.

11. N. B., however, the fact that during the recent conflict between India and Pakistan, units of the American Seventh Fleet were despatched to the Bay of Bengal.

12. N. B., Mr. Heath's comment during his speech to Common-wealth Heads of State at Singapore in January, 1971 that nineteen ships had been deployed in the Indian Ocean during 1970. As Geoffrey Jukes

has pointed out, however: "Reports on movements of Soviet naval units show that this was not a permanent presence—the numbers referred to ships which spent *any* time in the Indian Ocean in 1970, not to ships which spent all of 1970 there . . ." "The Soviet Union and the Indian Ocean," *World Review*, July, 1971 (reprinted in *Survival*, vol. XIII, No. 11, November, 1971, p. 370).

13. According to T. B. Millar, the Soviets have also been engaged in considerable activity in hydrography, oceanography and maritime intelligence. "Soviet Policies South and East of Suez," *Foreign Affairs*, vol. 49, No. 1, October, 1970, p. 73.

14. Hodeida and Aden are both alleged to be staffed by Russian technicians. Certainly Hodeida was built with Russian assistance.

15. "Soviet Policies South and East of Suez," *op. cit.*, pp. 71-72.

16. *The Times*, March 24, 1972.

17. Relations between the Gulf states and the implications of current and Soviet policy towards these states together with possible Western responses have been well analyzed from different points of view in two recent articles: R. S. Sullivan, "The Architecture of Western Security in the Persian Gulf," *Orbis*, vol. XIV, No. 1, Spring, 1970, pp. 71-91.

18. Millar, *op. cit.*, p. 75.

19. *Ibid.*, p. 75.

20. *Ibid..*, p. 76.

21. Traditionally the navy has been seen as a defensive force confined to operating in the local environment of the Soviet Union and accorded lower priority as compared with the Army in terms of allocation of resources.

22. Quoted in L. W. Martin, "Strategy of the Southern Oceans," *World Survey*, No. 11 (London: Atlantic Education Trust, November, 1969), p. 4.

23. See Jukes, *op. cit.*, pp. 371-72. Also MccGwire, "The Background to Soviet Naval Developments," *The World Today*, vol. 27, No. 3, March, 1971, pp. 93-103. Also "The Russians All at Sea," *The Guardian*, August 26, 1970.

24. *Poseidon* missiles with a range of two thousand five hundred miles represent the latest stage in the growing sophistication of American capability. These carry a larger number of warheads than their predecessors and "will in due course be individually guided to attack several targets simultaneously." Jukes, *op. cit.*, p. 371.

25. *Ibid.*,

26. MccGwire, "Russians all at Sea," *op. cit.*

27. Jukes, *op. cit.*, p. 372.

28. *Ibid.*, p. 372.

29. "Soviet Policies South and East of Suez," *op. cit.*, p. 79.

30. That Russian naval planners are aware of the need to design capacity appropriate for an interventionist role is clear from the recent

construction of two helicopter carriers, the creation of naval infantry and the development of float support capacity. *Ibid.*, p. 77.

31. N. B., MccGwire's comment: "The Royal Navy's withdrawal from East of Suez did not prompt the decision to deploy Soviet units to the Indian Ocean. More significant, I believe, was Britain's inability to meet India's request for modern diesel submarines; Russia's unprecedented action in supplying India with submarines of the up-to-date F. class gained Russia access to naval bases on the west coast of India." "The Russians all at Sea," *op. cit.*

32. See Dr. Millar's chapter on *Naval Armaments in the Pacific.*

33. For a detailed account of British military relations with South Africa see the author's "Strategic Significance of Southern Africa," London: Royal United Service Institution, 1970. Also "South Africa and the Defence of the West," *The Round Table* (London), January, 1971. (Reprinted in *Survival*, vol. XIII, No. 3, March, 1971, pp. 78-84.)

34. For a clear statement of conservative aspirations on this score see Geoffrey Ripon, "South Africa and Naval Strategy," *The Round Table*, No. 239 (June, 1970) pp. 303-9. According to Mr. Ripon, "NATO should broaden its maritime horizons . . . to give support and backing to our Portuguese allies and to the efforts of South Africa in her action as a bastion against the spread of communism in Africa and her commanding geographical position in two oceans." p. 308.

35. N. B., the remarks by the South African Minister of Defense, Mr. Botha in May, 1968: "Because of the apparent preoccupation of certain Western Nations with their own political objectives, with which they are saddled, we must ask ourselves whether the time has not come to encourage greater cooperation among friendly nations in the Southern Ocean area. . . ." Quoted in "Defence of the South Atlantic," *Background* (May/June, 1969). The timing of these remarks is interesting, coming as they did shortly after the first sighting of Russian warships in the Indian Ocean.

36. For a detailed discussion of South African attempts to promote closer ties with certain Latin American states see "The Strategic Significance of Southern Africa," *op. cit.*, pp. 28-32.

37. More sophisticated weapon systems such as Mirage jet aircraft have been acquired from external sources willing to defy the embargo and in this context France has been significantly active. South Africa's present naval capability consists of two destroyers carrying Wasp ASW helicopters, six ASW frigates, one ocean-going minesweeper, ten coastal minesweepers, five seaward defense boats and one fleet-replenishment tanker. In addition South Africa is in the process of taking delivery of three Daphne-type submarines from French shipyards at an estimated cost of eight million pounds each. The total strength of the navy is approximately three thousand five hundred.

38. R. D. Laing, "South Africa—A Bastion for an Oceanic Association," *Report from South Africa*, June, 1969, pp. 18-21.

39. Quoted in "Simonstown: Bastion of the Free World," *Background* (Johannesburg: South Africa Foundation), January/February, 1970.

40. Quoted in "Defence of the South Atlantic" *Background*, May/June, 1969, *op. cit.*

41. There is a good discussion of the difficulties the Soviets would face in trying to disrupt the shipping lanes in Jukes' article, *op. cit.*, pp. 373-4. He refers in particular to the obstacles confronting successful use of the Soviet submarine fleet and the dangers that would accrue from any attempt to sink tankers, a high proportion of which are owned by NATO countries friendly to the United States. *N.B.* his comment: "It is difficult to see sinking taking place outside a general war context; in any event it would also require a large force of submarines based nearer the scene than a port at the remote end of the Pacific." p. 373.

42. *N.B.* T. B. Millar's remark ". . . if the Simonstown Agreement, giving the British Navy access to the base's facilities, did not exist, it might be difficult to invent it: but seeing that it does exist, Britain (for mercantile reasons) and Australia (for mercantile and naval reasons) will surely wish it to be retained." "The Indian and Pacific Oceans: Some Strategic Considerations," *op.cit.*, p. 6.

43. Before 1968 British forces numbered eighty thousand in Singapore and Malaysia and thirty thousand in Aden and the Gulf. Some $650 billion were spent in South East Asia on a variety of defense functions.

44. For a good discussion of this subject see L. W. Martin, *British Defence Policy: The Long Recessional* (Adelphi paper, No. 61, London: Institute for Strategic Studies, 1969). Also T. B. Millar, *Britain's Withdrawl from Asia—Its Implications for Australia*, Australian National University 1967.

45. Only the French among the member states of the EEC have any strategic interests in the Indian Ocean by virtue of its harbor and base capacity at Djibouti and the military component of the Franco-Malagasy Agreement. The latter provides *inter alia* base facilities at Diego Suarez.

46. *Strategic Survey*, 1970 (London: Institute for Strategic Studies), p. 26.

47. R. P. Owen, "The British Withdrawal from the Persian Gulf," *The World Today*, vol. 28, No. 2, February, 1972, p. 80.

48. N. B. Jukes' comment, "Admittedly it would be difficult to verify compliance with a non-nuclear agreement, but *one* identification by Soviet Intelligence of a Polaris submarine between the Malacca Straits and the Cape would suffice to prove violation and sporadic identifications of this kind pose an intelligence demand well below that required for combat purposes, where the aim is to know where every submarine is at all times." *op. cit.*, p. 372.

49. *Ibid.*, p. 372.

50. Hedley Bull, *The Control of the Arms Race* (London: Institute for Strategic Studies), 1961, p. 75.

51. In this context I have in mind the fact that at the time of the signing of the Test Ban Treaty (and this would be arguably true of the non-Proliferation Treaty as well), both the United States and the Soviet Union could be said to be satisfied 'power' and therefore to continue testing was not seen as a crucial interest which it would be imprudent to relinquish.

52. See "The British Withdrawal from the Persian Gulf," *op. cit.*, p. 80.

53. Bruce Larkin, *China and Africa, 1949-1970* (Berkeley: University of California Press, 1971), p. 211.

7 Naval Armaments in the Far East

T. B. Millar

For many centuries maritime power has been important to the major countries of the Far East, and to the external powers active there in empire or in trade. Vast land distances, difficult terrain and poor communications separated the area from the markets or metropolitan capitals of Europe. Japan, the Philippines, the East Indies, Australia were all island states or groups, dependent on the sea for trade and communications and, where possible, security. Numbers of other islands or ports provided fueling stations along the sea lines of communication, and were thus essential elements of imperial rule.

World War I ended the German colonial empire in the Far East, and gave a further impetus to the expansion of the Japanese. The Washington naval agreements ensured that Japan would have maritime superiority in the Western Pacific, while the transfer of control of most of the German Pacific islands to Japan under the League mandate system provided opportunities for distant maritime facilities and a sense of being not simply an island but an oceanic power. The Pacific no less than East Asia lay open before them: 1941 was a logical, almost inevitable, successor to 1921.

World War II destroyed the Japanese and Dutch empires, and severely sapped the British. The changing configurations

of power in the East Asian region since that time have begun
to move to a more 'natural' pattern. While the Soviet Union
took hasty advantage of a defeated Japan in the few days
after Hiroshima, it was already a major Asian and Pacific
power, a function it has steadily strengthened. The United
States, dominant at sea in 1945, has been forced to retreat
substantially from a policy of continental intervention
towards a primarily 'off-Asia' position. Britain has departed,
leaving a useful aid mission behind in the archipelago and a
trade and information post at Hong Kong. Indonesia, after a
brief, economically disastrous adventure in chauvinism (in-
spired by China and made possible by the Soviet Union), has
settled down to try to cope with her massive internal
problems. The Indo-China civil war continues, but raising
fewer of the old 'domino' fears. China has begun to emerge
on the world stage, an uncertain giant, predominantly
localized by its low technology/population ratio. And the
Japanese, whose energy and wits were but briefly numbed by
the war, have re-emerged as the most dynamic and by far the
largest industrial and economic power in the region and
potentially the largest military power.

Within this overall, slightly uneasy, and still drifting
balance, navies have played and are playing a variety of roles.
The U.S. Seventh Fleet has kept Taiwan secure from the
People's Republic, made possible the containment of North
Korea, restricted North Vietnamese coastal operations against
the South, and carried out much of the allied bombing in the
Vietnam War. The modest Chinese fleet has also deterred
incursions from Taiwan. The British, Australian and New
Zealand navies dominated the seas of the archipelago during
Indonesian 'confrontation' of Malaysia, making Indonesian
success even more unlikely. And the Soviet navy, moving out
into warmer waters evacuated by the British, has engaged in
flottenpolitik which has given high psychological if somewhat
tentative political returns.

Maritime power of course includes a great deal more than
naval ships. In a maritime environment, shore-based aircraft

can engage in strike, interception and reconnaissance operations over large areas of the ocean. This paper will only touch on those aspects, and be primarily concerned with naval armaments and facilities in the geographical region of the western Pacific, including the Malay archipelago. For the same reasons, it does not distinguish land-based maritime air capacity from land-based continental air capacity.

Of the three local powers with significant navies, the most significant is the Soviet Union's.[1] An estimate of the average size of the Soviet Pacific naval forces (the 5th Fleet based on Vladivostok and the 7th Fleet on Petropavlovsk and Sovetskaia Gavan) is given in Table 1. At any time, these fleets may be augmented or depleted, just as the U.S. Seventh Fleet can be supplemented by the First operating in the Eastern Pacific, or depleted to send forces into the Indian Ocean or even the Atlantic.

For obvious reasons, the Pacific coast is nowhere near as important to the Soviet Union as its western and southern seaboards. It is much further from most major centers of industry and population, as well as from the seat of political power. It is a relatively uncomplicated coastline, without the disadvantages of the Dardanelles or the Baltic, but there are still some disadvantages. Reinforcement is not easy. Except during the few weeks of high summer, maritime movements between the eastern and western Soviet Union have to be around the Cape of Good Hope and through the Indian Ocean, unless Panama is used. The Sea of Japan and (to a lesser extent) the Sea of Okhotsk come close to being inland seas. All the ice-free[2] Soviet Pacific ports and bases are on the Sea of Japan, with exits only through one of the four narrow straits—Tartar (between Sakhalin and the mainland), Soya (Sakhalin/Hokkaido), Tsugaru (Hokkaido/Honshu), Shimonoseki (Honshu/Shikoku), or Tsushima (Japan/Korea). Tartar Strait is iced up for seven months of the year; Soya is only 25 miles wide, with Japan controlling the other side; Tsugaru and Shimonoseki are under Japanese control, and Tsushima is effectively dominated by Japan and South

Table 1   Operational Maritime Forces of East Asian Countries*

	Attack carriers	Escort/ ASW/ helicopter commando carriers	Submarines nuc. pow., nuc. arm.	Submarines nuc. pow. attack	Submarines convent. powered
Japan					11
China					30
Taiwan (Republic of China)					
North Korea					4
South Korea					
North Vietnam					
South Vietnam					
Thailand					
Philippines					
Malaysia					
Singapore					
Indonesia					4
United States 7th Fleet	4	2	3	7	
Soviet Union Estimated average Pacific deployment[3]			5	15	120
United Kingdom East of Suez deployment					1
Australia		1			4

*Compiled from various public sources and some private estimates whose accuracy can be neither proven nor disproven. It is recognized that some of the classifications are arbitrary and inadequate.

1.   These two figures are from *Jane's Fighting Ships* 1971-72. The I.I.S.S. Military Balance gives a total of 530 landing ships and craft, many being very small; Sekino (op.cit.) accords the Chinese navy 535 patrol craft and 305 amphibious craft.

Cruisers	Destroyers dest./ escorts frigates	Corvettes patrol vsls sub chasers	Missile/ torpedo/ fast gun fast gun boats	Mine- sweepers various	Patrol craft	Landing ships	Landing craft	Trans- ports
	40	20	10	41	27	4	48	
	24	24	400	27	22	29[1]	25[1]	
	29	25		19	50	46	29	6
		11	50	34	26[2]	NA	10	
	16	17		12		20	NA	
		2	4		39	NA	NA	
	4	9	22	12	900	15	24	
	3	8		4	20	4	5	1
	1	14		2	28	9		1
	2		4	6	24			
					4			
	7	10	20	10	35	5	8	1
1	30	NA[4]	NA	NA	NA	NA	NA	NA
4	34	50	30	120	130	30	70	
	6							
	12			4	20	NA	NA	1

2. This also is *Jane's*. Some other sources give a much higher figure.

3. The Japan Defense Agency White Paper of October 1970 lists the Soviet Far Eastern Forces as including about 600 naval ships, of tonnage 600,000 tons, with 20 nuclear-powered and 80 conventionally-powered submarines.

4. These 7th Fleet figures were not available to me in Australia.

Korea. All are relatively shallow, and suitable for minelaying. One of the factors in the Soviet decision to stay neutral in the Japanese war until the last moment must surely have been the vulnerability of the Pacific ports to Japanese naval power. The United States or, in years to come, Communist China might also derive advantage from this accident of geography. Since the war, having taken back southern Sakhalin, the Russians have built a base at Korsakov, on the southern tip facing the Pacific.

This situation is presumably one reason why the Russians have so far turned a deaf ear to Japanese demands for the return of the Etorofu, Kunashiri, Shikotan and Habomai islands in the South Kuriles (referred to by Japan as 'the northern territories'). These were seized by the Soviet Union soon after the end of World War II, and while they are of no great value to the Russians, in Soviet hands they are strategically embarrassing to the Japanese. The nearest Habomai island is less than three miles from Hokkaido, and Kunashiri is also clearly visible from Hokkaido. There has been a succession of fishing disputes between Japan and the Soviet Union, and the latter has used force majeure to intern hundreds of Japanese fishermen and confiscate their catches. Some observers believe that in the event of a Soviet conventional war with the United States, the Russians would attack and try to occupy Japan in order (a) to prevent the Americans from using the bases there, and (b) to protect its own eastern seaboard and outlets.

From the land, the largest Soviet Pacific base and port at Vladivostok, the somewhat smaller but developing facilities at nearby Nakhodka, and the industrial and communications city of Khabarovsk on the Amur River would be extremely vulnerable to a hostile China.

The roles of the Soviet Pacific fleets are presumably:

(a) defense of the Soviet coast, ports, shipping routes and fishing areas;

(b) surveillance of the seas to keep track of potentially hostile maritime forces;

(c) 'showing the flag' for political purposes.

The most potentially hostile forces are the American nuclear-armed, nuclear-powered submarines. So far as we know, neither the Russians nor the Americans have as yet developed a capacity to locate submerged nuclear submarines, or even to track them for any distance if they are discovered (e.g., on leaving base). Soviet maritime air reconnaissance is not yet capable of scanning the whole of the Pacific, because of the lack of aircraft carriers or forward bases. (In some situations, the Russians could perhaps use Cuba as a base from which to minitor the eastern Pacific waters.) The United States has no such limitations, except as they relate to submarines or to weather conditions. Both countries have observation satellites, so far imperfectly developed.

It is difficult to compare the Soviet and U.S. Pacific fleets. Both are capable of launching nuclear attacks on the other's territory. The American fleet includes several attack carriers. It is capable of much better reconnaissance, and much quicker reinforcement. It has its own bases in Honolulu and Guam, and access to bases (but see below) in Japan, the Philippines, Korea, Vietnam, Thailand, and Australia. The one great advantage which the Russians have over the Americans is in the surface-to-surface cruise missile, and in some highly sophisticated long-range air-to-surface missiles. By these means the Russians have overcome some of the disadvantages of not having fixed-wing carriers, and rendered extremely vulnerable the larger American vessels not under an air umbrella. Thus whereas American navies have operated successfully against nonexistent or relatively unsophisticated North Korean, North Vietnamese or Chinese forces, the balance would be very different against the Soviet Union in the Northwest Pacific. This would be true even if the Americans were matching the Russians in ship replacement, which they are not.

While the greater part of east-west internal Soviet trade

goes by rail, Soviet trade has increased with respect to most Asian states, including Japan. Soviet merchant ships have entered the Europe-Far East and Europe-Australia conferences. They cross the Pacific to Canada and the United States, and trade between Soviet east Asia and Southeast Asia. A large part of the Soviet and East European war supplies for North Vietnam have gone by sea, and Soviet naval vessels are continuously active in the Indian Ocean. The key straits—Suez, and the passages through the Malay-Indonesian archipelago—have thus become increasingly important. While not being able to get Suez opened, the Soviet Union has become the major external power operating along the Suez-Red Sea passage. It does not enjoy a similar position in the archipelago, but has begun a range of diplomatic and economic moves to improve its position. Indonesia earlier declared its sovereignty over the whole of the seas within its island chain. Malaysia and Indonesia have now announced their common view that the Strait of Malacca also, which they share, is not an international waterway. The right of innocent passage is conceded, but this raises the possibility of a fee for such passage (to pay for dredging) and implies a readiness to bar warships and other vessels whose passage might not be deemed 'innocent'. The Soviet Union has objected, and would like (as would Japan) to see the strait declared an international waterway by an appropriate international authority.

Throughout Southeast and East Asia the Soviet Union has not built naval facilities outside its own territory, nor apparently has it obtained privileged access to other people's facilities. This does not mean it has not tried or may not succeed. Reports indicate an attempt (unsuccessful so far) to build or obtain facilities at Singapore. It has begun to make use of Singapore's facilities. To use someone else's base offers low risk but for an easily interrrupted return. To build your own on his territory involves higher risk for a higher return. In Egypt, and apparently in Cuba, the first was a preliminary to the second. One can conceive of similar attempts being made elsewhere. And while the 1969 Brezhnev proposal for a Soviet-backed 'system of collective security in Asia' met little group response, the treaties which Iraq just signed—with India in August, 1971, following a similar one with the U.A.R.—at least hint that a series of bilateral arrangements could come to constitute such a system. The prerequisites for such a treaty are probably (a) a friendly relationship with the U.S.S.R. including extensive arms aid, and (b) a situation of external threat or exciting external opportunity where no other major power will help. Potentially, there are several such situations in the region.

Naval arms aid can clearly be a factor in the regional balance. North Korea was able to capture the Pueblo because of Soviet arms, just as the U.A.R. was able to sink the Eilat. It is interesting that Soviet aid to North Vietnam has been predominantly sophisticated ground and air equipment, rather than naval. This may have saved the United States considerable embarrassment. Supposing a Soviet-donated Vietnam-fired guided missile had sunk the Enterprise!

To the extent that there is a potential confrontation in the Far East, it is between the Soviet Union and the United States. Yet for the most part the American naval effort is not specifically directed against the Soviet Union, but rather is designed to safeguard Taiwan against the mainland, help fight the Vietnam War, and stand ready to defend Japan or South Korea.

South Korea is a much more sensitive area than Japan. A past and possible future enemy lies just across the cease-fire line, and has two powerful (if competitive) friendly neighbors. It seems to me that no one is going to attack Japan in the near future, and the task of the U.S.-Japan Security Treaty is psychological reassurance for the Japanese more than their physical protection. Psychological reassurance related mainly to possible nuclear attack (Soviet or Chinese), and for this the nuclear missiles on Okinawa and the nuclear weapons in the Seventh Fleet and in Pacific-based Polaris submarines have provided an effective public demonstration.

It would seem unlikely that Okinawa will continue to do so after it is returned to Japanese control next month. The irony of the Japanese position is that it wants to have as little as possible to do, publicly, with that part of American power on which it wants most to depend. We cannot assume that the naval facilities in the region to which the U.S. currently has access (and most of which she built) will continue to be available to her indefinitely. Guam, which is an American island, has a fairly small naval base, which will remain American. But in Japan the United States may well find herself becoming a junior partner, or even her presence unwanted and embarrassing, while invisible Polaris or Poseidon submarines continue to meet the requirements of deterrence. Despite the economic disadvantages it would suffer, the Philippines may before long have an administration which for domestic political reasons demands the return of Subic. American naval forces at present make very little use of Sattahip (Thailand) or Camranh Bay (Vietnam), but their accessibility for more than a few years is uncertain, to say the least. Some limited use of Singapore may be possible, because profitable to the Singapore government. Australian facilities are small, remote, and subject to industrial stoppage. The present general picture is of course not as bad as this chronicle suggests might be the case.

While Japan is the largest trading nation in Asia, the United States is the best customer of some East Asian states (e.g., Japan, Taiwan, the Philippines), the major supplier of others (Thailand, Australia, and Japan). It has been the largest provider of foreign aid. But in Europe and Asia (as distinct from Latin America) the deployment and tasks of the U.S. Navy and other defense forces since World War II have rarely been related to trade or economic aid or even investment; they have been predominantly strategic/political, the exercise of military strength for the political ends of power. In simple terms, these ends have been the containment of Communism, the defense of the free world, the expression of democratic power for righteous causes, etc.

This has been the American equivalent of the European imperial commitment, and was as clearly seen to constitute a national interest. The change in objectives and motivation characterized by the Nixon doctrine, coupled with a change in capacity due to a less powerful navy with fewer forward facilities, raises the possibility that within 3-5 years the U.S. Navy in the Pacific will have very different—and fewer—roles from those of the last two decades. Again, it could find life much more complicated, with the Soviet Union having access to many facilities at present denied it, with a more sophisticated and more widely ranging (and thus more competitive) Chinese navy, and with Japan once again using her naval forces to demonstrate her power and (potentially) to protect her steadily widening interests.

By its geography, Japan is a vulnerable country.[3] It is located within a few miles of a traditionally unfriendly superpower, the Soviet Union, and only about 350 miles from a potential superpower, the Chinese People's Republic. Both are armed with nuclear weapons, which Japan is not. It is extremely poor in natural resources, including food, which must therefore be imported and could be subject to interruption. Less than 1 percent of crude oil is home-produced, for example, and less than 2 percent of iron ore.

Japan is forbidden by its Constitution from having defense forces of any kind. The 1951 Peace Treaty, on the other hand, recognized Japan's 'inherent right' of self-defense, and the rationale of the development of the defense (technically, 'self-defense') forces is a progressive compromise in interpretation between these two documents, a moving frontier of definition invading prepared areas of ambiguity. The 1970 White Paper states under the interesting subheading 'Limits of the Constitution' (p.39):

(a) Since our military power is intended for self-defense, its size and scale must be that which is proper and necessary. What degree of defense power this means in concrete terms cannot be described categorically because of various conditions such as the progress and development of science and technology at a given time; but in any case Japan cannot possess weapons which will pose a threat of aggression to other nations, such as long-range bombers like B-52s, attack aircraft carriers, and ICBMs.

(b) Also, as our defense power is for self-protection, it cannot take action which exceeds the scope of self-defense. In other words, the cases in which the deployment of the Self-Defense Forces will be ordered are those where there are direct *or indirect*[4] attack against our country. Consequently, so-called overseas dispatch of forces will not be carried out.

Under the subheading 'Limits of Policy', the White Paper states (p.40):

(a) With regard to nuclear weapons, we adopt the three-point non-nuclear principle (no acquisition, development or hosting). Even though it would be permissible to say that in [a] legal and theoretical sense possession of small nuclear weapon[s] falling within the minimum requirement for capacity necessary for self-defense and not posing a threat of aggression to other countries, would be permissible, the government, *as its policy,*[4] adopts the principle of not attempting nuclear armament which might be possible under the Constitution.

While all this may sound clear and reasonable enough, it does not tell us a great deal about the navy, except that it is prevented by the Constitution from having attack carriers and by present government policy from having nuclear weapons. Otherwise it is a policy which could apply equally to (say) the Soviet Navy. By definition, navies operate 'overseas', and the Japanese Navy has been seen in waters extremely remote from the homeland. Commander Sekino, in his authoritative article, states the main tasks of the MSDF to be 'the defense of Japan against invasion from the sea by meeting and repulsing it upon the sea; and securing a supply of the necessities of life for the nation, as well as various raw materials for the continued conduct of war.' This could cover a very wide range of activities. Sekino says that the navy currently emphasizes the second task—'protection of sea communications'—but with its present strength it is 'able only to protect in convoys 20 to 30 percent of the nation's maritime transportation, for a distance of several hundred miles from Japan; that is, in the waters bounded by the mainland, the Nanpo (Bonin) Islands and the Nansei (Ryukyu) Islands'. In fact, few of the major trading nations would have a higher convoy capacity, but then few are as dependent as Japan on sea transport. Even within Japan, according to Sekino, 40 percent of goods moved travel by sea.

It is true that the Japanese Navy could not mount offensive operations associated with (say) an invasion of some remote and even moderately powerful state, but then one cannot see why it should wish to do so. Submarines are offensive weapons, but are not enough on their own. Japan's main concern must be protection of shipping against Soviet and/or Chinese submarines. Sekino is also concerned at the possibility of a Soviet invasion, and estimates that Soviet shipping in the Far East could probably lift and supply several army divisions in the event of war. He lists the following weaknesses in the Japanese Navy:

(a) almost all the shipbuilding and repair facilities are in the hands of private companies;

(b) research and development is inadequate;

(c) 'afloat support' capacity is very limited, restricting operations to home waters;

(d) although anti-submarine armaments are good, anti-aircraft capacity is weak, although supplemented (in the home environment) by land-based aircraft which would also be essential for defense against missile-firing ships;

(e) convoy capacity is so limited that in war merchant shipping would have to be cut by about 50 percent.

While all this may be true, the Japanese Navy—such as it is— is modern and efficient. The fourth five-year defense programme covering the period until mid-1976 envisages the construction of 103,000 tons of naval shipping, including two 8,000-ton heavy destroyers carrying helicopters, nine submarines, 14 high-speed missile ships, and 61 other vessels. One of Japan's great assets is her shipbuilding capacity which is quantitatively second to none, even though in naval terms it lacks some of the more sophisticated and specialized technology. While the Japanese Navy still does not have attack or ASW carriers, this is not (as mentioned above) a problem in the area within the range of land-based aircraft. Nor does Japan have the capacity to bomb China, whereas both China and the U.S.S.R. are capable of bombing Japan. The U.S.S.R. can also attack Japan with IRBMs or ICBMs, and China will be able to do so before long, if indeed it cannot already.

In these circumstances, Japan has various alternatives: to continue to rely on the United States for her ultimate conventional and nuclear protection; to greatly increase her own defense capacity including by nuclear weapons; to try to do both of these; or to end the U.S. Treaty and perhaps seek alternative friends or allies.[5] This is not the place to discuss the factors bearing on a Japanese decision to 'go nuclear', but the much-repeated argument that Japan is too vulnerable to do so seems to me to hold no water. Rather is vulnerability an argument working in favor (especially) of a deterrent such as submarine-launched ballistic missiles. Having successfully produced a nuclear-propelled merchant ship (the Mutsu), and various kinds of missiles, a Japanese "polaris" submarine could probably be managed within a few years of the decision to build it. Such a decision does not yet appear to have been taken. As is well known, Japan has signed the Nuclear Non-Proliferation Treaty, but has given no evidence that she will ratify it.

Without extending the political aspects of Japan's security unduly, one can say that Japan has been cautious about accepting both American advice to take a more active role in the region and Soviet inducements to engage in joint economic ventures, including further development of Nakhodka. Both appear designed in part as anti-Chinese measures, or at least are likely to be so seen in Peking. At the same time, the insufficiently sensitive American diplomacy towards Japan in recent times must have helped the cause of those Japanese who either want to 'go it alone' or would like to come to better terms with Moscow or Peking. A Soviet gesture over the southern Kuriles would further their cause quite dramatically, but is probably unlikely, partly because of the precedent it could offer for Soviet-Chinese territorial disputes.

Japanese naval bases are located at Yokosuka in Tokyo Bay, at Kure in the Inland Sea, Sasebo on Shikoku and Maizuru in central Honshu facing Korea, and at Ominato in Mutsu Bay in northern Honshu off the Tsugaru Strait. A small base is being developed at Yoichi on the Shakotan Peninsula in Hokkaido facing the Soviet Pacific coast. Japan has also taken over small naval facilities in the Bonin Islands returned by the United States, and is reportedly expanding them; presumably it will in time have access to and eventually control the much larger naval and air bases on Okinawa. Okinawa is of considerable strategic significance to Japan. It is on the oil route to the Middle East, and the iron-ore route to Australia. It is equidistant (400 miles) from Taiwan, the Chinese mainland, and Japan. Further, the Ryukyus of which Okinawa is simply the largest island have at times been considered to include the Senkaku (or Tiaoutai) islands northeast of Taiwan, which are reported to be above rich oilfields. While the Senkakus have been administered by the United States as part of the Ryukyus, will be returned to Japanese control on May 15th, and will still have a bombing range used by the United States, the U.S. government has not declared its position on sovereignty of the islands, which is claimed also by the Republic of China and the People's Republic.

Japanese dependence on imported oil—hitherto predominantly from the Middle East—has led it to take an interest in the Strait of Malacca and dredge it, to develop huge supertankers, to provide economic aid to Indonesia, and to engage in a number of offshore explorations. At present, restrictions by Indonesia or Malaysia on the passage of tankers would be economically and strategically harmful to Japan, while total restriction by Indonesia would force a detour of several thousand miles around Australia.

A potentially significant aspect of Japan's maritime position relates to Micronesia, in which Japan has been showing increasing interest over the past five years. Japanese fishing vessels now use the former Japanese bases at Palau and Truk; warships sunk in Truk lagoon are being salvaged; Japanese tourist traffic to the islands has multiplied; there have been visits by research ships and naval training ships; and Japanese commercial involvement is now an important factor in the economy of the territory. A plaque put up in Saipan by a visiting Japanese War Graves group reads (in English and Japanese): 'Devote yourselves to the creation of the Pacific Global Area—March, 1970 AD'. One cannot but wonder how long an independent Micronesia would remain independent.

Nearer to home, Japan has declared[6] that the security of the Republic of (South) Korea was 'essential' to Japan's own security, while the maintenance of peace and security in the Taiwan area was also 'a most important factor for the security of Japan'. Taiwan must have been downgraded since the Nixon visit to Peking, but South Korea has for centuries had a special place in Japanese strategic thinking. The Sea of Japan is an area of great potential turbulence, and irrespective of the Constitution or of current doctrine, no Japanese government would easily accept a change in the status quo on the peninsula. If Japanese forces are used to prevent it, the Maritime Self-Defense Force would almost certainly be the first.

The Chinese People's Republic is not profligate with information about its navy, and public Western sources are little better. *Jane's Fighting Ships* lists 35 submarines, but probably 8 to 10 of these are useful only for training. The four "Gordy"-class destroyers are all over thirty years old, and eleven of the escorts are not much younger. The Soviet "G"-class submarine, built at Dairen in 1964, has missile tubes but apparently as yet no missiles. The teeth of the navy are provided by the 'G'-class and the 21 'W'-class submarines, 7 'Osa'-class missile boats and 3 "Komar"-class with Styx missiles, 160 fast gun boats (some doing up to 40 knots), and some 240 hydrofoil fast torpedo boats (40-45 knots). Apart from the submarines, which are capable of operating over a radius of several thousand miles, the Chinese Navy is thus very much designed for coastal defense. And for the submarines to engage in unsupported aggressive operations far from home would make little sense on any basis. By all accounts, China's coastal defenses are extremely efficient, especially considering the length of the coastline.

Rumors about expansion of the Chinese Navy appear regularly in the West. Sisters for the 'G'-class submarine have had numerous press notices of conception but none of birth. *Jane's Fighting Ships* (1971/72) states: "It is reported that there may be up to three nuclear powered submarines in various stages of construction designed for a displacement of 3,000 tons and an armament of missiles and torpedoes. First vessel begun in 1969." It will be interesting to see whether the reports turn out to be accurate. Official statements in the Peking *People's Daily* and other journals indicate a desire to emulate the Soviet Union in expanding naval and merchant marine capacity, but intentions have yet to be translated into ships, and there is little naval tradition or experience. Reports of Indian sightings of Chinese naval vessels in the Indian Ocean, and of Chinese assistance to Tanzania to set up a small navy and base do not invalidate this general comment. (It may be significant that senior members of the naval hierarchy have not been purged as have generals in the army or air force.)

Nevertheless, in local terms China represents a sizeable threat to any naval power that might attempt to attack it. It has also apparently provided some small ships for the North Korean Navy. A number of naval bases are located along the coast, as well as on Hainan island. There have also been reports of a base, or port, being developed in the Paracels.

As could be expected, the Republic of China (Taiwan) has a different kind of navy from the People's Republic. It has no submarines, is almost wholly ex-U.S., and is geared to operate in conjunction with the U.S. Seventh Fleet. While a sizeable number of landing ships and craft give an ostensible amphibious invasion capacity, this is wholly dependent on American support, which for many years has been demonstrably lacking. Although the ROC Navy would put up strong resistance to an invasion from across the strait, it could scarcely on its own repel such an invasion.

No other country in the area has a significant naval capacity. North Vietnam, with Soviet-supplied missile boats, is perhaps the most able to respond sharply to intruders within its coastal environment.

Much of the coastal and island sea, being comparatively shallow, is susceptible to mining, both offensively and defensively, and to the installation of fixed underwater sensors. We can assume that China has engaged in the latter, to enable it to intercept Nationalist infiltrations.

The developing pattern of major naval deployment in eastern Asia is thus one where the Soviet Union is more active and more ubiquitous; Japan increasing in size but still limited in range; China slowly building but still tied to the continent; and the United States less certain of its role, less accessible to forward facilities, less committed to the defense of remote, smaller partners.

NOTES

1. Although I have consulted various sources for these comments on the Soviet Navy, I am particularly indebted to Siegfried Breyer, *Guide to the Soviet Navy* (United States Naval Institute, 1970).

2. Petropavlovsk, an important naval and air base on the Kamchatka Peninsula, is ice-free only from May to October.

3. A major source of information for this section is the article by Commander Hideo Sekino, "Japan and her Maritime Defense," *United States Naval Institute Proceedings*, May 1971; also the Japan Defense Agency White Paper, *The Defense of Japan*, October 1970 (English version).

4. Emphasis added.

5. Three days after Mr. Sato's last visit to the United States (January 1972), his Ambassador to Washington was reported as saying that the Nixon visit to Peking might be "the beginning of a process of unravelling our mutual security in the Far East."

6. In the Sato-Nixon communiqué of November 24, 1969.

8   Some Aspects of Sea-based Deterrent Strategies

Michael Rosenthal

Within the United States pressures to deploy new strategic systems are unremitting. The fiscal 1973 Annual Defense Department Report, by Secretary of Defense Melvin Laird, includes projected requests for a new bomber, the B-1, to be equipped with subsonic cruise armed decoys, SCAD, and short-range attack missiles, SRAM, and for a new submarine fleet, the undersea long-range missile system, ULMS, as well as for continued funding of the Safeguard ABM program. The steady deployment of new strategic systems is troublesome from several points of view. Accepting as the rationale for these procurements the concept of mutual reciprocal deterrence, one has the feeling that adequate levels of "assured destruction" have already been provided and that the great cost of new ventures detracts from the ability to resolve urgent domestic problems without any enhancement of the secure atmosphere in which these might best be expected to take place. Even more discomforting is the possibility that new deployments are not only unnecessary to provide an adequate deterrent force but are contraindicated, that constant alteration of the nuclear environment makes the possibility of the use of nuclear weapons greater, rather than smaller.

The purpose of this paper is to discuss the stability of

land-based and sea-based strategic systems. It will define technological and political concepts of stability, and then argue that land-based systems as they are currently deployed are metastable in both senses. The chapter then discusses the stability of the submarine systems and the way that they are currently deployed and argues that the stability of these systems can be improved by a simple alteration in the way they are deployed and without expenditure of new funds. It is also suggested that such alterations might serve as the basis for an arms control agreement.

Stability and Metastability of Strategic Systems

New strategic deployments may be disequilibrating for two different reasons. First, they may create political incentives rewarding those whose organizational interest also lies in the procurement of nuclear weapons systems and thus lead to a deployment by one's opponent of a substantially similar system, a response in kind to the initial deployment. This in turn may lead to new deployments from the first side. We may call this an arms race instability. The American deployment of MIRV, the Soviet and American ABM deployments and the magnitude of the American Minuteman force may be thought of as exemplary of arms race instabilities.

The second point is that the deployment of new systems, or the development of new or substantially improved technologies, may alter the incentives for either opponent to attempt a first strike. We may call this a first strike instability. The decision to abandon the soft ICBMs, deployed in the early 60s, in favor of the relatively secure Minuteman system, solid fuel missiles in hardened silos, was perhaps the first visible implementation of the ideas of first strike stability. This was the first deployment designed to correct an obvious instability, that is, to reduce the incentives for an enemy attack, not by diminishing the threat of one's own systems or by altering the political environment, but simply by making a particular mission, the elimination of American missile strength, technically impossible.

Though perceptions of a first strike instability may cause a reaction similar to an arms race instability, one cannot explain strategic deployments entirely in this way. Explanation of American and Soviet policy must include the political and bureaucratic mechanisms which fuel an arms race as well as the scientific and technological pressures which create a first strike instability. This section will examine some of the questions relating to first strike instabilities. This will be done by examining the land- and sea-based systems and contrasting the sources of their stability or instability. In order to do this, we will examine the concept of stability as it applies to land- and sea-based systems.

Stability is a dynamic, time-dependent state. Though it is often claimed that the nuclear environment since W.W. II has been stable, the evidence adduced for this consists primarily of three data; first, the absence of nuclear war since Hiroshima and Nagasaki; second, the successful defense of West Berlin; and third, the stand down of the Russians in Cuba.[1] But it is obvious that stability at any instant, or even over a period of time, does not imply that a system is stable for all time, and we may consider the division of systems into those which are metastable and those which are stable.

By this I mean that we can easily imagine systems which remain unused in time and thus have the appearance of stability, but which in fact may be driven into use rapidly and, perhaps, without warning. As an example, one can look again at the situation which evolved during the early development of the American and Russian strategic systems. Large, soft, strategic systems were deployed and never used. It was soon recognized that they were, in fact, metastable. Not having been used, it may be argued that they contributed to deterrence, but it is now realized that systems containing elements of softness, either in the weapon or in the command and control mechanism, do not necessarily contribute to deterrence, and, in fact, that under circumstances which do not seem to be unthinkable, they create precisely the opposite effect.

We can further divide the question of first strike stability into the separate categories, political and technological first strike stability or metastability. That is, in examining the stability of nuclear weapons systems we can imagine that they will be used for dramatically different reasons.

On the one hand, the military postures of a pair of opponents may indicate that one of them will find great advantage in a counterforce first strike or a damage limitation strike. This is the usual meaning of first strike instability. I characterize this as a technological instability in that the use of nuclear weapons arises from a rational calculation of the technical performance of one's offense versus one's opponent's defense and a presumed maximization of one's expected values.

On the other hand, there is a type of first strike instability which I will call a political instability, in that the use of nuclear weapons arises from internal political pressures and in which the rational calculation made in the first case is absent. This would include emotional responses and responses made for purposes of revenge rather than actions taken for damage limitation. The liability of various systems to become unstable in these ways is a function of both their intrinsic technical capabilities and the way in which the weapon is deployed. For instance, the bomber on air alert and circling the perimeter of the Soviet Union has a stability very different than a bomber grounded in the Midwest. The political stability of the airborne bomber is lower than the grounded bomber, while the technological stability of the airborne bomber is higher.[2]

Technological Stability of Land-based Systems

Though we may not be able to characterize the stability of modern systems with complete precision, it is possible to identify characteristics which force them to one end of the spectrum of stability, metastability, or instability. In this sense, the major distinction between land-based systems and submarine systems is in their visibility. Land-based systems, as they are currently deployed, are not invisible; in the case of the Minuteman system, the location of the missile silos is detectable by satellite inspection. The bomber forces are also locatable by satellite inspection and in any case the aircraft must be based at airports with capabilities sufficient to handle their takeoff and landing requirements. Further, the number of bombers which can be kept on air alert is low because of the high cost.

The result of these intrinsic visibilities is to force the present land-based systems into a position of technological metastability. This conclusion is based not only on the vulnerability of bomber bases to nuclear attack and by the possible future vulnerability of the Minuteman system, but is supported by the considerable literature dealing with controlled counterforce or limited strategic strikes. The small CEP of land-based missiles makes plausible counterforce scenarios. We are led to the conclusion that the presence of visible means of delivering nuclear weapons will have the effect of inducing one's opponent to target them. If they are targeted, then the possibility that they will be attacked is enhanced. The interaction of these asumptions leads to a continuous series of actions designed to lessen this threat and to a series of reactions designed to make one's own threats more plausible.

One would not find this process as discouraging as it is if it resulted in more effective and more stable deterrence. But actions designed to decrease the vulnerability of land-based systems may not be translated into greater stability. By their nature, improvements in the design of passive, or perhaps active, defensive measures are carried out in secret, and their capabilities are carefully concealed. And in the offense-defense race there are clear asymmetries in one's ability to determine the effectiveness of new engineering developments.

In general, the offense will have a greater ability than the defense to evaluate the effectiveness of new systems; offensive systems can be evaluated in extensive series of simulations and tests, and even after deployment, operational testing may continue. Further, the environment in which the offense is expected to operate may be comparable to that which exists during testing, for instance, during a first strike attempt or in a delayed response following a pre-emptive attack.

On the other hand, the defense of strategic systems cannot be effectively tested in the environment of the nuclear attack in which it will be expected to be successful. As long as the Partial Test Ban Treaty is respected, no offensive or defensive nuclear weapons system can be evaluated fully, but the strictures which this implies are more rigorous for the defense than for the offense. The defense must allow a complicated and sophisticated electromechanical system to perform at full effectiveness following a nearby nuclear explosion. However, the most difficult functions which an offensive missile system must perform will already have been completed by the time defensive measures will be met.

The active pursuit of aggressive technological programs designed to improve missile accuracies and to obtain multiple warheads illustrates the way in which a relatively secure deterrent balance may deteriorate, and, for certain systems, eventually vanish.[3] The combination of secrecy and offense-defense asymmetry lends special dangers to an action-reaction cycle based on the visibility of nuclear attack systems. In an environment in which the technological capabilities of opponents are large and in which they may be changing rapidly and at different rates, inhibitions against counterforce attacks on land-based strategic systems may be eroded.

Political Stability of Land-based System

Though, ultimately, any decision to go to war is a political decision, there is clearly a military, or technological, component which must be included. The Israeli decision to attack Egypt in the Six Day War must have been preceded by a careful analysis of the relative strengths of the Israeli air force and the Egyptian air defense. However, one can separate to some extent the political and technological components in the calculations of the defender. I have argued above that the visibility of the land-based systems implies that they are metastable in the technological sense, i.e., that they induce one's opponents through rational calculation to target them and thus enhance the probability that they will be attacked.

I also conclude that the land-based systems, as they are currently deployed, are metastable in a political sense as well. By this I mean that the presence of these systems within the United States is an intrinsic liability in that the political pressures to respond to any attack on them will be overwhelming. There can be little doubt that an attack on these forces, whether deliberate or accidental, will lead to the most extreme crisis. This is so for several reasons.

The strategic systems have been envisioned as the mechanism by which such attacks would be prevented from occurring. The failure of this deterrent mechanism would have a profound psychological shock and the resultant atmosphere would be characterized by extreme uncertainty. This would be heightened by the destruction of American lives and properties and by the knowledge that the inhibitions which had previously existed against the use of nuclear weapons had now vanished.

Second, one must also think that any attack on the continental United States by a nuclear power would create a crisis far greater than the mini-crises arising when American forces are attacked elsewhere. Loss of American lives due to attack at distant sites can be tolerated both by the American public and by the American government. The destruction of the U.S.S. Liberty and the EC-121 spyplane, the capture of the Pueblo, and the recent strafing of American vessels by Indian forces all call attention to the minimal response which can be expected following attack on a small American force operating overseas. In my judgement, however, the attack of any nation against forces stationed within the United States would create a political crisis of such proportions that a military response would be forthcoming. One need only look at the Cuban Missile Crisis to find a situation where it was the political implications of the Russian deployment which brought to bear on the administration—and on the President in particular—such potent forces that the President was forced to react strongly. There is little possibility that a rational analysis of the changing strategic situation would have evoked such a rapid and potentially violent response. As the Commander-in-Chief of the Armed Forces, the President is personally responsible for the protection of the nation, and any crisis in which doubt is cast on his performance in this regard will bring personal forces and emotions into play. One is struck by the difference between the constrained and calculating appraisal of Robert McNamara and the response of the President to the same events.[4] It is clear that McNamara was obliged to consider only the military and strategic implications while the President, at the center of a political tornado, had no choice but to become engaged personally.

In this sense, as a political crisis unfolds and becomes a military crisis, differently deployed systems may possess varying degrees of technological and political stability. The bomber and the ICBM forces, as they are presently deployed, fail to meet the requisites of both political and technological stability and must be considered metastable.

Stability of Sea-based Systems

Having examined the reasons for which the land-based systems may be classified as metastable, we will now examine briefly the factors which contribute to the stability of the sea-based systems.

First we will look at the factors which contribute to their

technological stability. The major factor is the essential invulnerability of the modern nuclear submarine. Traveling at depths down to 500 meters, the submarine is enveloped in a medium which is practically opaque to all high frequency electromagnetic radiation (in this context high frequency is greater than 100 Hz).[5] When traveling at speeds below five knots, the submarine may not be detected acoustically except with active devices[6] and the range of the devices presently deployed on ships is probably less than 20 kilometers.[7] Since the submarine may achieve speeds which are comparable or greater than most surface ships, it is possible for them to receive information locating surface traffic via low frequency transmissions and then navigate to avoid contact. This is perhaps the reason that the submarines do not assume fixed on-station positions but instead move about in a continuous fashion.[8] The Navy continues to claim that no submarine which has assumed its patrol depth has ever been located and tracked.[9] This inability to find and target the submarine makes it invulnerable, though once found it is a relatively soft target.

Second, the submarine systems enhance the stability of deterrence by their designed inability to deliver weapons with CEPs less than about 1-2 kilometers.[10] They are unsuitable for a first-strike or tactical use in which targets of interest are small and well hardened. Their nuclear weapons are clearly weapons of last resort; their use would thus imply that prior political restraints had been eliminated. It is difficult to imagine any scenario in which one posits the use of submarine missiles that does not include some elements of desperation or irrationality. Because of this and because we believe, or hope, that foreign affairs will be carried on with a semblance of rationality and in situations which are not desperate, the submarine systems appear to contribute to deterrence in ways which the land-based systems do not.

But the essential element of technological stability is not the invulnerability of the submarine, but its invisibility. Because it cannot be located, there are no plausible scenarios involving first strikes against a submarine fleet. The submarine fleet will retain its technological stability as long as it remains invisible.

For the submarine fleet to achieve maximum political stability, the submarine system should be deployed in a manner such that the political and emotional pressures which might develop in a crisis situation would not greatly enhance the probability that major reprisals will be made quickly and without substantial deliberation. The fact that the submarine is stationed at sea clearly obviates the possibility of a political instability similar to that described for the land-based systems. An attack on a patrolling submarine would not be an attack on the continental U.S. and thus would entail a considerably reduced fear of immediate escalation due to emotional responses. On the other hand, this reduced emotional response creates the new fear that its deterrent value has diminished. This is precisely the reason that it is possible for the Air Force to argue that the total reliance on a sea-based deterrent will *not* increase the effectiveness of deterrence but will reduce it, and therefore that we should maintain the Triad.[11]

On what assumptions do they base their claims? Their argument relies entirely on the feasibility of a war of attrition waged only at sea, one in which American sea-based strategic forces are slowly eliminated, with the result that only the Soviet Union, having retained its land-based systems, maintains a viable and now unilateral nuclear strike capability. I will discuss this possibility because it illustrates some of the implications of current American deployment tactics for the Polaris-Poseidon system and suggests desirable alteration of these tactics.

Though the sea war of attrition is more realistic than the comparable campaign waged against land-based systems, for it to remain plausible one must assume that the Soviet ASW systems are of comparable or greater effectiveness than the United States systems and that only the U.S.S.R. land-based systems are retained; that is, that the U.S. eliminates land-based systems entirely and that no major reallocation of these funds is made to submarine systems, either defensive or offensive. In addition, it assumes that throughout what would be a lengthy campaign, the pressures arising from fear and confusion and from domestic political opposition will be insufficient to generate an emotional and perhaps irrational escalatory response. It must also assume that one would not escalate through rational calculation.[12]

While these assumptions, by themselves, may be so unrealistic as to preclude any attempt to wage a war of attrition, any such possibility rests almost entirely on a third assumption made implicitly in the arguments against a blue-water strategy, one which is crucial in discussing the tactics of submarine strategic forces. This is that the submarine forces of the U.S. must always remain within striking distance of their targets in order to remain an effective deterrent against attack by the Soviet Union. This has the following implications for submarines with a missile range of 3000 miles, the generally accepted figure for the Poseidon system: On-station patrols are possible only within a small fraction of the total area of the North Atlantic, in the Mediterranean, or in a small triangular-shaped section of the Arabian Sea, assuming that all targets are located in Western Russia. Though patrols in the Pacific were instituted in 1964, submarines based in Guam and patrolling the Pacific or Indian Oceans cannot target cities in Western Russia. In addition, submarines in the Arctic Ocean will be within range of targets in most of Russia. While the presence of a permanent ice cap is a problem, missile firing is possible if the submarine surfaces through the ice or in open areas.[13]

(Though the total land and sea area within a three thousand mile distance of Moscow is approximately 27 million square miles, only about six million square miles is sea area. However, the available sea area increases approximately quadratically with missile range and an increment of 1000 miles increases the available sea area by a factor of about two and dramatically increases the attack perimeter.

Submarines with missiles of 4000 miles range could attack Moscow from all of the Arabian Sea and part of the Indian Ocean, including the Bay of Bengal. From the Pacific, Moscow would be within range from a narrow strip along the coast, including the Sea of Japan, the Yellow Sea and part of the South China Sea, the Sea of Okhotsk and part of the Bering Sea. Almost all of the North Atlantic would now be part of the attack zone on Moscow and submarines stationed in the northern part of Maine would be able to target Moscow as soon as they left base, unless they traveled southwest.)

The assumption of in-range stationing is implicit because it would be impossible to wage a war of attrition, in the present technological circumstances, unless one knew that submarines were limited to the specific regions noted above and that they would not leave these zones even *after* a campaign of attrition had begun. For if the submarines are free to roam the entire sea area of the world, one would have to presume that the months to years in which the scenarios[9] of attrition take place would then be multiplied by the ratio of the newly available area to the formerly prescribed area; a ratio which is about 14:1 given the 3000 miles missile range and about 7:1 if the missile range were increased to 4000 miles. With this increase (these would be lower bounds since the increased distances may make it impossible for ASW units to have any substantial capability in some regions) the attrition time would become comparable to the lead time for the construction of new submarines or other strategic systems, if this was felt necessary, and thus the war of attrition would stretch out to infinity, hardly an attractive future for the initiator. Unless the war of attrition were abandoned it could be ended only by an attack against land-based systems and facilities, precisely what was to be avoided in the first place. Under the circumstances, a war of attrition hardly seems a plausible proposition.

This demonstrates how a change in tactics may drastically alter the outcome of a war of attrition. Given the feasibility of a successful war of attrition taking place in a time, *t*, the alteration of tactics changes the time to at least 14*t* for presently deployed systems. This lengthening tends to reduce the feasibility of such an engagement and demonstrates the advantage of utilizing the entire ocean area for patrol.

I would now like to argue that it is advantageous to adopt a variant of this policy and deliberately station one's submarines in sea regions which are a distance from their targets greater than the missile range. These advantages are distinct from those involving a war of attrition, though the adoption of such a policy would increase the patrol area by 13 and also effectively reduce the possibility of such a war to zero.[14]

The additional advantages gained by stationing nuclear submarines at distances further from their targets than their missile range lies in the question of political stability discussed above. Given that the nuclear submarine has little or no counterforce capability, there is little reason for them to be stationed within range of their soft targets, for in general, these will not move. The actual U.S. policy of on-target stationing implies that the submarine has tactical capabilities and that there are targets of urgency which must be attacked quickly. If the averred policy of the U.S. is to avoid systems which have a counterforce or tactical capability, then the implications of the actual use of the Polaris-Poseidon fleet are contradictory.

By stationing submarines beyond range of their targets, one will strengthen the stability of deterrence in two ways. First, by announcing and carrying out a policy of extra-target stationing, one would be demonstrating, in fact as well as rhetoric, that the submarine was not considered useful as a tactical weapon and that the threat of nuclear attack had been rolled back. In this sense, the rollback should have a psychological value similar to the refusal to place nuclear weapons in fixed orbits as agreed to by the U.S. and the U.S.S.R. in the Outer Space Treaty. This move, as is the Outer Space Treaty, would probably be uninspectable and yet might still form the basis for an arms control agreement.

The second advantage lies again in countering the internal political pressures which one expects in crisis situations. The deployment of missile submarines beyond their target range increases the flexibility of the President in dealing with demands for military action. This is done by reducing his options by one, i.e., eliminating the option of attacking immediately. In this way, one is guaranteed that a hiatus exists between the perception of a threat and a nuclear submarine response, a span in which negotiation with internal and external pressure groups may lead to restrained and responsible measures. The Cuban missile crisis illustrates the considered response one expects when a threat is perceived but not actualized. One can imagine that a considerably more aggressive response would have resulted if the missiles had not been discovered until after they were thought to be operational rather than some days before.

By mitigating the pressures for an immediate nuclear response, one is more likely to be able to focus discussion on diplomatic measures and military responses at a lower level. At the same time, one has not eliminated the possibility of using submarine nuclear weapons at a later date. Though it may seem unusual to argue that flexibility will be increased when options are eliminated, the elimination of military options will tend to increase the political efficacy of those who favor political responses. The elimination of options which are the fruition of fear or desperation will tend to reduce the fears themselves.

The adoption of these tactics can only be carried out if it does not substantially weaken the deterrent value of the submarine fleet. To examine this question, we must look at two separate issues. One of them is strictly technical while the other is political and psychological. One is the ability of the submarines to achieve on-station positions if so ordered. The other is whether the knowledge that retaliation will be delayed for at least the time which it takes the submarines to achieve on-station positions weakens the credibility of retaliation. That is, whether or not deterrence with a guaranteed delay is weaker than deterrence with a capacity for instant response.

The first question may be reduced to the problem of the effectiveness of a barrier defense along the target range perimeter. This is not precisely defined since there is a multiplicity of targets, but one may easily map the area which is more than *n* miles from any point of the Soviet Union. For simplicity I will assume that the only target of interest is Moscow. Thus the defense perimeters are circles. This also makes the defense perimeter much smaller and the problem of penetration more difficult. The penetration of such a barrier will be made simpler in direct proportion to the length of such a perimeter. For the missile system with a range of 3000 miles, the defense perimeter is roughly 4000 miles long. If the missile range is increased to 4000 miles, the defense perimeter triples to approximately 12,000 miles. (It increases more rapidly than the area because the 4000-mile arc includes a narrow strip of the Pacific along the coast of China and the Soviet Union.) While such a barrier seems more feasible than ocean wide ASW, it seems unlikely that it could be wholly effective over a long period of time, especially during periods of active hostility.

According to Robert Frosch, "If a submarine is willing to creep around at a few knots and patrol quietly, the passive range of detection is small. The only thing you can do is to use active surface sonar, from surface ships or helos, and the best sonar range we have in the best destroyer sonar we have is sometimes under the right oceanographic conditions about (deleted)."[8] In a discussion of the Soviet threat to the bomber force, Colonel Trapold stated, "The way he (the Soviet Union) operates now he has a terrible problem keeping a larger number of submarines on-station because he has to spend so much time traveling. While the submarine travels, if he wants to keep down the probability that we will detect it, he must operate at very, very slow speeds, like on the order of five knots or so."[6] The implication of this testimony is that the defense of an ocean perimeter must be done with active sonar, assuming that the submarine will be able to travel slowly towards its attack stations. Given this, we must then question whether the submarine can deal with active sonar searches, either alone or in conjunction with surface ships and aircraft. The problem of penetration then becomes a question either of sea control or of the ability of the submarine and surface ships to effectively negate active sonar search by taking sonar counter measures. The problem of sea control is too large to deal with in the context of this discussion, but it is clear that, if necessary, the submarine fleet, itself, may contribute to this mission if we assume that nuclear weapons may be used at sea. Each submarine is a potent area clearance weapon, given that large ships are relatively soft and that the air wing of air-capable ships is softer than the ship itself. Surface fleets without air capability will be unable to cope with a submarine attack unless the number of ships is large. Since the submarine is as fast as most surface ships, it may take advantage of air reconnaissance or satellite information to navigate a path through or around a waiting fleet.

Avoiding active sonar search, either from shore-based installations or from shipboard sonar, may be done either by overloading the searching sonar, jamming, or by confusing the detection system with a multitude of false targets. While the "entire ocean basin can be rung like a bell,"[16] this capability is not restricted to the searcher. The plethora of techniques developed for radar jamming and avoidance may also be applied to sonar searches. In addition, the search problem is complicated by the variability of the ocean medium and the searchers' inability to determine the exact state of the ocean over a long period of time. It would be difficult to maintain the viability of fixed installations over a long period of time in a situation of active hostility. Their locations may be established during noncrisis periods and they may be attacked without using nuclear weapons. Sea-based installation must be linked to shore-based evaluation centers and the link as well as the evaluation center may be vulnerable during periods of hostility. It seems unlikely that any nation could defend an ocean perimeter 12,000 miles long.

The final question to be answered is whether the strength of deterrence is weakened by an inability to retaliate instantly. Psychologically, I think that the answer is "no." When the retaliation to be applied is overwhelming, deterrence is not necessarily diminished by the imposition of a delay. A well-known and effective deterrent procedure is the murder of stool pigeons among organized crime. The "rule of silence" is rarely broken, and the effectiveness of the deterrence does not lie in the threat of instant retaliation, but in the certainty that it will be executed at a later time even if thwarted in the short run.

It is important to note that this question does not arise only with systems in which delay is guaranteed. As soon as we abandon the principle of certain and instant relatiation, as soon as we eliminate the doomsday machine from consideration, we allow the same question to be asked about every strategic system. "Will there be any retaliation if it is not immediate?" Once the concept of "assured destruction" is operationalized, but the tactic of launch on warning or some equivalent is eliminated, the possibility that contemplation will not be followed by counterattack must be entertained. This applies with equal force to both the Minuteman system and the off-station Polaris submarine. Even today it is not the threat of guaranteed retaliation that deters, for no such guarantee exists. What deters is the high probability that retaliation will take place. The fact that delay is guaranteed, rather than likely, would be a slender threat upon which an aggressor would hang hopes of gain.[17]

In the context of mutual reciprocal deterrence, the arguments above tend to the conclusion that American policy should evolve slowly into one in which primary if not total reliance should be placed upon sea-based strategic forces. One is also drawn to the conclusion that the Polaris-Poseidon force as it now exists may be significantly enhanced, in the sense of assured survival, by utilizing the entire ocean for concealment, ignoring the stricture of remaining within range of targets. Even without insisting that every submarine remain beyond target range, stability would be significantly enhanced by stationing submarines randomly, leaving open the possibility that one or two would be within target range.

In the short run, the facts of geography indicate that it may be desirable to retrofit the Polaris-Poseidon fleet with the new ULMS-1, 4000-mile-range missile. This increase in missile range would allow all targets in Russia to be reached from any ocean touching the Eurasion continent. However, the desirability of procuring the ULMS system is cast into doubt since one of the major arguments for procuring a follow-on to the Polaris fleet is the increase in the sea room available for concealment and the consequent reduction of the probability of discovery, and we may obtain these features as well as other desirable characteristics by redeploying the Polaris fleet, without the projected expenditure of $1 billion per ULMS boat. Since the average age of the Polaris fleet is only eight years and since the projected threat when it is deployed in the present mode is very low, there is little reason to go beyond the initial research and development stages in developing a follow-on fleet.[18]

NOTES

1. These are also the major arguments used to support the case for American superiority by those who believe that this has been the key to successful deterrence. If Soviet planners take these beliefs seriously, they may well believe that the American withdrawal from Vietnam has been forced by Soviet superiority in land-based missiles.

2. Two-step procedures or procedures in which there is a clear change of role during implementation, for instance, a bomber on approach to a target changes role as it crosses a hostile frontier, are politically more difficult to implement since they require either two decisions or bargains to be made or else they provide a clear demarcation at which the routine may be stopped.

3. See D. G. Hoad, "Ballistic Missile Guidance," in *Impact of New Technologies on the Arms Race*, ed. B. T. Feld, Cambridge, Mass. 1971. Hoag projects missile or MIRV CEPs of 30 meters without using terminal recognition guidance systems.

4. For an exceptional description of the Cuban Missile Crisis see Graham T. Allison, *Essence of Decision* (Boston, Little Brown, 1971) or also Elie Abel, *The Missile Crisis* (Philadelphia, Lippincott, 1966).

5. H. O. Berktay and B. K. Gazey, "Communications Aspects of Underwater Telemetry," *Electronic Engineering in Oceanography*, IERE conference, September 12-15, 1966, IERE, London, 1966.

6. Testimony of Col. Augustine C. Trapold, III, Air Force Director, Strategic Offensive and Defensive Studies. In hearings, Committee of Armed Services, U.S. Senate 92nd Congress, First Session on S.939, pt. 4, p. 2869, 1972.

7. John Marriott, quoted in "ASW, Some of the Issues and Some of the Programs," Edmund J. Gannon, 9/2/71, Library of Congress, Congressional Research Service report 71-203F.

8. Dr. R. A. Frosch, Assistant Secretary of the Navy (Research and Development) in Hearings on Military Posture and HR. 3818 and HR. 8687 before the Committee on Armed Services, House of Representatives 92nd Congress, First Session, Part 2, p. 4300, 1971.

9. George Wilson in *Washington Post*, May 31, 1971, quoting Rear Admiral Levering Smith.

10. Admiral Thomas H. Moorer, Chairman, Joint Chiefs of Staff has stated, "None of our current SLBMs are designed to be launched on a

depressed trajectory. Neither are they planned for attack against hard targets. The Poseidon, with its many MIRVs, was specifically employing long-range exoatmospheric missiles such as Galosh deployed around Moscow, relying upon exhaustion of inerceptors rather than upon penetration aids." Submarine missile accuracy is complicated by difficulty in determining initial coordinates without signaling the position of the submarine. This may be done using undersea topographic features or via satellite communications. Missile CEP is probably not limited by navigational errors and may be better than the 1-2 kilometers quoted above. Nevertheless, Moorer's statement indicates that they are not suitable *currently* for use against hard targets. Hoag (see ref. 3) claims that there is no technical reason for submarine missile accuracy to be greater than land-based missiles. If one moves to a sea-based strategy, incentives for highly accurate missiles may be largely removed.

11. See paper provided by Major General W. F. Pitts, Director of Budget, Headquarters, USAF, and reprinted in hearings before a subcommittee of the Committee on Appropriations, House of Representatives, 92nd Congress, 1st Session, Research, Development, Test and Evaluation, pt. 6, p. 297ff.

12. I assume that port facilities are not attacked. This will eliminate pressures of the type described for land-based systems. However, even with such an attack, one could argue that in conjunction with an attack on parts of the submarine fleet it would be of such limited geographic scope and of such clear specificity that it would create a signal strong enough to make the response of major retaliation unlikely. It is also likely that the operation of port facilities could be seriously impaired using conventional weapons and thus also signal that the use of nuclear weapons is undesirable, thus reducing the probability that they will be used.

13. Numerous polar expeditions beginning in 1957 have established the feasibility of discharging Polaris type missiles in Arctic regions summer or winter. In summer there are numerous open areas and in winter frequent wind opened regions which refreeze at about 6'/hour. The submarine locates open regions using television and may surface even through three feet of ice. See *New York Times* especially **August 13, 1958, p. 1; March 28, 1959, p. 1; April 8, 1959, p. 7; and February 11, 1960, p. 8.**

14. I have not discussed the question of a war of attrition waged against commercial shipping and designed to disrupt economic life. This involves attack and hunter-killer submarines and involves a different set of considerations. In any case, the strategic nuclear submarine has little if any capability against shipping and little defensive capabilities and thus would not be involved in this type of action.

The arguments above will clearly not be true if the war of attrition may be waged effectively at chokepoints, i.e., regions through, near, or from which submarines are compelled to travel for reasons of transit or replenishment. If a substantial fraction of submarines can be destroyed as they pass through or from these points, the increased operating area available after they are clear is of no use. There are several reasons for supposing that the U.S.S.R. and especially U.S. SSBN forces may not be effectively countered at chokepoints. The U.S. has no geographical chokepoints similar to the Greenland-Iceland-Faeroe Island alley which Soviet forces must transit. But the Soviet Union is not compelled to transit SSBN forces during crisis periods, and in the Pacific they are reported to be moving SSBN bases onto the Kamchatka peninsula from which they may depart to the Pacific with ease. In the region around bases, all defensive forces available may be brought to bear. The local region may be swept of mines or hunter-killer submarines at the times when submarines are departing or returning to base.

In addition, the nuclear submarine may operate for extended periods of time without returning for replenishment. The normal tour for U.S. SSBN patrols is 60 days and there is probably no reason that this could not be extended substantially during periods of great crisis or war. The limiting factors are probably human requirements for food and rest; food may be replenished almost anywhere and during crisis or war periods one may ask for and expect considerably greater sacrifices from submarine personnel. For the SSBN fleet, where the expenditure of munitions and fuel is not cause for replenishment, a war of attrition at chokepoints is difficult and probably not feasible. The problems for hunter-killer submarines are clearly greater because of the need to replenish spent munitions.

(While conditions of attack and defense are clearly different than during World War II, experience there shows that even with the technical superiority of Allied forces, and control of both the air and sea, the attempt to choke off submarines as they left their bases in the Bay of Biscay was not convincing as a method of terminating the campaign of U-boat harassment. During a period of intensive activity from May to December of 1943, 32 U-boats were sunk as a result of this campaign. Elsewhere, as a result of the intensive and active protection of convoys, 183 U-boats were sunk. Less than 4-1/2 percent of the U-boats in transit were sunk or damaged, and after they began new tactics in which they took advantage of the safety of waters near the Spanish mainland, the percentage of kills was even lower.) See Samuel E. Morison, *History of United States Naval Operations in World War II,* Volume X, p. 105 (Boston, Little Brown, 1959.)

15. The successful resolution of the Cuban Missile Crisis without escalation from beyond the limited force involved in the blockade is due in large part to the fact that the option of attacking immediately was eliminated from consideration very early. Ironically, this may have been due in large part to the Air Force and Joint Chiefs of Staff themselves. Allison (see note 4) argues convincingly that the Joint Chiefs, determined to use massive air strikes or nothing, incorrectly claimed that a surgical strike, eliminating only the offensive missiles, was impossible. The option of massive air strikes and invasion was

politically unacceptable and thus the air strike option was abandoned completely, only to be revived when it was realized that the blockage might not be effective and that the Air Force may have overstated the difficulties of a surgical strike.

16. Victor Anderson, "Ocean Technology," in *Impact of New Technologies on the Arms Race* (Cambridge, Mass., MIT Press, 1971), p. 203.

17. The effect of operationalizing a Capacity for Delayed Response (not a guaranteed delay) has been studied by John R. Raser and Wayman J. Crow, "A Simulation Study of Deterrence Theories," reprinted in *Theory and Research on the Causes of War*, Dean G. Pruitt and Richard C. Snyder, editors (Englewood Cliffs, Prentice-Hall, 1969). They examined some effects of CDR; when possessed by only *one* bloc in a bipolar world,

1. Need not retaliate upon warning.
2. Need not retaliate if the source of attack is unknown.
3. Need not promise to retaliate on warning.
4. Not under pressure to strike pre-emptively.
5. Given extra time, it can centralize and rationalize decision-making process.
6. Need not retaliate on a pre-programmed basis.
7. With delay, it can establish responsibility for attack.
8. It can retaliate when the attacker's defenses are weak.
9. It can retain deterrence capability after attack.
10. Since it need not retaliate reflexively, it might not retaliate at all.

Options 1-4 are part of any assured destruction capability. Options 5-9 are those introduced by a CDR. At least one, option 5, would be strengthened by the introduction of a guaranteed delayed response (GDR). To the extent that options 5-9 have the effect of strengthening the appearance of their possessor, they contribute to deterrence, while the result of option 10 is clearly the opposite.

They concluded that:

I. "When (a nation) had a known CDR she was perceived as stronger than when she did not."

II. "Accidental, pre-emptive, and catalytic wars were less likely when (a nation) had CDR than when she did not."

III. "When (a nation) had CDR there was a strong tendency for her opponents to be more deterred."

To the extent that GDR strengthens CDR, and to the extent that we trust the validity of such simulation studies, we conclude that GDR will strengthen the effect of deterrence. Apparently the effect of options 5-9 negates the influence of options which tend to diminish the probability of retaliation.

It would be interesting to repeat such a simulation to see whether the hypothetical strengthening of deterrence by changing CDR to GDR is verified. It might also alter one of the other conclusions which they drew, namely, that "strategic war was much more probable when (a nation) had CDR, primarily because (they were) more belligerent and more ready to make war . . ." While an agreement to implement off-target stationing implies a lack of belligerence, a simulation study might examine the probability that such agreements would be broken and contrast this probability of war with the situation in which there are no agreements.

18. The average age of the U.S. SSBN fleet, from the date of commission, is:

	Boats	Average Age
LaFayette class	31	7.24
Ethan Allen & George Washington class	10	10.7
TOTAL	41	8.1

Only the 31 LaFayette class boats are scheduled for conversion to the Poseidon system.

9 International Law, Ocean Regimes, and Threats to Peace at Sea

Gerald J. Mangone

Long before railways, automobiles, and aircraft existed, the streams and rivers carried both armed men and peaceful trade to the estuaries and the seas. The early superhighways of modern civilization were the oceans. Christopher Columbus sailed across the Atlantic to America aboard the 100-ton Santa Maria with a crew of thirty-nine officers and men in 1492 and returned to Spain with the tiny Nina, a vessel no longer than seventy feet bearing sixty tons with a crew of about twenty-five men. Five years after Columbus landed upon the island of San Salvador, John Cabot laid the great claim of England to America aboard his little 50-ton Matthew with a crew of only eighteen men. Lumbering across the vast seas, guided by crude quadrants and astrolabes, with sailors who sometimes gulped a gallon of beer a day, the European three-masted ships first linked the continents into a one-world society.

In ancient times the growth of transport and trade in the Mediterranean Sea had gradually led to a large body of maritime practice and law which was collected in scrolls and books, such as the famous Byzantine rules known as the *Rhodian Sea Law* codified about 700 A.D. Other well-known codes of later periods were the *Rolls of Oléron*, an island in the Bay of Biscay, and the fourteenth-century *Consolato del*

Mare of Barcelona. Such maritime law mainly dealt with the construction or sale of ships, the care and insurance of cargoes, the rights and duties of master and crew, and other mercantile matters of title, contract, and tort. Many of these legal principles and practices were adopted by the consular courts located in continental ports in the Middle Ages and during the development of the modern nation-state.[1] The practices and judgments of the early English mercantile courts passed into the Black Book of the Admiralty and special courts of admiralty were established in England in the sixteenth century.[2]

Admiralty law has had an important history in adjudicating matters, both national and international, affecting vessels and seamen and continues to be a special type of law in the United States. It also contributed to strengthening the rights of neutral property aboard vessels captured as prize by a belligerent on the high seas, which touched upon public international law and was a grievous cause of international controversy for centuries. But today the world needs more than admiralty law to regulate the use of the oceans. Indeed, the general principles of law recognized by civilized nations as applying to the oceans and the customary practices of states with respect to the seas and the seabed have long been inadequate to those problems raised by twentieth-century technological developments in navigation, in the harvesting of fish, and in the recovery of underwater mineral resources. Today public international law for the oceans, as evidenced by treaties, is archaic, confusing, and incomplete.

Territorial Seas

Fifteenth-century sovereigns naturally sought to extend their dominion over the seas, as they had the land, by discovery, conquest, or uncontested use. The "English" channel is a semantic record of the day when England claimed sovereignty over the channel, the North Sea, and the Atlantic between North Cape (Stadland) and Cape Finisterre; the Danish-Norwegian kingdom looked upon the northern Atlantic Ocean, especially between Iceland and Greenland, as its own sea. Less than two months after Columbus announced his discovery of the Indies to Ferdinand and Isabella, Spain proceeded to divide with Portugal all the oceans and land not yet held by a Christian prince to be found south and west toward India beyond the Azores and the Cape Verde Islands. In 1513 Balboa crossed the Isthmus of Panama, waded with full armor into the Pacific Ocean, which he called the South Sea, and took possession of it in the name of his Spanish sovereign. In 1577 Spain loudly protested to England against the passage of Sir Francis Drake through the Straits of Magellan and his entry into the Pacific as a violation of Spanish sovereignty. Fifty years later the Dutch were still paying the English for fishing rights in the North Sea. As late as 1674 Holland acknowledged its obligation to salute the English flag on British seas.

Although the twenty-three-year-old Hugo Grotius had written a brilliant chapter on the freedom of the seas for the navigation and commerce of all nations,[3] a part of his vindication of a seizure of a Portuguese ship by the Dutch East India Company near Malacca, his views, published in 1609, gained acceptance very slowly in the face of then-prevailing opinions and the greedy political ambitions of new dynastic states. Only gradually, over the course of one hundred and fifty years, did the great maritime powers, especially Great Britain, find more advantage in both their military movements and their commercial trading through a doctrine of freedom on the high seas than through a pretentious claim to sovereignty over waters far from their own shores.

In 1793 Secretary of State Thomas Jefferson informed the British and French ministers that American officials would, for the present, enforce their orders in marginal waters only to the distance of one sea league or three geographical miles from the coast of the United States.[4] A year later Congress gave the Federal district courts jurisdiction over complaints against capture made within a marine league from the coasts or shores of the United States. Since then, for almost 180 years, the United States has been observing a three-mile territorial sea.[5] Great Britain, France, Italy, Japan, and almost all other states generally exercised their jurisdiction from 1900 to 1930 no further than three miles or one league out to sea as customary international law.[6] But since 1930, slowly but surely, technological changes coupled to security concerns and economic opportunities have been edging the states of the world toward larger claims of sovereignty over their marginal waters.

The first public international conference to deal with the breadth of the territorial sea and attempt to fix a universally agreed upon boundary was held at The Hague in 1930. No agreement was reached, but only eight of the thirty-eight states attending had actually asserted jurisdiction beyond a league from shore. The second international conference on the law of the sea, held in Geneva in 1958, with an additional session in 1960, also failed to reach agreement on the limits of territorial sea..[7] By then, although the three-mile limit was still the most widely practiced rule, twenty-seven out of the seventy-three states at the conference claimed jurisdiction beyond that limit. By 1970, fewer than one-third of the states of the world still held to a three-mile territorial sea; by 1972 a majority claimed complete jurisdiction over the air, water, and submerged land column from four to twelve miles beyond their shores; and more than a dozen states had asserted either complete jurisdiction or partial control from twelve to two hundred miles out to sea. The trend to more extravagant claims by states to their marginal seas has been unmistakable.

Historically, of course, the three-mile seaward limit to jurisdiction never was universal or absolute. States have generally taken the view that threats to their security or violations of their laws may require the exercise of authority beyond territorial waters. The Territorial Waters Jurisdiction

Act of 1878 in Great Britain, for example, stated that the Crown could exercise control "over the open seas adjacent to her coasts to such distance as is necessary for the defense and security" of British dominions. The United States in 1799 claimed the right to board and search any vessel, if bound for an American port, up to four leagues out to sea; in 1922 the U.S. Tariff Act provided the same authority to revenue cutters to prevent the importation of alcoholic beverages, and in 1935 the President was authorized to declare a customs enforcement area up to 50 miles beyond a twelve-mile customs zone. Aircraft proceeding to the United States must identify themselves at least one hour's flying time before reaching the American coast. Many other states have similar regulations for control of various activities in the contiguous zone beyond their territorial seas. In 1958 treaty form was given to the right of coastal states to exercise authority beyond their territorial waters, but not exceeding a distance of twelve miles seaward, by the Geneva Convention on the Territorial Sea and the Contiguous Zone. Under the Convention, a state can establish such contiguous zones "to prevent infringement of its customs, fiscal, immigration, or sanitary regulations within its territory or territorial area."

The three-mile territorial sea, therefore, no longer has credence as customary international law. But neither the contiguous zone limited to twelve miles nor the twelve-mile territorial sea has obtained universal acceptance. In recent years states have been claiming new and broader contiguous zones for protective purposes, such as the Canadian assertion of jurisdiction in 1970 over Arctic waters one hundred miles from the coast in order to regulate pollution, and Iceland's assertion in 1972 of control over all fisheries within 50 miles of its coast. And some states, such as Chile, Ecuador, and Peru, have asserted complete jurisdiction over maritime zones not less than two hundred nautical miles from their coasts excepting only "the innocent and inoffensive passage of ships" of other nations. The effect of these actions if sustained by international law, would be far-reaching upon the navigation of the oceans and the passage through various international straits; they would also bear upon the access to fisheries, presently on the high seas, which some nations have enjoyed for long periods; and they would affect the potential recovery of petroleum and hard mineral resources from the seabed.

International Straits

The innocent passage of foreign vessels through the territorial seas of a state has been widely recognized in customary international law. It was given positive form by Article 14 of the 1958 Geneva Convention on the Territorial Sea and the Contiguous Zone. Passage is innocent "so long as it is not prejudicial to the peace, good order, or security of a coastal state." Fishing vessels are not making an innocent passage unless they are observing the laws and regulations of the coastal state to prevent such vessels from fishing in territorial waters. Submarines are required to navigate on the surface and to show their flag. Thus, innocent passage is only an abatement or easement, very carefully circumscribed, of the sovereign's right over his territory and narrowly limits the activities of both private and public vessels travelling through an offshore zone. Innocent passage itself may be suspended by a coastal state, temporarily and without discrimination, if such suspension is considered essential for the protection of its security. Extending the territorial sea to 200 miles would put millions of square miles of the high seas, as well as the air above and the ground below them, under national jurisdiction.

A universal extension of territorial waters from three miles up to twelve miles under international law will have a significant legal effect upon passage through international straits. Some 52 straits would come completely under the jurisdiction of coastal states with the recognition of a six-mile territorial sea by a multilateral treaty; some 116 would fall under national jurisdiction with a twelve-mile territorial sea. The United States has become alarmed at the prospect of both the navigation and overflight of several important international straits, such as the Strait of Gibraltar, being subject to the jurisdiction of other states except for the easement of innocent passage.[8]

On August 3, 1971, therefore, the United States submitted to the UN Sea-Bed Committee draft articles for the Law of the Sea Conference proposed for 1973 under which a state could establish a territorial sea up to twelve miles in breadth. But the articles provided that in straits used for international navigation between high seas or between the high sea and a territorial sea, foreign ships and aircraft in transit would pass through international corridors, enjoying therein the same freedom of navigation and overflight as on the high seas. In submitting the articles the U.S. Department of State Legal Adviser and chief of the American delegation stated that the United States would be unable to conceive of a successful Law of the Sea Conference that did not accommodate their objectives.

On July 28, 1972 in Geneva the Legal Adviser further argued that the concept of free transit through international straits did not mean the right to navigate unsafely or pollute, and that the United States would be willing to accept safety standards established by the Intergovernmental Maritime Consultative Organization and the International Civil Aviation Organization for the transit of international straits—but not those imposed unilaterally by coastal states.

The policy of the United States to secure international guarantees for the free transit of international straits stems from the Department of Defense's interest in rapid surface and covert submarine naval deployment around the world. Innocent passage not only is subject to a coastal state's interpretation of threats to its national security, but could be suspended or delayed by many peripheral questions such as damage to the marine environment. For example, the Strait of Malacca is poorly charted, and with some points in the channel less than 75 feet deep, yet it has been carrying 90% of Japan's oil imports in some giant oil tankers. Such passage is difficult to consider as "innocent" in view of the perils to the coastal state.

If nuclear attacks were launched by either the United States or the Soviet Union against each other or any of their vital allies, the legal nuances over straits would not deter their use by warships. To avoid this catastrophic possibility, the free-ranging, difficult-to-detect submarines armed with missiles that can instantly strike the interior of Russia provide inhibitions against a Soviet first-strike atomic attack. By mid-1976 the conversion of 31 U.S. submarines to Poseidon missile systems, with multiple independent reentry vehicles (MIRV) will be completed while ten submarines will be armed with the Polaris A-3 single warhead system. The submarine launch of the ballistic missiles is not designed for attack against hard targets, but such missiles can already reach most Soviet urban centers from open seas. The new underseas long-range missiles (ULMS) expected to be operational in 1978, moreover, will greatly increase the range of destruction.[9]

An examination of some sixteen major straits that might be affected by the widening of territorial waters shows that five of them are in the Caribbean and one lies between Canada and the United States. Of the remaining ten major straits, three (Ombai, Lombak, and Sunda) are located within the Indonesian archipelago and one (Western Chosen) lies close to South Korea. The Dover Strait between Britain and France, through which three to four hundred ships pass daily, controls the English Channel; the West Bering Strait, between a Russian island and the Soviet mainland, links the Pacific Ocean to the Arctic seas; Iran has a vital interest in the shallow Hormuz Strait which provides access to the Persian gulf and the oil-rich sheikdom. French Somalia and Yemen face Bab el Mandeb between the Arabian and Red Sea with the Suez Canal. Finally, the busy Malacca Strait flows between Indonesia and Malaysia and Singapore while Spain and Morocco stand at the rather narrow water gate between the Mediterranean Sea and the Atlantic Ocean.

It is noteworthy that not a single continental Latin American state and not a single African state, other than Morocco, lies directly upon one of these major straits. If the Dover Strait and the Bab el Mandeb were disregarded because a NATO power controls at least one shore of those straits, the status of Western Chosen, lying between the shores of allied South Korea can also be ignored. The shallow West Bering Strait so close to Russian shores cannot be traversed furtively. And in any case the Soviet Union already adheres to a twelve-mile territorial sea in which the passage of naval vessels must be "authorized." That leaves Indonesia, Singapore, Malaysia, Iran, Spain, and Morocco as the only states that might take action under present international law to restrict or suspend innocent passage through international straits that would fall under their jurisdiction by widening the territorial sea to twelve miles.

From the point of view of international politics, it would seem quite unnecessary for the United States to make the free transit of international straits a non-negotiable condition for a Law of the Sea conference. Suspicion and animosity have already been raised by both the United States and the Soviet Union, who both want the right to send vessels on the surface or below the surface of such straits, regardless of their mission, type, or cargo. The military advantages seem dubious and the fears of the coastal states for their safety must be considered. It may be asked why Washington should seek a tedious, temper-raising, risk-filled road through a Law of the Sea Conference of 130 or more nations in order to gain a multilateral treaty for free transit when specific bi-lateral arrangements with five states or regional accords involving the major interests in particular international straits could probably obtain all the minimum guarantees required for the surface navigation of both commercial and navy ships.

The Continental Shelf and Seabed

The agreement or nonagreement of the nations of the world on the maximum extent of the territorial sea will not only affect the status of international straits, but will bear heavily upon the exploitation of the mineral and living resources of the oceans. The value of mineral resources lying upon or within the seabed adjacent to coastal states first gained political attention during World War II when a tremendous drain upon American petroleum reservoirs took place. Although underwater drilling had been initiated in the 1890s off the coast of California, it was not until the 1930s that offshore oil recovery from independent pile-supported platforms in the Gulf of Mexico at great distances from the mainland became both technologically feasible and economically viable.

No question in international law had arisen about the right of states to recover resources from the waters and submerged land within their territorial seas, at that time widely regarded as three miles from the low-water mark on the coast. But foreseeing that technological developments would soon make more distant and deeper drilling possible, the United States moved to give a legal basis to American mining of the seabed beyond territorial waters. On September 28, 1945 President Harry S. Truman proclaimed that the United States regarded the natural resources of the subsoil and seabed of the continental shelf beneath the high seas, but contiguous to its shores, as subject to American jurisdiction and control. Other states quickly followed the lead of the United States by their own unilateral declarations, decrees, or legislation; some went further in assuming complete jurisdiction over the area of the adjacent shelf, regardless of depth, and a few took this opportunity to assert sovereign control over both the shelf and the waters above it to a distance of two hundred miles out to sea.

The continental shelf, of course, was a geographical expression, not a legal norm. Its contours and its depth around the world lack regularity. Wide areas of submerged shelf extend from the northeastern shores of America, the eastern coast of Argentina, around New Zealand, Australia, Indonesia, off the coast of China, in the Bering Sea, and off almost all the coasts of the Soviet Union. The continent of Africa, however, has a comparatively narrow continental shelf, as do the western coasts of both North and South America. Edges of the continental shelf occur anywhere from 60 to 1600 feet under water. Although the United States in 1945 unofficially considered submerged land contiguous to the continent and covered by no more than 600 feet of water as continental shelf, that figure is an arbitrary average, not scientifically accurate nor demonstrably equitable.

From 1950 to 1957 the UN International Law Commission discussed a regime for the high seas and drafted articles for a Convention on the Continental Shelf, as well as conventions on the territorial seas, the high seas, and fishing, all of which were signed in Geneva in 1958. Some experts had felt that the legal limit to a coastal state's exploitation of its adjacent continental shelf beyond territorial waters should be determined by its capability of exploiting that shelf. In the 1950s virtually all the recovery of offshore petroleum still occurred in shallow waters under one hundred feet in depth. Other experts had felt that the 200-meter isobath ought to be a definitive legal limit to a coastal state's exploitation of the continental shelf. In the end a political compromise prevailed. The Convention, which had been ratified by some 47 states, describes the continental shelf as the seabed and submarine areas adjacent to the coast, but outside the territorial sea, to a depth of 200 meters, or beyond that limit to where the depth of the superjacent waters admits the exploitation of the natural resources in that area.

Fears that coastal states, particularly the United States, would rapidly march out to sea with the flag planted on monstrous drilling platforms dividing the oceans into national lakes still exist, but they are tempered by an increasing set of political constraints upon arbitrary state claims. There is now a consensus among the nations of the world, which was given legal-evidence form by the United Nations on December 17, 1970 by declaration of the General Assembly, that the seabed and subsoil beyond the limits of national jurisdiction, with their resources, are a common heritage of mankind; that no state may claim or exercise sovereignty or sovereign rights over the international seabed area; and that no state or person can claim, exercise, or acquire rights incompatible with an international regime, including appropriate international machinery, to be established.

The problem facing the governments of the world has been to create an international legal structure with an international agency that will realize the principles recommended by the UN General Assembly. Since 1971 the UN Sea-Bed Committee has been trying to develop articles of a treaty that would provide machinery for the orderly exploration and recovery of mineral resources of the seabed. Considerations of technology, the requirement of adequate capitalization, fair pricing, reasonable incentives, and the special needs of coastal and developing states to share in benefits from seabed resources, have been some of the complex factors demanding study, long discussion, and cautious negotiation.

The United States precipitated consideration of the issues of an international regime for the oceans by laying on the table on August 3, 1970 a bold, imaginative draft convention to establish an International Seabed Area comprising all areas of the seabed and subsoil of the high seas beyond the 200-meter isobath adjacent to the coasts of continents or islands in which no state would have or could acquire any right, title, or interest except as provided in the convention. However, the draft convention provided that the zone between the 200-meter isobath and the edge of the continental margin would be denoted as the International Trusteeship Area in which the coastal state would issue, suspend, or revoke all mineral exploitation licenses, establishing the conditions for work in the area, but remitting to an

International Seabed Resources Authority between one-third to one-half of any revenues from fees and licenses in the Trusteeship Area. Draft articles for a comprehensive seabed treaty were also submitted by Tanzania, by the Soviet Union, by a group of eleven Latin American countries plus Jamaica and Guyana, and by Japan. None of these drafts specified the limits of national jurisdiction or the international seabed area, but all provided some scheme for international machinery for licensing or exploiting the resources of the ocean floor. A luxuriantly detailed and overarching draft convention submitted by Malta introduced new concepts of ocean space; national ocean space would extend 200 miles seaward from a coastal state, but innocent passage could not be suspended beyond a twelve-mile seaward zone nor in international straits essential to commerce pending an agreement within five years between the coastal state and the International Ocean Space Institution. Beyond national ocean space there would be the international sea administered by and for the benefit of the international community.

All the drafts provided for international councils and assemblies as policy-making organs. The Soviet Union assured the veto power of the socialist bloc; the United States draft guranteed equal power of the few developed countries with the many developing countries; while the Tanzanian and Latin American drafts insisted that decisions be taken by simple and two-thirds majorities of states regardless of size, wealth, or maritime importance. Both the United States and the Malta drafts made detailed provision for the adjudication of conflicts that might arise out of the proposed conventions.

Other working papers have been submitted by the United Kingdom, France, Poland, and notably a group including Afghanistan, Austria, Belgium, Hungary, Nepal, the Netherlands and Singapore which recommended an international area of the seabed and subsoil outside the territorial sea and beyond the submarine area measured either by a depth of 200 meters of water or 40 miles from the coastal baselines for the territorial sea. But it was clear from the discussions of the UN Sea-Bed Committee in 1972 that general agreement upon details of a draft convention to regulate the exploration and exploitation of ocean floor mineral resources had not been reached.

Mineral Resources

Meanwhile the enormous increase in the demand for energy throughout the world has sent entrepreneurs in search of profits from petroleum and gas out to sea. During the 1960s offshore crude oil production from the Middle East multiplied seven or eight times. Latin America—apart from its long draining of the long-established reservoirs in Lake Maracaibo—and Africa began offshore drilling on a large scale during this decade. The United States, which had obtained production from wells located no deeper than 150 feet underwater in 1960, was drawing oil from a well under 340 feet of water by 1970. Offshore production by 1972 was supplying about 17 percent of the world's gas and oil requirements. Within the next twenty years offshore production may supply more than half the world's demand for petroleum energy. Thirty-eight new rigs were scheduled to join the world's offshore drill fleet in 1973. One self-propelled rig under construction in Avondale Shipyards, New Orleans, will carry a crew of 90 men and be able to drill through 25,000 feet of the seabed under 1,000 feet of water. A 445-foot drillship, built in Japan at a cost of $16 million with twin screws and 8,500 horsepower and launched in 1972, was equipped to drill below 2,000 feet of ocean waters. Four other drillships and barges are known to be under construction in shipyards around the world.

Technical progress, moreover, in recovering ferromanganese nodules with their nickel, cobalt, and copper, has advanced to the point where their commercial extraction might be feasible by 1974. The nodules seem to be strewn rather abundantly in the deepwater basin of the north Pacific, off the coasts of Georgia/Florida in the north Atlantic, northeast and southwest of New Zealand in the south Pacific, and in the south Atlantic from Brazil to South Africa. With an airlift pump and dredgehead, Deepsea Ventures, a subsidiary of Tenneco, retrieved in the summer of 1970 ferromanganese nodules approximately 170 miles east of the coast of Georgia/Florida under 2,700 feet of water. In 1971 the same company used a chemical hydro-metallurgical process to produce pure manganese, nickel, copper, and cobalt from nodules that had been taken in the mid-Pacific Ocean at depths of 18,000 feet. The Hughes Tool-Global Marine Company in 1972 ordered a 600-foot, 35,000-ton deepsea mining ship.

Other nations have also been interested in hard mineral resources on or in the ocean floor. The Japanese in 1971-72 used a continuous bucket dredge to capture ferromanganese nodules in 12,000 feet of water about 200 miles from Tahiti. The Russians sent the Akademic Kurchatov research vessel to the Pacific in 1968-69 and the Vitraz in 1969-70 to explore for nodules, taking samples in 1971 at depths up to 13,000 feet, while the Germans took thirty tons of sludge probes for copper, zinc, lead, and silver ores from the bed of the Red Sea.

The world-wide search for new sources of petroleum energy and hard minerals, of course, touches the quick of national security and international politics. Minerals policy cannot be separated from defense policy in the United States where there is also a domestic paradox between the enjoyment of cheap energy and the complaint against pollution. Moreover, the defense policy of the United States must take account of the vitality of non-Communist Europe and Japan which have become increasingly dependent upon the importation of oil. Between 1950 and 1970 European oil consumption multiplied ten times to 12 million barrels a day; Japan in

1972 was consuming close to four million barrels a day, nearly all of which was imported, and may consume three times that amount daily within the next decade.

It is hardly appreciated by the American public that the fundamentals of economic and political relationships between the oil producing and the oil consuming states have been profoundly altered since 1960. The formation of the Organization of Petroleum Exporting Countries (OPEC) has led to aggressive demands for the termination of acreage concessions to the international oil companies as well as an increased scale of taxes or royalties upon their production. The petroleum exporting countries obtained in 1972 direct participation in the capital structure and management of the companies themselves. Settlements by the companies with OPEC have inevitably led to very large increases in the energy costs of both Europe and Japan as well as to general uncertainty about these vital supplies in a future under the control of the leaders of Iran, Iraq, Kuwait, Saudi Arabia, Libya, Venezuela, and other oil-producing countries.

The importance of new offshore petroleum exploration and recovery around the world can be seen in the light of the immediate dependence of Japan and Europe upon the reserves of the Middle East and North Africa, by far the largest reserves known anywhere and estimated at some seventy years. Moreover, although the United States draws only a little more than ten percent of its own oil requirements from OPEC countries, chiefly Venezuela, American oil companies have a great stake in the extraction, transportation, refining, and marketing of petroleum products throughout the non-Communist world. Beyond the consideration of business profits, however, lies the fact that the American people and their armed forces will require larger imports of petroleum energy in order to maintain even modest growth patterns. In 1972 about 26 percent of U.S. crude oil and 12 percent of total American energy requirements came from foreign sources. By 1985 it is estimated that 40 to 55 percent of U.S. crude oil and 23 to 32 percent of total energy needs will come from abroad. In sum, the control of petroleum reserves by unfriendly governments would not only affect the foreign relations of the United States with Japan and western Europe, but reach the core of the American economy.

The value of hard minerals upon the ocean floor both to entrepreneurial profits and national security cannot be easily calculated. Uncertainty still exists about the economic yield from the mining of ferromanganese nodules which may depend upon processing and marketing the cobalt, nickel, and copper within them. Moreover, mineral prices tend to be subsidized and regulated both by public bounties and private cartels, so that the results of competition of prices between present land mining and sea mining are unknown. Another factor that could become a major inhibition of mining is environmental damage. Mining for diamonds, tin, and other near-shore minerals presents certain technical-economic problems, but the probability of reaching and processing the ferromanganese nodules that lie beyond the present claims to jurisdiction by states poses politico-legal problems similar to the issues raised by the recovery of petroleum in deeper and deeper offshore waters.

One hundred and eight members of the United Nations have already expressed their belief that some area of the seabed beyond national jurisdiction is the common heritage of mankind and that benefits from the resources to be found in that area should be shared equitably by states. The United Nations is seeking rational management of the international seabed area through machinery to be agreed upon by an international treaty of a universal character. But there is little agreement on the precise limits to national jurisdiction over the seabed and even less on the form and powers of the international machinery. Pending a signed treaty and its ratification by many states, which by the most optimistic estimate might require another three years, mining enterprises and naval security interests will continue to assess their futures in view of rapidly changing marine technology.

International Seabed Authority and the UN

The American draft of an international seabed treaty in 1970 was an ingenious arrangement.[10] It provided a very wide international trusteeship area in which the superjacent waters would retain their character as high seas while granting authority to the administrative coastal state for licensing the exploration and exploitation of mineral resources in the area. Thus, the flexibility of navigation for the United States fleet on the world's oceans, the control of offshore mining all the way down to the continental margins of the United States, and the opportunity for American firms to make application for offshore mining permits directly to other coastal states were all protected. Shares of the income from the mining activities in the trusteeship area, however, were conceded to an international development program.

The international trusteeship proposed by the United States has not gained many adherents, but the idea of an intermediate zone or an economic resource zone between territorial waters and the high seas has been favored by many states. Such a zone would be controlled by the coastal state, but could be subject to international standards by multilateral agreement. For the exploitation of the seabed, however, it has been argued by some petroleum interests that the United States would be better advised to follow the 1958 Geneva Convention on the Continental Shelf by simply taking jurisdiction over the adjacent seabed as far out as the depth of water permits exploitability. But in the long run a shifting boundary of the seabed is a conflict-breeding device, triggering national claims over the superjacent seas and inevitably provoking disputes over vital resources. The Geneva Convention, moreover, offers no help at present for a legal framework for deepsea mining. To stand pat on its prescriptions simply ignores the opportunity for building world order under international law for the oceans and seabed.

Another tack was taken by the American Mining Congress through the U.S. Senate Interior and Insular Affairs Committee via a bill introduced in November 1971. With the intention of providing the Secretary of the Interior authority to promote the conservation and orderly development of the hard mineral resources of the deep seabed pending adoption of an international regime, the bill would have enabled the Secretary to issue licenses to develop surface and subsurface blocks of the deep seabed to citizens of the United States or corporations organized under the laws of the United States. Such licenses, for a fee and requiring active investment by the licensee to develop his claim, would be exclusive as against all other persons subject to American jurisdiction. The claim could also be maintained against other states that might reciprocally agree on a similar system for licensing their nationals. The bill was designed to be an interim arrangement until the regime under study by the UN Sea-Bed Committee received treaty sanction. The United States would guarantee the entrepreneur the full term of his lease and reimbursement for loss of his investment or increased costs due to conditions that might be imposed by the international regime more burdensome than the United States Act.

Advocates of a strong international authority for the oceans and seabed, which would have the power to explore and exploit the mineral resources for the benefit of all nations, decried the American Mining Congress bill. Delegates from some of the developing countries who have notions of a well-capitalized, internationally managed enterprise under the policy control of those states participating in the international regime regarded the bill as a move by the developed states to gain rights and profits from an area acknowledged as the common heritage of mankind. But even officials of developed states questioned the wisdom of granting such licenses to the deep seabed under national authority with the certainty that only a few states could participate as reciprocating grantors and the likelihood that entrenched rights and regulations would make the establishment of a future international regime more difficult.

The behavior of the UN Sea-Bed Committee in 1971 and

1972 disappointed many high hopes of 1970 that the nations of the world could reach agreement on some basic treaty articles for the seabed. Experienced observers of the UN system recognize its shrill rhetoric, procedural clumsiness, and exasperating diplomatic maneuver as symptomatic of the difficulty of bridging differences between peoples of greatly diverse culture, wealth, and power. Nevertheless, very slow progress toward the drafting of any convention was made in two years. To wait forever for consensus on international machinery for the seabed, of course, runs contrary to the march of technology and irrepressible national ambitions to recover and use valuable resources that are plainly available. Although the American Mining Congress bill aimed to give some protection to entrepreneurs who must take risks to mine the deep seabed in the absence of positive international law, it practically ignored the 1970 declaration of the UN and sours present negotiations for an international regime in the Sea-Bed Committee. A wiser course is to allow the UN system a few years—not many—to recognize that the demarcation of the international seabed is imperative and to understand that unless agreement is reached on some international machinery soon, there may be no international authority at all.

The program of work for Sub-Committee 1 of the UN Sea-Bed Committee includes the status, scope, and basic provisions of an international regime as well as the powers of the international machinery. Despite some thirty meetings of the Sub-Committee during the New York and the Geneva sessions of the UN Sea-Bed Committee in 1972, and despite the formation of a working group which endeavored to prepare a working paper showing the areas of agreement and disagreement among member-states, to be followed by an effort to negotiate disputed issues, the results have been meager. Although the usual encomium of "substantial and encouraging progress" has been applied to the work of the Sub-Committee, it was still far from the realization of draft articles for an international regime or an international agency. Part of the delay was due to the interlocking import of a seabed treaty with critical agreements on the limits of territorial seas and the rights of states to fish the high seas.

Living Resources of the Sea

Conflict between nations over the catch of fish has a very long and bitter history.[11] In North America, for example, altercations between the British and the Americans went on for a century. Following the Peace of Ghent in 1814, the British seized at least thirty American vessels between 1815 and 1818 in their determination to exclude New England ships from Nova Scotia, Newfoundland, and Canadian waters; again in 1843 and 1844 American ships were seized while fishing off Nova Scotia; and from 1877 to 1880 Newfoundland natives threatened and attacked American vessels catching herring within their coastal waters despite the treaty privileges that had been accorded to the United States. When the fisheries provisions of the British-American Treaty of Washington in effect between 1873 and 1885 lapsed, the two states had to go back to a treaty of 1818 for guidance. Arguments over the interpretation of those articles finally led to an international arbitration of the North Atlantic Coast Fisheries question in 1910. On its part, the United States had seized three Canadian sealing vessels in 1886 about sixty miles from shore and again arrested several Canadian sealing vessels in the Bering Sea in 1887, which finally led to arbitration with Great Britain in 1893 and eventually the Fur Sealing Convention of 1911 that included Russia and Japan.

In more recent times Britain and Iceland quarreled over their fishing rights in 1958 when Iceland first extended its territorial sea to twelve miles. Another confrontation occurred in 1972 as Iceland further extended her authority over fisheries to fifty miles from her shores. Japan and Korea had feuded for several years over fishing grounds until their Fisheries Agreement of December 18, 1965. A seething controversy between the United States and some Latin American states began when more than seventy American ships fishing for tuna were seized between September 18, 1951 and June 28, 1963. All the vessels were arrested beyond three miles from the shore and sometimes fifteen to thirty-five miles out to sea. The international friction has not been eased either by exhortations, conferences, threats, or the actual curtailment of American economic-military assistance. In 1971 the Ecuadorean Navy alone seized 51 American fishing vessels whose owners were forced to pay licenses and fines totaling $2.4 million to obtain the release of their ships. Trouble arose between the United States and Brazil when the latter sought to exclude distant-water American shrimp fleets from Brazil's coasts and was only resolved by a conservation agreement in 1972 that left the legal determination of territorial seas and contiguous fishing zones unsettled. At the same time the dwindling fishing stocks off the northeast Atlantic coast, attributed to the presence of Russian factory fleets, so incensed New England fishermen that many called upon the United States to extend its own exclusive fisheries zone from 12 to 200 miles from shore.

The complexity of international fisheries disputes defies an easy or early solution. Changes in fisheries technology, new economic development patterns in both wealthy and poor nations, and domestic politics all batter the traditions, customs, and old international accords about living marine resources and create many conflicts for diplomacy to measure and moderate. The stakes are large. Gross revenues from the world-wide annual harvest of fish and other living resources of the sea have been estimated as high as nine billion dollars. In recent decades the catch of fish for human consumption has risen at an average of 4 percent annually while the catch for fish meals has soared at the phenomenal rate of 12 percent annually. But world averages are useless, if not misleading, without a recognition of particular national interests in the fish stocks of the ocean in areas that lie beyond present national jurisdiction.

The nature of U.S. fishing interests can be quickly perceived by the fact that of a fleet of 80,614 vessels in 1968, there were 66,654 motor boats under five tons. The largest vessels were the tuna ships ranging up to 1000 tons which in 1970 landed 180,000 tons of that fish worth more than $74 million. Shrimp, however, has been the single most valued American marine harvest, and was worth about $130 million in 1970. In general the United States has an aged fishing fleet with the exception of the modern boats and equipment to be found in the king crab, shrimp, and tuna sectors of the industry.

By contrast with the United States, the U.S.S.R. has close to 3000 fishing vessels larger than 100 tons, which is about half their total fleet in tonnage. The Japanese have almost 2500 fishing vessels, about 15 percent of their total fleet tonnage which are larger than 100 tons, but they also utilize some 227,000 motor and 116,000 nonmechanized boats in their diverse catch. In addition to the exploitation of their own inland waters and offshore areas, both the Russians and the Japanese are distant-water fishermen, catching tuna, salmon, crab, lobsters, and other species off the coasts of other nations, including the United States.

Some clues to the international fisheries policy of the United States can be seen by noting that the greater part of American fresh fish supply now comes from foreign countries. Except for tuna, a greater exploitation of nearby high-priced coastal stocks by relatively small vessels seems the most likely drift of the industry. Thus, most American fishermen would prefer wider zones of exclusive fisheries jurisdiction. Although little more than 200,000 people are employed primarily or secondarily in the whole industry, they have considerable political power in regions like New England or Alaska. But wider coastal zones of fisheries jurisdiction raises for Washington the spectre of other nations asserting control over American vessels traversing offshore waters far out to sea and interfering with the passage of both United States merchant and warships through presently recognized high seas. For their own good reasons both the Soviet Union and Japan also wish no abridgment of their navigation or their distant-water fishing activities. On the other side, several Latin American countries like Chile, Peru, Ecuador, Costa Rica, Argentina, and Brazil, some African, and some Asian countries, alarmed about the depletion of the fishing resources off their coasts, have resolved to maintain and renew their wealth of living marine resources by controlling the vessels and conditions of catch in maritime zones up to 200 miles from their coasts.

At Geneva in 1960 a joint United States-Canadian proposal to the Law of the Sea Conference tried to limit the further widening of the territorial sea by offering a compromise under which a six-mile, instead of a three-mile, territorial sea would be permitted and would allow states to establish an exclusive fishing zone in the high seas contiguous to their territorial sea to a maximum of 12 miles from their coasts. Within the contiguous zone, however, those states which had been fishing there during five years before 1958, would have been permitted to fish there another ten years. Since the proposal failed to receive a two-thirds majority by one vote, the status of the territorial sea has remained open to interpretation by customary international law. The 1958 Geneva Convention on Fishing and Conservation of the Living Resources of the High Seas, however, had specifically emphasized the special interest of the coastal state in maintaining the productivity of the living resources in any area of the high seas adjacent to its territorial sea. After the failure of the 1960 conference to produce an international convention, individual states that had maintained a three-mile territorial sea began to proclaim jurisdiction over a fisheries zone up to 12 miles from their coasts as a matter of practice. Thus, the Fisheries Limits Act of Great Britain in 1964, the Territorial Sea and Fishing Zone Act of New Zealand in

1965, and, finally, Public Law 89-658 of the United States in 1966 all extended jurisdiction of those coastal states for fisheries either partially or exclusively. The problem, therefore, now lies in the high seas adjacent to a coastal state beyond twelve miles from its shoreline. But the issues are complicated by the evidence that species of fish recognize no territorial limits in their feeding, migrating, and spawning habits; that coastal fishermen wish to exploit their coastal fish exclusively; and that distant-water fishermen insist upon access to fish on the high seas beyond national jurisdiction as a common property resource.

An International Regime for Fisheries

The depletion of fish stocks is not a new concern of man. Indeed, the office of the Commissioner of Fish, forerunner of the National Marine Fisheries Service, was established by the U.S. Congress on February 9, 1871 to investigate the apparent diminution of the food fishes of the eastern coast of the United States due to overfishing by more than one state or more than one country and to suggest practical remedies. The International Council for the Exploration of the Sea, established in 1902 after the first international conference on the exploration of the sea in Stockholm during June 1899, was primarily founded to aid the fishery industry in the northeast Atlantic, the North Sea, and the Baltic Sea. Today a network of bilateral conventions, such as those between the United States and Canada, Russia, and Japan deal with the conservation of such species as salmon, halibut, and crab. And a score of international councils or commissions, such as the International Whaling Commission, the International North-East Atlantic Fisheries Commission, the Inter-American Tropical Tuna Commission, or the Indian Ocean Fishery Commission, either attend to a single species of fish or a group of species within certain geographical fishing grounds. International fisheries agreements can be categorized three ways: conventions that are primarily to foster scientific investigation of living marine resources; second, conventions that are designed to conserve fish resources by prescribing minimum mesh size for nets, periods or seasons when certain species cannot be fished, or quotas of the catch that may be taken; and third, some agreements that deal with the conduct of the vessels themselves, requiring marking of ships and equipment, priorities in making a catch, and so forth. Enforcement of all agreements is always a problem since nations have been extremely cautious about permitting the arrest, boarding, and search of their flag vessels on the high seas. Moreover, the actual prosecution and punishment of the nationals of one state by another state for a fisheries treaty infraction on the high seas is denied.

Whether the present claims of a number of states to protective jurisdiction over their marine resources and seabed to a distance of 200 miles from shore can be maintained under future international law or not, the question of providing fish conservation responsibilities for coastal states in their offshore waters beyond the territorial sea must be faced. The policy objectives of the United States are, first, to avoid a zone of exclusive fisheries jurisdiction beyond 12 miles from shore; second, to protect its own coastal and anadromous species from outside depredations; and, third, to engage as freely as possible in the catch of highly migratory oceanic species, notably tuna and tuna-like fish.

In July 1971 the United States first presented a number of draft articles on fisheries to the UN Sea-Bed Committee at Geneva. They envisaged international regional regulation in which a coastal state would have an annual preferential allowable catch in the contiguous zone of the high seas up to its ability to harvest fish in that zone—excepting only that the percentage of the total allowable catch that had been traditionally taken by distant-water fishermen of other states would not be allocated to the coastal state. The draft articles also called for special commissions of five members for the settlement of disputes between the parties to an international or regional fisheries organization. In the event, however, that the states concerned with a particular fishery were unable or felt it inadvisable to establish a regional organization, the coastal state, after consulting with other states interested in the fishery, would be empowered to set up its own regulatory system.

Between 1971 and 1972, however, a marked shift in U.S. fisheries policy occurred, especially under criticism by American fishing interests that had protested against the State Department's exclusion of their views. After reiterating its basic belief that regulation by species was the soundest way of managing fish stocks, Washington indicated in new revised draft fisheries articles submitted to the UN Sea-Bed Committee on August 4, 1972 that it was prepared to consider a greater role for coastal states by placing upon them primary responsibility, including powers of inspection and arrest, for the conservation and management of coastal and anadromous species, such as salmon. The regional organizations proposed earlier were shunted aside. Moreover, the United States explained that the traditional distant-water fishing quota to be allocated was a matter to be negotiated between the coastal state and the distant-water fishing state in the UN Sea-Bed Committee and in the forthcoming Law of the Sea conference. Finally, the United States offered to consider some limitations of the commissions that it had suggested for compulsory arbitration, especially while a dispute was under consideration.

Both changes in technology and the logic of geography argue in favor of the responsibility of coastal states for the conservation of coastal and anadromous species of fish, which together constitute three-quarters of the world's marine catch. Evidence of the need for an expansive and exclusive fisheries zone either for conservation or to obtain economic rent by the coastal state, however, is not compelling *if* there is an international convention to provide a framework for sustaining the species and for the allocation of the catch, and *if* there is a certain, third-party arbitral or judicial remedy to interpret agreements and resolve disputes. What is lacking for world order in virtually all the diplomatic approaches to rational fisheries management is a recognition that salmon or tuna or whales are not the property of any single state; that the right to catch free-swimming creatures by any state also entails a responsibility for a replenishment of the resource; and that any group of states gaining wealth from marine life beyond present national jurisdiction rightfully owes a rent to the rest of mankind.

Philosophic or poetic as these prescriptions may be, the political and legal instrumentalities are already available. Regional fisheries arrangements could provide representation of nonfishing states in their councils and arbitration while rents could be charged both by coastal states responsible for certain coastal and anadromous species or by regional international organizations for quotas of a catch. Finally, all these fisheries arrangements, which should be local, regional, and specialized, since they do not involve all states in all areas, must be supervised by a UN Fisheries Authority with power to receive reports, publicize problems, and bring the weight of world opinion against any plunder of the living resources of the oceans.

Marine Pollution

One other issue of international law and evolving ocean regimes requires examination for its potential as a threat to peace: marine pollution. The contamination of the oceans by radioactive wastes, toxic metals, chlorinated hydrocarbons, and, in particular, petroleum has received much public attention, but states have moved carefully toward the creation of new international rules and regulations in this area.[12]

About 90 percent of ocean pollution comes from the runoffs from pipes and rivers into the seas, and the blow-offs through the atmosphere of contaminants arising from agriculture and industry within a country. Thus, most of ocean pollution could rather immediately and effectively be curbed by a national consciousness of the problem and a national will to enact appropriate controls. Although coastal states have generally injured their own health, marine life, and shore values by their pollution, the discharges of one state through its outlets or estuaries to the water can no longer be regarded as unrelated to the welfare of other states in seas like the Baltic, the North, and even the Mediterranean. Moreover, the insecticides, with chlorinated hydrocarbons and polychlorinated biphenyls sprayed upon agriculture in one country can be wafted out to sea by the wind to inhibit photosynthesis in phytoplankton or cause reproductive failure in the fish and birds, thereby affecting other countries. Too little is yet known about the durability, circulation, and effects of marine pollution spilling or flying from the land into the sea, but it has now reached a level of international concern as indicated by the Stockholm UN Conference on the Human Environment in 1972.

Traditional remedies for one state to recover damages from another due to its polluting activities may be available under the legal doctrine that each state has a responsibility to protect other states against injurious acts by individuals within its jurisdiction. But such remedies will not suffice for an increasingly advanced technology in production, distribution, and marketing of global dimensions. In the long run states will probably seek to establish minimum international standards for the control of pollution, and, thereafter, pledge to consider or to act upon such standards through their own domestic legislation. Failing such progress, the usual diplomatic protest and litigation for damage will be an awkward and unsatisfying way to meet a serious environmental challenge.

A more tractable international problem has been the dumping of wastes by ships into the oceans that lie beyond the jurisdiction of any state. For centuries the seas had been used as a great sink for mankind with little heed to the consequences. Indeed, with time, both chemical process and bacterial action transformed, recycled, and reused the spoils and sewage of men. But the dumping of radioactive wastes, agents of biological or chemical warfare, nondissolving plastics, and thousands of tons of oil strains the cycle of nature and endangers the marine environment.

As early as 1950 the UN Economic and Social Council had noted the threat of oil pollution to the seas. In the following year studies were undertaken that led to a 1954 London conference, attended by 42 states, which resulted in the International Convention for the Prevention of Pollution of the Sea by Oil. Five years later the Convention was deposited with the newly constituted Intergovernmental Maritime Consultative Organization (IMCO). The Convention, amended in 1962 and in 1969, provided that oil may not be deliberately discharged upon the high seas by the vessels of any of the states party to the Convention except at certain rates, certain distances from shore, and under certain conditions. Controls lie in ship designs to prevent leakages and in the records of discharge that must be kept by the captain of the ship and the right to inspect such records in port. Another IMCO conference was scheduled for 1973 with the main objective being to achieve the complete elimination of the willful and intentional pollution of the seas by oil and noxious substances other than oil by 1975, if possible, and certainly by 1980.

Elimination of the deliberate dumping of oil, however, does not address the problem of accidental oil or other hazardous spills upon the seas. The wreck of the Torrey Canyon, carrying 119,328 tons of crude oil off the southwest coast of England on March 18, 1967 precipitated diplomatic action and the convening of an international legal conference by IMCO at Brussels in November 1969. The result was two new international conventions: the first—Convention Relating to Intervention on the High Seas in Cases of Oil Pollution—gives the coastal state a clear legal right when faced by grave and imminent danger from oil pollution to take necessary measures in adjacent waters beyond national jurisdiction, and it provides procedures for consultation or, in the event of a dispute, arbitration with other interested states. The second—Convention on Civil Liability for Oil Pollution Damage—provides strict liability for damages irrespective of fault; however, an owner not actually at fault in cases of collisions, fires, sinkings, or other disasters from natural causes is liable up to about $14 million. It should be obvious that these conventions still leave a great uneasiness among the poorer coastal states who do not have the expertise or equipment to intervene in the event of oil pollution disaster along their coasts and raise questions as to whether there should be any limit to the compensation for damages in an age of mammoth tankers and deep, gushing drillholes in the continental shelf.

Under the 1958 Geneva Convention on the Territorial Sea and the Contiguous Zone states may take measures in the contiguous zone to enforce their sanitary regulations, but the contiguous zone is understood to extend no further than twelve miles from the coast. Under the 1958 Convention on Fisheries and Conservation of the Living Resources of the High Seas, states may also take measures beyond national jurisdiction for the conservation of fish, but the objective of that article was hardly contemplated marine pollution. The 1958 Convention on the High Seas placed states under a general duty to adopt regulations to prevent marine pollution from oil due to pipe breaks, vessel discharges, or exploitation of the seabed and called for the cooperation of states with international organizations in order to prevent pollution of the seas or the air space above in measures taken for the disposal of radioactive materials and other harmful agents.

None of these early efforts to regulate marine pollution is adequate for the rapid increase and dispersion of contaminants that has taken place in the last twenty years. Canada moved unilaterally to establish a marine pollution control zone in waters 100 miles north of its shoreline in 1970, despite the protest of the United States, but the problem called for co-operative action by states and multilateral agreement to protect the oceans of the world from abuses that would eventually harm mankind.

In 1970 the U.S. Council on Environmental Quality issued a report, *Ocean Dumping–A National Policy*, which gave original and valuable statistics on the waste dumped by the United States into the sea. The report urged national legislation to curb disposal of some wastes at sea and recommended that the United States take the initiative in achieving international cooperation by developing proposals to control ocean dumping to be presented in such forums as the 1972 UN Conference on the Human Environment at Stockholm. The U.S. submitted its first draft convention on ocean dumping to the Intergovernmental Working Group on Marine Pollution, which was preparing work for the Stockholm Conference, in June 1971. This draft was severely criticized for leaving all discretion to the individual states in identifying substances which could or could not be dumped under national legislation with the only obligation being a report to an international registry on the nature and location of substances dumped under national permits.

Just before the second Working Group meeting in Ottawa in November 1971, a dozen European ambassadors had gathered in Oslo and drafted a convention designed to end the dumping of poisonous wastes by ships or planes into the northeast Atlantic Ocean. All parties to the convention, which was signed by eleven states, pledged to end the dumping of halogen or silicone compounds, mercury, cadmium, cancer-producing substances, and durable plastics; they also promised to control the dumping of such substances as arsenic, lead, tar, copper, fluorides, and containers by requiring special permits for their registered ships or for other ships leaving their ports with such wastes.

In the Ottawa meeting and successive consultations of the Working Group in Reykjavik (April) and London (May) 1972, the Oslo convention became a dominant influence over the U.S. drafts and a model for the far more comprehensive

Convention on the Dumping of Wastes at Sea signed in London by 57 states on November 13, 1972. In itself the Convention was a substantial achievement in gaining international cooperation even though dumping accounts for only a small part of marine pollution and even though all enforcement and penalties under the Convention are left to the individual states under somewhat indeterminate scientific standards. The issue of a pollution zone ranging from 50 to 200 miles off shore and subject to the control of the coastal state has not been settled and new interpretations of the Convention itself, which provides for no international regulatory authority or adjudication, are bound to sow conflicts that must be contained.

In conclusion, to save man from the absurdity of despoiling his own environment and from battles over fish, energy resources, and the utility of the highways of the world, international law for the oceans and seabed will be needed in the coming decade as never before, not only to provide equitable standards for the peaceful uses of the oceans and seabed, but to create agencies—administrative, regulatory, and judicial—in order to moderate the abrasive claims of nations and guarantee peace with justice.

NOTES

1. Eula McDonald. "Toward A World Maritime Organization," *Department of State Bulletin*, 2 parts, Vol. XVIII, No. 447, No. 448, January 25, 1948, and February 1, 1948.
2. Arthur Nussbaum, *A Concise History of the Law of Nations*, rev. ed. (London, The MacMillan Co., 1953), describes briefly early mercantile and maritime law, pp. 27-34, and has good footnotes for further reference.
3. Hugo Grotius wrote *On the Law of Spoils* in the winter of 1604-05 for the Dutch East Indian Company, a chapter of which, "The Free Seas," was published in 1609, but not "discovered" until its republication in 1864.
4. For Jefferson's actions in establishing a U.S. three-mile territorial sea, Marjorie M. Whiteman, *Digest of International Law*, Vol. 4, p. 36 (Washington, 1965) has the background.
5. *Protocol of Proceedings of the International Marine Conference Held in Washington, D.C.*, 3 vols. (Washington, D.C., U.S. Government Printing Office, 1890).
6. International Hydrographic Conference, London, 1919, *Report of Proceedings* (London, His Majesty's Stationery Office, 1920) and *International Hydrographic Bureau*, Report of the Proceedings of the Second International Hydrographic Conference, Monaco, October 26-November 10, 1926 (Cannes, Imprimerie Robaudy, 1962).
7. Documents, meetings, committee reports of the 1930 Hague Conference are in League of Nations, *Acts of the Conference for the Codification of International Law*, The Hague, 1930. The Law of the Sea Conferences of 1958 and 1960 can most quickly be studied in Arthur H. Dean, "The Geneva Conference on the Law of the Sea," *American Journal of International Law*, Vol. 52 (1958), p. 607, and "The Second Geneva Conference on the Law of the Sea," *Ibid.*, Vol. 54 (1960), p. 751. The conventions signed are UN Doc. A/Conf. 13/L.52, L.53, L.54, and L.55.
8. I have drawn on the original releases from the U.S. delegation on international straits as presented in Geneva by John Stevenson, the Legal Adviser of the Department of State, and I was present in both 1970 and 1971 when the statements were made to the delegates of the

UN Sea-Bed Commission. The Office of the Geographer, U.S. Department of State, issued a map in 1971 showing "world straits affected by a 12-mile territorial sea."

9. For material on U.S. submarine range and striking forces, see the U.S. Secretary of Defense, *Annual Report to the President*, as well as the statements of the Chairman of the Joint Chiefs of Staff before the U.S. Armed Services Committee.

10. *The UN International Law, and the Bed of the Seas*, Woodrow Wilson International Center for Scholars, 1971, treats the background of the issues and the development of law and organization for the seabed. See also the *Yearbook of the UN International Law Commission* from 1950 to 1957 and the *Reports of the Ad Hoc Committee to Study the Peaceful Uses of the Sea Bed* (A/7230), 1968, and the *Report of the Committee on the Peaceful Uses of the Sea-Bed* (A/8021), 1970 and (A/8421), 1971

11. Data on early fisheries have been drawn from Raymond McFarland, *A History of the New England Fisheries* (New York, D. Appleton & Co., 1911) and T. W. Van Metre, "American Fisheries" in Emory R. Johnson and others, *History of Domestic and Foreign Commerce of the United States* (Washington, D.C., Carnegie Institution of Washington, 1915). For some of my statistics on the fishing industry, size of vessels, technology, and so forth, I have used the FAO, *Fishery Country Profiles* prepared by the Department of Fisheries. On the international management of fisheries I am indebted to Albert W. Koers, "The Enforcement of Fisheries Agreements on the High Seas," University of Rhode Island, *Law of the Sea Institute*, Occasional Paper No. 6, June, 1970 and to Donald L. McKeman, Coordinator of Ocean Affairs, U.S. Department of State, who presented the first American draft articles on fisheries to the UN Sea-Bed Committee in Geneva in August, 1971; revised in August, 1972.

12. A valuable study of ocean pollution describing the types, intensities, and diffusion of pollutants as well as the legal remedies available and the international organization active in controlling pollution is UN Economic and Social Council, *Report of the Secretary General, The Struggle Against Pollution of the Seas*, E/5003, May 7, 1971. For the background to the Convention on the Dumping of Wastes at Sea in 1972, with an analysis of the draft's limitations and the texts, see Lawson A. W. Hunter, *The Question of an Ocean Dumping Convention*, American Society of International Law, Washington, D.C., August, 1972. I am also indebted to members of the U.S. delegation to the Intergovernmental Working Group on Marine Pollution in Ottawa in 1971, which I attended as an observer, for their advice and counsel.

THE CONTRIBUTORS

John T. Hayward, Vice-Admiral, U.S. Navy (retired), is a Vice-President of the General Dynamics Corporation. While on active duty, he served as President of the Naval War College, and was a command participant in the blockade of Cuba, as well as in naval operations in the Mediterranean and along the Viet Nam coast.

George H. Quester, Associate Professor of Government, Cornell University, is serving as Director of the Cornell Program on Peace Studies. He is the author of *Nuclear Diplomacy: The First Twenty-five Years.* (New York, Dunellen, 1970)

Arnold M. Kuzmack is a Senior Fellow of the Brookings Institution. He served formerly Deputy Director of the Naval Forces Division, Office of the Assistant Secretary of Defense (Systems Analysis), and is the author of *Naval Force Levels and Modernization* (Washington, Brookings, 1971).

Barry M. Blechman, is a Research Fellow of the Brookings Institution, working as a specialist on Soviet defense and naval policy.

Curt Gasteyger, Deputy Director-General of the Atlantic Institute, Paris, was formerly the Director of Programmes of the Institute for Strategic Studies, London. He is a specialist on NATO defense policies, and the author of *Conflict and Tension in the Mediterranean* (London, ISS Adelphi Papers, 1968).

Jack Spence of the Department of Political Theory and Government, University College, Swansea, Wales, is a specialist on defense policy in sub-Saharan Africa and the waters of the Southern Hemisphere. He is the author of *South Africa's Defense* (Los Angeles, University of California Press, 1966).

Thomas B. Millar, Professorial Fellow in the Department of International Relations of the Australian National University, Canberra, has written extensively on Australian defense policy and the balance of power in the Indian Ocean-Far East region, including *Australia's Defense* (New York, Cambridge, 1968).

Michael Rosenthal, is a Research Fellow of the Program on Peace Studies and the Program on Science, Technology and Society, Cornell University, and is working on studies of the cost-effectiveness and conduciveness to arms control of aircraft carrier and submarine weapons systems.

Gerald J. Mangone, a Senior Fellow of The Woodrow Wilson International Center for Scholars, Washington, D.C., is an expert on legal questions pertaining to oceanic and seabed matters: among other works, he is the author of *The Elements of International Law* (Homewood, Dorsey, 1967).

Index

125, 150
Cuba, 5, 37, 165, 116
Cuban missile crisis, 5, 11,
  17, 29, 34, 82, 128, 181,
  186, 192
C.V.A., 6-7, 46
C.V.S., 46
Cyprus, 101-102, 103, 111,
  114

Dardanelles, 161
Defense, Department of, 8,
  43, 53, 209
De Gaulle, Charles, 106
dependence effect, 37
deployment, naval, 66, 67,
  69, 71, 75, 76, 81, 82,
  82, 85, 86, 87, 88, 102,
  112, 114, 118, 124, 130,
  133, 147, 176, 179, 180,
  181, 186, 188, 209
destroyers, 4, 5, 18, 21, 25,
  26-27, 46, 55, 56, 59, 69,
  70, 85, 104, 105, 111,
  125, 142, 171, 174
deterrent capacity, 12, 13,
  14, 15, 23, 30, 31, 80,
  87, 129, 139, 160, 168,
  172, 181-182, 183, 185,
  187, 188, 192, 193
deterrent equation, 11
disarmament: multilateral,
  146-147; unilateral, 9
Dominican Republic, 17
domino theory, 160

East Africa, 123, 150

East African States, 132
East Indies, 159
East Pakistan, 127, 151
Ecuador, 207, 224, 226
Egypt, *see* United Arab Re-
  public
electronic defenses, 4, 14,
  50, 56, 60
escalation, 19-20, 21, 22,
  23, 24, 25, 38
Essex, 48, 49
Ethiopia, 126, 144, 145
Ethiopian-Somalia conflict,
  126

F-4, 46, 60
F-14, 46, 60
Fifth Fleet (Soviet), 161
First Fleet (U.S.), 161
first strike stability,
  180-182, 187
fishing, 5, 13, 81, 86, 208,
  223-230
Five Power Agreement, 142
French navy, 18, 106-107,
  108
frigates, 5, 14, 105, 106,
  107, 142

Geneva Convention on Fish-
  ing and Conservation
  (1958), 226, 233
Geneva Convention on the
  Continental Shelf, 220
Geneva Convention on the
  Territorial Sea and the
  Contiguous Zone (1958),